πολλά, ἔχων ὄνομα
MANY HAVING A NAME

γεγραμμένον ὃ οὐδεὶς
(HAVING BEEN) WRITTEN WHICH NO ONE

οἶδεν εἰ μὴ αὐτός, καὶ
KNOWS EXCEPT HIMSELF AND

περιβεβλημένος ἱμάτιον
(HAVING BEEN) CLOTHED [WITH] A GARMENT

βεβαμμένον αἵματι, καὶ
(HAVING BEEN) DIPPED IN BLOOD AND

κέκληται τὸ ὄνομα
HAS BEEN CALLED THE NAME

αὐτοῦ ὁ λόγος τοῦ
OF HIM THE WORD —

θεοῦ.
OF G·D.

"REVELATION" XIX, 11–13

THE VICIOUS AND THE VIRTUOUS HAVE NOT INDEED POWER OVER THEIR MORAL ACTIONS; BUT

AT FIRST THEY HAD THE POWER TO BECOME EITHER THE ONE OR THE OTHER, JUST AS ONE WHO

THROWS A STONE HAS POWER OVER IT UNTIL HE HAS THROWN IT, BUT NOT AFTERWARDS."

ARISTOTLE

Last Journey

Atlas & Co.
New York

Last Journey

A Father and Son in Wartime

Darrell Griffin, Sr.

Copyright © 2009 Darrell Griffin, Sr.

Interior design by Yoshiki Waterhouse

Typesetting by Wordstop Technologies (P) Ltd.

Skip was studying Greek, a form of homage to some of his favorite philosophers. In his journal, he copied passages from a Greek translation of the Bible. Reproductions appear on the endpapers of this book.

Excerpt from *Out of the Labyrinth* by Erich Kahler (New York, George Braziller, 1967) on pages 164–65 appear courtesy of George Braziller Publishers.

Atlas & Co. *Publishers*
15 West 26th Street, 2nd floor
New York, NY 10010
www.atlasandco.com

Distributed to the trade by W. W. Norton & Company

Printed in the United States

Atlas & Company books may be purchased for educational, business, or sales promotional use. For information, please write to info@ atlasandco.com

Library of Congress Cataloging-in-Publication Data is available upon request.

ISBN: 978-1-934633-16-8
13 12 11 10 09 1 2 3 4 5 6

This book is dedicated to my son SSG Darrell Ray Griffin, Jr. This is the book that he and I were going to write together, but on March 21, 2007, an insurgent bullet robbed us of this opportunity. I finished the book as my last gift to him.

I would also like to dedicate it to Darrell Jr.'s fellow warriors of the 1–5 Infantry of 1st Stryker Brigade Combat Team, 25th Infantry Division and the 2–3 Infantry of 3rd Stryker Brigade Combat Team, 2nd Infantry Division.

Finally, I would like to dedicate it to all of our men and women in uniform who help keep our country free.

Contents

Chapter 1   *Getting the News*   1

Chapter 2   *Skip's Dust Bowl Lineage*   12

Chapter 3   *Darrell R. Griffin, Jr., Is Born*   26

Chapter 4   *Skip Finds an Angel*   56

Chapter 5   *A Just War?*   67

Chapter 6   *Preparing for War*   72

Chapter 7   *Iraq*   88

Chapter 8   *Bloody Days in Tal'Afar*   130

Chapter 9   *Home*   164

Chapter 10   *The Second Tour*   167

Chapter 11   *Home Again*   190

Chapter 12   *The Last Tour*   197

Chapter 13   *The Battle of Najaf*   224

Chapter 14   *A Spartan Warrior Comes Home on His Shield*   235

Chapter 15   *Last Journey*   259

Chapter 16   *A Father's Last Gift*   275

Appendix: *Skip's Incident Reports*   294

           Military Abbreviations and Acronyms   298

Acknowledgments   301

Chapter 1

Getting the News

May 2007—Los Angeles National Cemetery

DARRELL RAY
GRIFFIN Jr
S SGT
US ARMY
IRAQI FREEDOM
MAR 13 1971
MAR 21 2007
BSM w V PH KIA
BELOVED HUSBAND
SON AND BROTHER

I am standing at the grave of SSG Darrell Griffin, Jr., my son, reading the same words I have read every Sunday for the last month. BSM stands for Bronze Star Medal, w V means that the Bronze Star was awarded under circumstances of valor, PH stands for Purple Heart, and KIA stands for killed in action. It took about a month after Skip's death for his headstone to be carved and placed at his grave. While waiting for his headstone to arrive, the cemetery placed an index-sized card in a green, waterproof frame at the head of his grave. It said: *Grave No. A 15, Section 89A, Darrell R. Griffin, Date of Death, 03/21/2007.* Too brief a grave marker and too brief a life.

Darrell's family called him Skip; his wife, Diana, called him Darrell; and his military comrades called him Griff. Not only did Skip get stuck with my complete name with a "Jr." at the end, but he also got stuck with my nickname. When he was younger he was called Little Skip and I was called Big Skip. Skip grew to be six foot two and two hundred forty pounds of solid muscle. Then the family referred to him as Big Skip and me as Old Skip.

I normally come to visit Skip's grave every Sunday before church. Kim, Skip's mom, often comes with me. I have only missed a couple of weekends since he was buried.

The smell of his favorite incense, Nag Champa, which I just lit and placed in front of his headstone, wafts in the air. I like that fragrance. He loved to burn incense in his study while he was reading books by his favorite authors—John Calvin, Friedrich Nietzsche, Reinhold Niebuhr, St. Augustine, Nikolai Berdyaev, Jacques Ellul, and the other philosophers and theologians whose works he pored over with a graduate student's zeal—though he'd never finished high school. Sometimes I'll bring one of his favorite books and read out loud to him if no one is around.

I wrap the lighter and remaining incense and put it in the "Skip Toolbox." This is a small gardener's toolbox that contains all the items we need when we come to visit Skip: pruning shears, paper towels and spray cleaner to wipe off the bird droppings, clippers for trimming the long grass from around the headstone, and, of course, incense and a lighter. I got the idea of the Skip Toolbox from watching the other families that come regularly to visit their sons here. Since we come to visit Skip every week, we keep the toolbox in the trunk of the car.

Last Sunday, I noticed that the man parking next to me had a similar toolbox. He had the same basic accessories, but he also had a number of cigars. When Skip was in Iraq, Diana and Kim used to send cigars to him every month. Most pictures of Skip taken in Iraq are of him smoking a cigar. So I decided to buy some cigars and occasionally smoke one when I visit his grave. These small acts make me feel closer to Skip.

A lot of graves only have flowers on them during the first week. I assume many of these are the graves of soldiers whose families live out of town. Or maybe the first week is enough for most people. Skip was buried beside Christopher Dwayne Young, who did not have his headstone when we buried Skip next to him. Now his headstone reads that he was killed during Iraqi Freedom a few weeks before Skip, when he was twenty-one years old. He was old enough to die for his country and old enough to have a beer if he wanted one. Since Skip was buried, he and Christopher have been joined by another soldier, Walter Freeman, who was killed on April 4, a few weeks after Skip. Walter was also a casualty of Iraqi Freedom. He was just a couple of months younger than Christopher.

The Los Angeles National Cemetery is a United States National Cemetery in West Los Angeles, at the intersection of Wilshire Boulevard and Sepulveda Boulevard. Soldiers and their spouses whose graves date back to the Civil War are buried here. Interred also are veterans from the Spanish-American War, World War I, World War II, the Korean War, and other American conflicts. One of my son's "neighbors" is Nicholas Porter Earp (1813–1907). He was the father of Old West lawmen Wyatt Earp, Virgil Earp, and Morgan Earp. Section 13 grave A-18. More than 85,000 soldiers and spouses are buried here.

We had the option of burying Skip at Arlington National Cemetery in Arlington, Virginia. We selected the Los Angeles Cemetery so that we can visit him weekly. We have a good friend who lost her son in a helicopter crash in Iraq in 2005. He was buried in a group grave at Arlington with four other soldiers who had died in the crash because they couldn't tell which body parts belonged to which soldier. She wishes she had buried him in Los Angeles. I didn't ask her, but I was curious if she had a choice of where he was buried since he was in a group grave. Two of the other people buried with him were Iraqi soldiers.

Kim likes to drive to the hill in the cemetery that overlooks Skip's grave. When we get out of the car and stand looking at his grave site from the distant hill, for an instant it's as if it hadn't really happened, as if he were still alive.

I always expect to see a lot more flowers. It seems like the same few graves always have flowers on them. Skip gets fresh flowers every weekend, and so do a couple of his graveside neighbors. Today, Kim is placing flowers in front of Skip's headstone in one of the little cones that the cemetery provides for this purpose. She also brought some for Christopher. We often find on Skip's grave the same bouquet of flowers that has been put on Christopher's. We assume Christopher's family has been bringing Skip flowers, and we often reciprocate the gesture. We have varied the times we come to visit Skip to increase the chances of meeting them, but we haven't seen them yet. Although we may see the same people at the cemetery, there seems to be an unwritten rule that we don't talk to each other. There is the normal quiet and dignified nod as we pass one another, but rarely any conversation.

We always take a photograph with our cell phone of the fresh flowers we just placed on Skip's grave and then send it to Diana, Skip's wife. Since she lives at Fort Lewis, Washington, and can't visit Skip's grave very often, it seems to give her some comfort every time we send her a picture. She likes knowing we are taking care of Skip.

Besides Christopher's family or friends sometimes putting flowers on Skip's grave, another odd thing we have noticed is that there are often three or four new pennies, always face up, on top of Skip's headstone. We know they are new because the "tail" sides that aren't exposed to the elements are still shiny. I have noticed this a few times on other soldiers' headstones, but they are fairly consistently placed on Skip's.

These are the little questions that perplex me.

There are also bigger questions.

Questions such as *Why did my son have to go to war?* And *Why did he die?* And *What did he die for?* These seem like simple, straightforward questions, but they are not. They were the subject of numerous conversations that Skip and I had over the course of several years. Philosophy, theology, and politics were our favorite topics. Most fathers and sons like to go hunting and to sporting events together; they like to talk about cars. Our favorite father-son activity was to spend an entire evening talking about books—once Skip was old enough, over a bottle of merlot. We called it *The Great Conversation.*

I was sixteen when Skip's sister Rene was born, and eighteen when Skip was born. I spent most of my time doing jobs like washing dishes while finishing high school and college. Because these jobs never paid very well, there wasn't much money to buy toys. A good, cheap form of entertainment was for me to take Skip and Rene to the library or to buy them used books. They both loved to read.

I say good-bye to Skip and stand up to walk back to my car. I notice that the incense has burned a hole in the little army flag that someone had placed by Skip's headstone. Now it says: "United States Arm."

As I get in my car, I remember a favorite quotation of Skip's: "Of all the sorrows that afflict mankind, the bitterest is this, that one should have consciousness of much, but control over nothing." —Herodotus.

At four o'clock on March 21, 2007—I remember the exact time—Kim called me at work to tell me that Skip had been shot. He had been wounded a couple of times before while on tour in Iraq, so I asked her how bad it was. All she could say was, "He's gone." I threw the phone against the wall and ran out of the building. The only words I could get out of my mouth as I ran to my car were the words Kim had told me: "He's gone."

Kim asked me to get home as soon as I could. Diana had called to tell her that Skip had been killed and casualty assistance officers (CAOs) were trying to reach us. The army assigns CAOs to go to the houses of family members designated on a soldier's deployment papers and notify them in the event that he is killed. These papers are completed by all military personnel before deployment to a combat zone.

As I was racing home, I called Rene, Skip's sister, and told her. Her husband had to take the phone from her.

Then I called his brother, Christian, and his other sister, Sommer.

After I hung up the phone, the car was silent except for the white noise of the traffic around me on the Ventura Freeway. I was almost grateful that the traffic was as congested as it normally was during the work week. It gave me time to collect myself and try to be strong for Kim and the kids when I got home. As I turned off the Ventura Freeway onto the Santa Monica 405 Freeway, I saw a dilapidated old travel trailer being towed by a pickup truck. The trailer was about twenty feet long and ten feet wide. It was chalky white and appeared to have several layers of tar on the roof, probably from years of patched leaks. It reminded me of the trailer I lived in when I brought Skip home from the hospital after he was born. Rene had been born a year earlier. I was just finishing high school and entering college, so the little trailer was the best I could do.

Kim's car was already sitting in the driveway when I got home. I walked in the house and gathered Skip's younger half sister Alexis, his younger half brother Jordan, and Kim into a circle so we could all cry together. Kim got us each a glass of wine and we sat and waited for the CAOs to knock on the door. There are so few things that Hollywood portrays accurately in war films. But it's dead-on when there's a scene showing the unwanted knock at the door by two soldiers in dress greens.

It was 7:00 p.m., about three hours since Kim had called to tell me about Skip. The knock at the door startled us, even though we were expecting it. I opened the door and one of the soldiers said, "The President of the United States regrets to inform you that your son, SSG Darrell Ray . . ." I interrupted him mid-sentence: "Please come in." They could tell from the redness of our eyes that we already knew what had happened. Kim and I were so consumed with our own grief that it wasn't until later that I thought about the awful time Diana must have been having, being by herself when they came to her door at Fort Lewis.

One of the CAOs handed us a used white three-ring binder with pages in it. While I was grieving with one part of my brain, the other part of my brain was wondering how callous these guys were for giving us such beat-up copies of "What to Do When You Lose a Loved One in Combat."

At such a time, it's as if your brain is a separate entity from you, trying to help you survive the fact that you have just heard the worst possible news: your son has been killed in the sands of Iraq, halfway around the world. It must be part of a self-defense mechanism developed over eons of time. This would have been a good topic of discussion for Skip and me.

We sat and listened to what help the army could give us now that we had lost our oldest son in combat, but I wasn't really listening. I was thinking to myself, *Is there anything they can say that will make any difference now that my son is gone?* After they delivered their canned speech, we all sat in silence for a few minutes. The only sounds were occasional sniffling, the ticking of the clock on the living room wall, and a police siren in the distance.

I asked one of the officers how it had happened. He said, "I was told very little other than he was shot in the back of the head by a sniper."

"Did he suffer?" I asked.

"I don't think so, given the nature of the wound," said the other soldier. I could tell they didn't really know. They were from the local National Guard armory. Neither one had served in a war zone. But I knew they were just trying to help us.

They got up to leave and shook our hands. They explained that an officer would be assigned to work with us to arrange for funeral and burial services. They gave us the name of Sgt. Holifield and said he would be contacting us that day or the next. I thanked them as I closed the door behind them.

Later that night I pulled some of Skip's journals down from my library shelves. I opened up one of the journals he had kept in Iraq and sniffed it to see if there were traces of Skip that I could smell.

From the start, he had been troubled about the idea of going to Iraq. Given his constant studying and reading of philosophy, I knew he would have a lot of thoughts about the war. I had encouraged him to keep a journal; he was going to write a book about his experiences when he got home.

From Skip's journal:

I am attempting to create an account of two tours of combat in Iraq as an infantryman. I am trying to make sense of a world that I had never known until the first time that I had to kill a man. A world where men wanted to kill me and a world where friends didn't just move away but died violent deaths on the field of battle.

With all of the attenuated emotional, psychological, and spiritual trauma that has come with seeing death and dealing it out, I have also been plagued with the unanswered questions that our government is asking itself concerning solutions for the complex situation that we have put ourselves in [in Iraq]. *With no clear strategy politically, the consequences have a direct effect on how we, as the sword of our government, engage not only the "enemy" but also how we engage the various political/religious blocs in this complicated world of intrigue and shifting loyalties. As of late I have started to wonder whether or not we are killing insurgents or merely combatants fighting each other in a "war of all against all." At this stage of the war, I choose not to use the word "insurgent" as a description of who I am trying to kill.*

If nothing else, this attempt at a book will hopefully put to rest the demons that I have courted by killing and living in this chaotic world for two years. I want anyone who reads this to remember the anonymous tens of thousands who have died as a result of being caught in the middle of the storm created here when we chose to invade this country. Is this a moral attempt at redemption or a political, clinical description of my experience here? I do not know. This being said, I will give an account, in the most broad terms, of the people of this country that I have spoken with and what they feel the answers are to the life and death situation that they face on a daily basis. I have spoken with Christian and Muslim alike. I have spoken with the most sectarian of Muslims and the most progressive of their religion. It seems as if they could care less who runs the country as long as they can have their lives back and not have to worry about being torn to pieces going to the store to buy milk. I have spoken with members of the Iraqi military and this is where you begin to see the friction point that lurks underneath their uniforms. Staunch religious loyalty proven by the gun is the rule of the day.

Skip wasn't able to complete his book. A sniper's bullet saw to that. I am going to finish the book that my son started—the book that Skip was born to write.

Chapter 2

Skip's Dust Bowl Lineage

It was August 1945 when my grandpa—Darrell Jr.'s great-grandpa—loaded my grandma, my mother, her younger sister Patsy, and their younger brother Bobbie Joe into his Model A and headed for California—the Promised Land. He had worked the zinc, lead, and coal mines in Oklahoma until his lungs became infected. Safety conditions in the mines of 1937 were sorely lacking. Miners worked below ground and out of sight, so the corporate owners were the face of the mining industry. It was more than cave-ins that killed miners. Many of them died slow, lung-damaged deaths.

Aunt Pat (Patsy) liked to tell us about this trip out to California. According to the story, Grandpa, an Ottawa Indian, stopped at a liquor store somewhere in New Mexico to buy a small bottle of whiskey. He came back out to the car kicking the dirt. He got in the old Model A and slammed its frail door. "They won't sell to Mexicans, niggers, or Indians. Especially Indians." Grandma got out of the other side of the car. "I'll get it." Minutes later she came out with "Grandpa's medicine." There were actual laws on the books then barring the sale of liquor to Indians.

They made it as far as Arizona, where Grandpa used up his last gas ration coupon. He pulled into a gas station to get gas and fill up the radiator with water. As Grandpa got out of the car, he told the kids, "This is the last pee stop till we get to California so you better go now." He walked over to the attendant who was sitting on the front porch and started to explain that he was out of coupons. The attendant said, "It don't matter, the Japs surrendered a couple of days ago." Grandpa paid the attendant, gathered up the kids, and headed for California.

They drove on to the San Pablo region, near San Francisco, and found an old wooden caboose to live in while they worked the fruit fields. It had electricity and running water, and it didn't leak. San Pablo was a little industrial town. There were foundries spewing out black smoke that coated everything with grime and gave Grandpa a hacking cough. Grandpa got a job working in the smelting plant. This was the last job he ever had. When he got too crippled to work anymore, he and Grandma packed up the family and moved to Stockton, California. Grandma was able to get welfare for me and my sisters. She found a job working at a local school as a cook's helper.

At times I hated Grandpa. But as I got older, I began to understand his sour attitude toward people and life in general. He was a proud six-foot-two American Indian, but he had a stoop from arthritis that made him almost a foot shorter. I remember watching Grandma drag Grandpa in an old wooden chair to the bathroom so he could relieve himself. We couldn't afford a wheelchair because any benefits we had from Grandpa's medical insurance plan had long since run out. He went from slamming a forty-pound sledgehammer on the closing pin of a fiery foundry blast furnace to having his bride drag him in a broken chair to the toilet.

My dad, David "Ross" Griffin, got my mom, Shirley Ann, Grandpa's firstborn daughter, pregnant when they were both sixteen years old. The only way he could see to support my mom was to join the Navy. They were married on the base at the San Diego Naval Training Center. At seventeen, he was in the Navy serving in Korea aboard the USS *Iowa*. After about a year in the Pacific, the *Iowa* steamed into Norfolk, Virginia. Ross got tired of the "Navy way" and went AWOL. He was lucky. Instead of getting a dishonorable discharge, he got a general discharge under honorable conditions. The Korean War was ending and the U.S. government was going through a general military force reduction, so he got swept up with all of the other seamen being discharged. He and Shirley set up housekeeping after he got out of the brig at Treasure Island, the Naval station.

The only fatherly skill that Ross had was getting my mom pregnant and keeping her that way for five straight years. I was born in 1952, my three sisters were born in the following three years, and then Mom got pregnant again.

Ross wasn't into working, so Shirley had to get a job at the Windmill Pub in downtown Rodeo. On October 18, 1956, on a narrow highway in Richmond, California, Shirley's boss, Dip, was driving her and a couple of customers home when he had a sudden stroke and hit a telephone pole. Everyone in the car died, including my mom. At the age of twenty-two, Ross found himself a single father with four kids, ages six months to four years old. He wasted no time shopping us around to his family. No one would take all four of us, so he turned to Shirley's parents, the Moxleys. He figured that they were "good Christians" who had done an okay job raising my mother, and they would keep us all together. To this day, I can't understand how they were able to take us in. Grandpa was very sick, out of work, and they were broke.

Dad was known around San Pablo as a bar-brawling tough guy. His reputation was worse now that his first love had died and he had given up custody of his kids. He was drinking in a local bar when a Hell's Angel came up to him and asked if he would like to ride with the Angels. Ross had just gotten a motorcycle from his brother-in-law's brother, who had to sell it fast because he was on the run for a bank robbery in another state. All Ross had to do was get his "colors" (the official Hell's Angel insignia). Becoming an Angel was the biggest accomplishment of his life.

I was about seven years old when we moved to Stockton, following my Aunt Pat, who had moved there with one of her husbands. We only had one car and my sisters and I were too young to be left at home alone. Grandma would get us up at 5:00 a.m. and load us in the backseat of his 1951 Hudson with our blankets and pillows. Grandpa never had a car that was less than ten years old. This one was big enough so that my sister Sharon could sleep on the back window dashboard; Sheila and Sandra got the backseat floorboard, and I got the seat.

At times there were eleven people living in Grandma and Grandpa's house. Aunt Pat and her three kids lived with us when she was between marriages. To help make ends meet, Aunt Pat got a job waiting on tables for tips only. At thirteen, I got my first full-time job as a dishwasher at the Rare Steer, working with Grandma. Every few years, my dad would come around and get me and my sisters excited with all of his empty promises, only to disappear again. He still owes me a bike.

The girl I got pregnant, Linda Sanchez, was Darrell Jr.'s mom. I remember her being the only kid at school who drove a car that was one color and didn't have any part of it painted with primer. She wasn't supposed to be going to Franklin High School in Stockton because she lived in Lodi. Her mom was single and worked in Stockton, so Linda was dropped off at her Grandma Zuniga's, who lived close to the school. We met during our junior year. Linda's mom was always at work, so we spent more time at her big house out in the country than we did at school.

Spending days at her house with our raging hormones and no parents around created the perfect setting for Linda getting pregnant.

Grandpa wasn't too happy when he found out. He felt a lot of his troubles in life were related to his being an Indian in a white man's world. He was proud to be part of the Ottawa Nation, and he looked just like the Indian on the face of a buffalo nickel. He didn't have much use for anyone else of color, and it bothered him that I would have a Mexican girlfriend.

"Are you telling me that you couldn't find a decent white girl?" screamed Grandpa Moxley. He got his crippled legs under him, grabbed his cane, and pushed himself up. His legs had been frozen into a sitting position from his years of severe arthritis. As he hobbled toward my bedroom door, he turned and said, "You're messing up bad. I had hoped that you could have moved up from busboy to fry cook." He shook his head. "You're just like your no-account dad. He never was anything and never will be and neither will you." He gave me a month to move out.

I had to get permission from the Juvenile Justice Department in San Joaquin County to set up a household with Linda. Since we were both under age, we had to demonstrate to the assigned probation officer that I had a job and a plan to finish high school. We were married in July 1969. I was working full-time as a dishwasher and completing my junior year of high school. It was hard to find a place we could afford to rent, and it was even harder to convince any landlord to rent to a sixteen-year-old boy who looked fourteen. I hadn't even begun to shave.

We finally found a place to rent. The Brown Top Trailer Park was a place where only desperate people lived. There were about thirty trailers in the park. Two washer and dryers were located in the center of the park. Next to the laundry was a trash bin that was always overflowing with garbage and liquor bottles. Our little eight-by-twenty-foot trailer was across from the garbage bins. On hot days the sound of the buzzing flies would almost drown out the noise of the busy road that was about twenty feet from our trailer. Behind the trailer was a fence that was held up by six-foot-high weeds.

The trailer was old. It had layers of tar on its roof to stop the rain from coming in, and a little two-step splintery stoop in front of the door. A dilapidated storage shed stood on the concrete slab that served as our porch. I talked the landlord into letting me sand down the splinters and paint the shed and the steps. I found a paint store, Paul Cox Studio, that sold its mixing mistakes for next to nothing. Mr. Cox gave me two quarts for free. Soon the stoop and shed were a light purple (the only mixing mistake the store manager had at the time), but at least there were no more splinters.

November 21, 1969

I was sitting in my eleventh-grade English literature class when a runner from the attendance office came in and handed the teacher at the front of the room a note. Mr. Bentley looked directly at me. "Darrell, can you please come here for a minute?" I was so absorbed in coming up with an excuse for not having my homework assignment ready that I forgot that today was the planned due date for our baby to be born. With a disgusted look on his face, Mr. Bentley said, "Well, Darrell, it looks like your *wife* is going into labor. You are excused from class." I went back to my desk to pack up my books. "Before you leave, the attendance office wants to see you." As I walked out of class, the guys who thought they were cool gave me the "thumbs-up" sign. The smart kids just looked at me and shook their heads.

When I got to the attendance office, the attendance lady and my guidance counselor were in a huddle, obviously talking about me. They broke apart the instant they saw me through the glass of the office door. The attendance lady said, "Darrell, before we can officially let you off campus you have to bring back proof that your wife is in labor. You need to bring back a note from your wife's doctor or at least from your wife." I rushed home, had Linda write me a note, and took it back to school, then ran back home and took her to the hospital. Later that day, Darlene "Rene" Griffin, Darrell Jr.'s older sister, was born. Linda and Rene came home two days later. Rene slept in a bassinet in the living room.

I stayed home from school for a couple of days to help Linda with the baby. Neither of us knew what we were doing. There wasn't any glamour in midnight feedings and changing full diapers. I remember sitting up late one night thinking that if Linda and I put our ages together—thirty-two—it would be a good age to have a child.

Every week, I went to the California National Guard offices to see how my application was going. The United States was deeply involved in the Vietnam War, and the National Guard didn't get sent to Vietnam. It wasn't the idea of fighting in Vietnam that bothered me; it was the fact that there didn't seem to be any reason for it. I had a copy of my completed National Guard application on the headboard of my bed, along with brochures for Canada. There was no way I was going to Vietnam to fight in Nixon's war.

April 30, 1970—Stockton, California—Brown Top Trailer Park

I had just gotten home after a long day at school and an afternoon shift of washing dishes at the Hoosier Inn. I was lucky to have this job. The owner, Charlie Dyer, always let me adjust my schedule to accommodate my school schedule. The staff was like a second family. On occasion, Charlie or Mrs. Dyer would help me with my math homework.

I grabbed a soda and some chips and turned on the television. There was Nixon with his five o'clock shadow, looking nervous:

> Good evening, my fellow Americans. Ten days ago, in my report to the nation on Vietnam, I announced a decision to withdraw an additional 150,000 Americans from Vietnam over the next year. I said then that I was making that decision despite our concern over increased enemy activity in Laos, Cambodia, and in South Vietnam. After full consultation with the National Security Council, Ambassador Bunker, General Abrams, and my other advisers, I have concluded that the actions of the enemy in the last ten days clearly endanger the lives of Americans who are in Vietnam now and would constitute an unacceptable risk to those who will be there after withdrawal of another

150,000. To protect our men who are in Vietnam, and to guarantee the continued success of our withdrawal and Vietnamization program, I have concluded that the time has come for action. Tonight, American and South Vietnamese units will attack the headquarters for the entire Communist military operation in South Vietnam.

My first thought was: *How cold does it get in Canada?*

I changed the channel and adjusted the rabbit ears on our hand-me-down TV. The scene was a bunch of unshaven, tired-looking young men walking a trail through a Vietnam jungle. There was napalm burning in the background. The only sound coming from the TV was the deadly noise of machine guns and helicopters swooshing by overhead. The words over the scene were: "and today's body count is . . ." I switched the channel again. I mouthed Walter Cronkite's "and that's the way it is on April 30th, 1970" as he closed *CBS Evening News*.

The country went crazy over Nixon's announcement. Students protested at Kent State University in Ohio. On May 2, the Kent State R.O.T.C. offices were burned out. The next day, the Ohio National Guard was sent to the campus. Ohio Governor James A. Rhodes promised to use "every force possible" to maintain order. Rhodes denounced the protesters as worse than "brown shirts" and vowed to keep the National Guard in Kent "until we get rid of them."

On May 4, fifteen hundred student protesters gathered on campus. Four students were killed and nine others were wounded when a contingent of guardsmen suddenly opened fire during a noontime demonstration.

June 1970—Fort Ord, California
Finally, my application to the National Guard came through.

It was raining the day I arrived at the processing station at Fort Ord. A stern sergeant lined us all up in a loose formation and laid it out: we would be processed over the next few days and assigned to our various basic training units within a week. There would be haircuts, shots, tests, more shots, more tests. On the first day, we all got haircuts. I could really feel the morning Monterey breeze with my new buzz cut. Later on that day, we were issued army boxers, T-shirts, socks, a duffle bag, army greens, fatigues, boots, and other gear. We were beginning to look like we belonged in the army. National Guardsmen (NGs) were trained alongside the regular army draftees, but you could always tell them apart. The NGs knew they were going home after their training and didn't pay a lot of attention; the regular army trainees were eager to learn all they could because most of them would be sent to places where their lives depended on it.

Basic training wasn't that tough. I was assigned to unit A13 (Company A, First Battalion, 3rd Brigade) and issued a punch card. If we did something above and beyond the call of duty, we could get our merit cards punched by a training officer. It didn't take much to get our cards punched; things like looking sharp at morning roll call, sporting extra shiny boots, or demonstrating a good shot pattern at rifle training often did the trick. The whole merit card system was somewhat juvenile. If we got enough merit points, we could actually go home for a weekend during basic.

One morning toward the end of August, Linda called to tell me she was pregnant. I was stunned. I had been gone for two months. I didn't have a job and had just signed up for college; our only income was the meager pay I was getting from the army while in basic training. Linda was living with my grandparents.

After nine weeks of basic training, we were promoted to Advanced Individual Training (AIT) and assigned a Military Occupational Specialty (MOS). My MOS was 94B20—cook's helper. Hardly a "tough soldier" MOS, but soldiers need to eat. I was never told why I was selected to be a cook, but two weeks after basic I was one of forty future army cooks standing in front of a stove. The first thing we learned that day was how to crack two eggs at the same time. I also learned how to make jelly rolls from scratch. In nine weeks, I went from not knowing how to flip an egg to being able to cook a meal fit for a general. But I was glad to be going back home.

November 1970—Stockton

I arrived home in time for Rene's first birthday. We lived with Grandma and Grandpa for a couple of weeks while we looked for a place we could afford. Grandpa had softened his negative attitude toward Mexicans while Linda was living with him. So much for the racist old Indian.

We ended up at the Brown Top Trailer Park again. All the old tenants were still there, probably because of the low rent. This gave a homecoming atmosphere to our return. We had moved up to a bigger trailer on the other side of the park, away from the heavy traffic. It was a lot roomier, and had a small dining room table that would accommodate two place settings. We also liked the fact that the built-in heater could be turned on without a match. There was a front and a back door. I had to have a place to study, so I nailed a piece of wood across the back doorway. That was my desk. I could sit there and study in the fresh air. Above the door I built a shelf for my reference books. I'd never had a study before, and it was magical.

The trailer was older than our first one but in much better shape. The paint was fresh and there was a small yard. We didn't worry much about theft. Any burglar who wanted anything of value would just keep driving past Brown Top. We could open the curtains along the front end of the trailer and let the sunlight in once in a while. The landlord had paved the dusty dirt road in the trailer park. Life was good.

In February 1971, I started at Delta Junior College. I had never personally known anyone who had gone to college. I still had my job at Paul Cox Studio, the paint store whose owner had once given me free paint for the shed out in front of our trailer. Mr. Cox was a retired executive from a major Northern California furniture chain. He had worked himself up to a mid-level management position and taken early retirement to start his own business.

One night, Mr. Cox invited Linda and me to his home for dinner. He and his wife—"the love of my life, Betty"—lived in the nicer area of town. I had never had a reason to go into this area before. I parked my '57 Volkswagen in front of his house. We got out of the car quickly so that Mr. Cox wouldn't come out and see the piece of junk we were driving. I was afraid he would notice the bald tires or the peace symbol that was standard issue for all VW bugs. I really needed this job, so I didn't want to make any political statements.

I was in awe of the Coxes' house: no broken windows, no peeling paint, a lawn that covered all the dirt in his front yard. It made me see what could be possible with a little luck and a good education. At the same time, it seemed to push those possibilities further from my reach. How would we get from a trailer in a dusty trailer park to a house like this?

Chapter 3

Darrell R. Griffin, Jr., Is Born

A bomb explodes in the men's room at the U.S. Capitol; the Weather Underground Organization claims responsibility. U.S. Army Lt. William Calley is found guilty of twenty-two murders in the March 16, 1968, My Lai Massacre and sentenced to life in prison. A Los Angeles jury recommends that Charles Manson get the death penalty. A lot of bad stuff happens in March of 1971. But one really good thing happens: Darrell Ray Griffin, Jr., is born.

Years later, he would ask me if I named him Darrell because it was cheaper. To this day, I cannot remember why we gave him that name—my name. But I'm glad we did. Having the same name always made us feel closer.

We brought him home to the Brown Top Trailer Park. His sister, Rene, was now sleeping on the fold-out couch-bed in the living room part of the trailer. Skip had a bassinet that Linda got at her baby shower.

August 6, 1971—Stockton
It was near closing time and Mr. Cox had his feet on his desk reading the *New York Times*. I had mixed my last gallon of paint and was cleaning and shutting down the paint machine for the evening. As I walked into the

office to say goodnight to Mr. Cox, I noticed a headline: "'72 Draft Lottery Assigns No. 1 to Those Born Dec. 4." In 1971, anyone who had a selective service lottery number lower than 125 had a good chance of being drafted. The draft lottery number for my birthday, June 21, was 296. This meant that I would never be drafted. I had taken a gamble back in May of 1970 and joined the National Guard. Now I was locked into six years of bimonthly meetings and two weeks of service every summer, but I was pretty sure that I wasn't going to Vietnam. I didn't really mind being in the Guard. It was like a weekend job. I always felt a little guilty about the guys that got drafted and went through basic training with me at Fort Ord. I knew I was going home after basic while they were going to try to stay alive in Vietnam. I would attend NG meetings twice a month and get paid for it. It wasn't much, but since I was making close to minimum wage it definitely helped the family budget.

Winter 1973—Stockton, Brown Top Trailer Park
Linda and I tried to keep it together and make a pleasant home for Skip and Rene, but it wasn't easy. One night we had a really bad argument. I said something to upset Linda, and she threw a jar of Vaseline at me. We started screaming at each other while Rene and Skip sat on the couch trying to watch TV. After about an hour the screaming died down. Linda went to the bedroom and slid the door closed. I sat down between Rene and Skip and gave them each a hug. Rene looked up at me and asked, "Do I have to get married when I get older?"

It was getting cramped in the trailer. Skip and Rene could play out in the front yard until someone drove past our trailer and kicked up dust. When the weather was bad, they had to play inside. Doing homework was impossible at times. While I was sitting at my desk trying to study, Rene and Skip would be playing fifteen feet away, and Linda would be watching TV. It was winter, so the kids had to play inside most of the time.

On a Saturday just after Christmas, I was doing my homework when I heard a knock at the door. It was Mattie Rivas, Linda's mother. She got right to the point: "How would you guys like to move into a bigger place?"

"I would love to," I answered, "but right now this is all we can afford."

"Look, Darrell, I know you don't like to take help from people, but I have a deal for you." She had sold her house and land out on Jack Tone Road and made enough to buy a couple of houses in town. She was going to rent one out. "It looks great on the inside, but the outside needs a lot of work. If you agree to fix it up, I'll let you live in it for what you're paying here."

Given our current situation, it sounded like a good offer. It was a small two-bedroom house just down the street from the Bachelor Adult Bookstore. The backyard was overgrown and looked like a thicket where hobbits lived. But the house itself was huge by our standards. It was newly painted and carpeted. The kids were still sharing a bedroom, but at least they were in a normal house. This didn't stop our bickering— Linda and I were two kids trying to raise two kids, so it was only a matter of time before we started up again.

Cleaning up the property was good therapy. I would work in the yard while Skip and Rene played in the overgrowth. Out behind the house was a corrugated metal shed, which proved to be a perfect place to grow marijuana. I hung some black lights from the ceiling and lined the shed with tinfoil. I had never had a green thumb, but before long the shed was full of six-foot-tall plants.

I invited my sister Sandra and her husband over one weekend for dinner and to sample some leaves from my "garden." I had been working hard and I needed a little rest from school. After dinner we all went out to the garden shed and picked a bunch of leaves. We put them on a cookie sheet, dried them out, and rolled them into joints. I didn't get much homework done that weekend. Soon this became a regular ritual. Then the stress of keeping up with my classes started getting to me, so I picked up the habit of smoking a doobie or two during the week as well. Within three months, I had to drop all my classes at Delta.

One day, my Franklin High School yearbook arrived in the mail. I lit up a joint, grabbed a glass of wine, and started flipping through the pages. How cool, I actually graduated from high school! So now what? I was lousy at skilled-labor jobs. I used to get Grandpa Moxley boiling mad because he would be under the car working on it and ask me for something like a seven-sixteenth box wrench. The instant I heard him yell, "Skip, bring me . . ." I would panic and start rummaging through his toolbox on the garage floor. I could never find what he wanted. Where I grew up, a man was measured by the size of his toolbox and what was inside it. If you had a robust collection of Snap-on or Craftsman tools, you were at the top of your game. Maybe part of the reason I felt inadequate as a young man was that my toolbox had only a few tools, and they were the ones I bought at the local auto supply store's 88-cent bin.

It occurred to me that, since I wasn't very good at skilled labor, maybe I should take college more seriously. Whenever I went to check on Rene and Skip Jr. while they were asleep, I felt guilty. They always looked so peaceful, knowing in their little hearts that Dad had it all together. Dad would be a good provider. Dad wouldn't let them grow up poor. The image of Skip sitting on the couch imitating me as I did my homework—underlining passages, drawing circles around paragraphs, and dog-earing pages—made me smile. I didn't want him to imitate me smoking weed, so one night I just quit.

It wasn't easy. Most of my relatives were stoners. At Christmastime, thirty or forty family members would gather at Grandma and Grandpa's house for the annual gift exchange and Christmas dinner. There was always a room set aside for getting high. It was tough to avoid that room. But then I would talk to some of my cousins about their money difficulties and how their unemployment checks didn't even cover their dope costs and their regular bills. Suddenly it got a lot easier.

May 1975—Turlock, California
Linda and I were still married—barely. I had left San Joaquin Delta Junior College with a B+ average and gone back to school. I was entering my last year at California State University, Stanislaus (CSUS), in Turlock, working toward a

degre in accounting that would lead to my becoming a certified public accountant. I was able to take most of my classes on the Stockton campus of CSUS, but during my last year I had to take all of my classes on the Turlock campus, forty miles away. I moved into the dorm for the last semester so that I could wrap up my degree requirements. Skip and Rene loved to visit the university library. They were already big readers, and we would spend hours there.

This was my last semester, and it was a good thing because I was out of money, out of energy, and out of time. I knew a divorce would have stopped my pursuit of a degree, so I tried to hang on as best I could, but the marriage just collapsed under its own weight. Both Linda and I were eager to move on with our lives. Graduation rolled around and I was totally stoked. It was almost over. I could get a real job. No more dishwasher positions, no more sales clerk positions. I was actually going to be qualified as a "professional." I remember standing in the Stanislaus State University Stadium as Skip and Rene watched me walk across the stage and get my degree. It was one of the biggest rushes I have ever had. It would be our ticket out of poverty, out of doing without. Maybe now I would no longer be considered "white trash." And even if I were still white trash, I'd at least be making more money. I would be white trash with a checking account, credit cards, and a mortgage.

December 1975—Stockton
Linda and I finally filed for divorce. There was a new preacher at my Grandma's church and he had a daughter. Marty

was young and pretty. Grandma thought it was the perfect combination: her grandson the college graduate and a preacher's daughter.

Grandma's church, The Church of God, had about forty parishioners, most of them older than she was. It was the same church I had attended as a child. I hadn't remembered everyone being so old. I think the core member group stayed with the church and grew old with it. It was in the center of an area of Stockton called Little Oakie Town. It got its name from the fact that most of the people who settled there came from Oklahoma during the Dust Bowl era.

I lived down the street from the Bili Liquor Store. You could go there any time of day or night and there would be a number of unemployed men standing around with socks (the preference was white gym socks) in their hands or dangling from their back pockets. This was their gear for sniffing glue. They would put gobs of glue in the socks and stick their noses in them and get so high they would forget their names. Oakie Town didn't have sewers or sidewalks. At times during the winter you could see soap suds bubbling up from the backyards of houses when their septic tanks got full and their washing machines were flushing out the dirty wash water. Another thing about Oakie Town was that it didn't have any minorities. Poor whites tended to live with other poor whites, just as poor blacks tended to live with other poor blacks.

We always felt we'd been forgotten. I remember wishing I was black. If you were black, you had an identity. You had a rallying cry. Mexicans had "Viva la Raza!" and blacks had "Black Power!" As poor whites—"Oakies" or "white niggers," as we were variously called—we were lumped into the white majority. But middle-class and upper-class whites didn't want us in their neighborhoods any more than they wanted blacks or Mexicans.

The Church of God was a Pentecostal, holy-roller, fire-and-brimstone little church full of Oakies. Most of the ministers who came through would stay a year or so and leave once they found that the pickings were pretty slim at this little church, where the sole career aspiration of most of the young men was to become truck drivers. Reverend Laws's kids dressed better than the other kids in the neighborhood, not because the members paid their tithes, but because he worked full-time as a carpet layer and his wife, Bonnie, made most of their clothes by hand. (Reverend Laws used to say he wanted a "silent" offering—he didn't want to hear change rattling; he only wanted dollar bills.)

Marty and I were married by Reverend Laws after a whirlwind courtship. I had just gotten my first professional job at an accounting firm. This was scary. All the other new hires at Bowman, Fong, McKnight, Horst, Hubbard, Anderson, and Murphy Certified Public Accountants looked as if they belonged there. They were dressed in Brooks Brothers suits and had golf clubs in the backseats of their BMWs and Mustangs. I wore plaid polyester sports jackets from Kmart, and drove a primer-painted Ford Maverick that I parked a block away.

The first day all the new hires showed up for work, we were lined up outside of Mr. Horst's office so that he could trot us around and introduce us to the other partners and staff. He was an impeccable dresser and expected the same from his new staff. He went down the row of accountants, shaking our hands and welcoming us by our first names, until he got to me. He may not have been able to remember my name, but I know my Kmart suit and plastic-soled shoes left an impression.

Mr. Horst had a number of tax forms lined up perfectly on the counter outside of his office. While in line with the other accountants, I leaned my hand on a stack of IRS 1040 forms and left a sweaty palm print. He grabbed the form, looked me in the eye for a few seconds, crumpled it up and threw it in a trash can. That's when I knew I would be lucky to survive the week.

Sure enough, a few days later I got a call from Mr. Horst asking me to come to his office. I was hoping that maybe I had crawled out of the hole I dug on my first day and that he wanted to congratulate me. But when I walked in, he said in a somber voice, "Have a seat, Mr. Griffin."

He paused. "Your work this first week has been adequate at best. But you are sloppy. When you draw your lines under figures you are drawing from right to left and leaving the little tail on the left-hand side of the lines when you lift your pencil. I want you to start drawing your lines from the left to the right so that the ending tail, if it is necessary to leave one, is on the right side of the numbers. Do you understand what I am asking?" As I walked back to the bull pen, I wondered why I had switched my major from art to accounting.

December 1976—Stockton
The first thing Marty and I did after getting married was move out of Oakie Town. We found a nice apartment complex,

the Hacienda Inn Apartments. It wasn't exactly the high-rent district, but the complex had no graffiti and almost all of the residents had jobs. Rene and Skip would stay with us every other weekend.

My last weekend in the Army National Guard was in December 1976. I took Skip with me to the armory to turn in my equipment. He was so excited that you would have thought we were going to Disneyland. He got to climb inside a helicopter, explore the supply room where all the weapons were locked up, and watch a bunch of soldiers engaged in a field exercise. He asked me how old he had to be to join the army.

One weekend Linda brought the kids over for what I thought would be their usual visit. She asked me if I could take care of them from now on. There were things in her

life that she needed to get done and it would be better if the kids stayed with us. I immediately said yes, but I wanted to make it legal, so I had an agreement drawn up transferring custody of the kids to me. We had gone through a particularly tough divorce. I was thankful that there were no assets to fight over, which could have made it a lot worse. Rene was seven and Skip was five.

Summer 1981—Turlock

Skip and Rene's half brother and sister, Sommer and Christian, were born while we were living in Stockton. I had gotten a job on the internal audit staff at Foster Farms, a large poultry company in Turlock. It was a fifty-mile drive from Stockton, so we decided to move there. Turlock is a little agricultural town nestled along Highway 99, which runs north and south in the Central Valley of California. When we moved there, Turlock had a population of about twenty thousand. Most of the people in town worked at California State University (known as Turkey Tech) or at Foster Farms, about fifteen miles south on Highway 99.

Marty and I should never have married. A lot of people thought we had a perfect marriage. I was becoming a successful accountant and she was a tall, attractive wife and mother. The truth was the marriage was a bad idea from the beginning. We almost broke it off the day before the wedding, but both of our parents talked us into going through with it. When Skip and Rene came to live with us, it just made things worse. Skip and Marty never got along, and it infuriated her when I took Skip's side in arguments. She also complained that I neglected her; I was always studying for my master's degree. She was probably right. After spending time with the kids, working, and studying, I didn't have a lot of energy left over. Instead of planning to spend the rest of my life with Marty, I was calculating how much, emotionally and financially, it would cost to go our separate ways.

Spring 1984—Turlock

One day that spring I came home to find Marty gone, along with Christian and Sommer. Her parents had helped move her out while I was at work. I was amazed at how many of our accumulated belongings she could remove from the house in such a short period of time. I was thankful that the microwave was built-in or it, too, would have been gone. That night, not having any food in the house or anything to eat it with—Marty had even taken the silverware—we got in the car and went down to Burger King.

We had agreed that Christian and Sommer would go to live with Marty; Skip and Rene would stay with me. Money was a little tight due to divorce attorney expenses, MBA-related expenses, replacing furniture, child support, and the usual costs of raising two teenagers as a single father—but we were happy.

Toward the end of 1984, I hired a bright young Japanese woman named Kim Tomomatsu into the internal audit department at Foster Farms, where I was working as an accountant. One day I got up my nerve and asked her out for lunch. It was Friday, Clam Chowder Day at the Swinging Door. In between my first and second bowl of chowder, I got up the nerve to ask her out on a real date.

That night, when I got home, I told Skip and Rene that I was thinking about asking out a lady at work. I hoped they wouldn't feel it was too soon to start dating since my divorce wasn't even final. They both gave me their blessings. My relationship with Kim quickly became serious. She moved in after a couple of months, and we began to have a normal household, a real home. Our meals were balanced and served at the same time most days, and we seldom dined at Burger King.

One evening Kim went shopping for groceries. Skip picked up the phone. "Dad, it's Mom. She wants to know if you need anything special from the store." Mom. He had called her Mom. When Kim got home, I told her. It turned out he had been calling her Mom for weeks.

We got married a few months later.

Winter 1984—Turlock
One morning, Kim went to her closet to get a coat before she left for work. In a hurry, she flung open the closet door and discovered to her amazement that all of her coats were gone. "Darrell, do you know what happened to my coats?" she called to me.

I looked in the closet and all I saw were empty hangers. "Kim, did you pack them away?"

"Why would I pack them away? It's still cold outside."

"Are you sure that you put all of your coats into the closet?"

"Never mind. I'll ask the kids." A few minutes later, Rene shouted from the yard, "Dad, you have to see this!" I ran outside, and there, lying on the ground, were Kim's missing jackets.

Skip came around the corner and stopped in his tracks the instant he saw the three of us standing there. "All right, all right, I did it," he said as he watched us pick up the jackets.

"You did what?" Kim asked.

"I loaned your jackets to a couple of kids at school."

Shaking my head, I asked, "Why?"

"Because they were cold," Skip said.

"Tell me the whole story," I said as we walked into the house.

"I told them Mom didn't mind loaning them jackets until they could buy their own and that she used to own a clothing store in Los Angeles. I got them all back except for one."

I explained that it was nice that he wanted to help his friends, but that he couldn't just take other people's property, especially his mom's. He knew it was wrong, but he held his ground: it was also wrong, he argued, that these kids had to go to school without coats. "Who really determines what is right and wrong anyway?" he asked.

Skip's questions often had more universal application than simply the matter at hand. It was as if he were filing them away for future use. One day, when he was about twelve, I brought up Plato's dialogue, *Euthyphro*, in which the character Euthyphro is challenged by Socrates to define what he means by "right." If you *pretend* that what you are doing in some particular case was decided not by you, but by someone else, you can create the appearance that you are not responsible. But to say that you are acting in a certain way because of someone else's decision is always a lie. I told him that the government does not decide what is right and what is wrong.

"If the state says a man is declared dead after five years, does this mean the man is dead?" Skip asked.

"Of course not. If he later walks into town, he is obviously still very alive. Right and wrong is defined by self and by society."

It was getting late. Skip and Rene had to get to school, and Kim and I had to go to work. I knew this question would come up again.

About a month later, I was helping Kim do the laundry. I walked into Skip's room to put away some of his clothes and caught a whiff of cigarette smoke. I opened the window and noticed below, behind a row of rose bushes, some cigarette butts scattered around in the dirt. Tucked between his bed and the wall was a pack of Marlboro Reds and a Zippo lighter.

As soon as he got home, I went into Skip's room. He was already doing his homework. This was an unusual sight because he hated doing homework. He loved to read as long as it wasn't part of an assignment. He was always reading. I told him I knew he was smoking. He just looked at me and then looked back at his schoolbook. I told him he was grounded for a month.

The next morning, I opened his bedroom door to wake him up for school. He was gone. I called the police and they said the only thing I could do was file a missing person's report.

Later that day, Skip called home and left a message telling us he was okay and would be back in a couple of weeks. *A couple of weeks?* He wasn't even a teenager. *How would he survive? Where would he sleep? How would he eat?*

That night, we got a call from the Oakland Police Department. They had picked him up trying to sell bags of oregano as marijuana at the Oakland airport. Just as I was arranging to go retrieve him, the police department called again and told me that he had run away. A few days later, he was picked up in Colorado by the police. They told me to come and get my son. By this point I was pretty frustrated, so I told them he got there on his own and he could get home on his own. They sent him back to Oakland.

Skip was pretty upset that I wouldn't pick him up in Colorado, so he told the Oakland police that I had beaten him. They put him into the Child Protective Services (CPS) system and he ended up at a foster home. He had been there for about a month when I got notice of a hearing that I was required to attend in Oakland. I drove the three-hour trip from Turlock to Oakland. The purpose of the hearing was to see if I should get custody of Skip or if he should stay in the CPS system. The attorney for the CPS read from a report where Skip had testified that I had beaten him. I was so furious that I got up to leave the courtroom.

The judge said, "Please sit down, Mr. Griffin. We are not finished with you yet."

"Your Honor," I shot back, "I have nothing to say. Let him stay where he is."

Suddenly Skip sprang to his feet and yelled, "I lied! I lied! I just want to go home with my dad!"

We didn't talk much on the way home. I started to ask Skip some questions about why and how this all happened, but he asked if we could talk about it later. I agreed. I was just happy to have him back.

We never did talk about this episode in Skip's life, but after we got home I went to my library and got out the Bible. I wasn't a Christian in those days, and I read the Bible more as literature than as a guide to life. After blowing off the dust and opening it to the index, I discovered the Bible was replete with exhortations about discipline:

> Folly is bound up in the heart of a boy, but the rod of discipline drives it far away.
>
> —Proverbs 22.12

But did this mean the rod of discipline as a stick or as the entire arsenal that a parent has at his disposal? I wasn't able to find anywhere in the Bible where children were given time-outs or told to stand in the corner or restricted from television. I took this to mean discipline, not beating.

> Do not withhold discipline from your children; if you beat them with a rod, they will not die. If you beat them with the rod, you will save their lives from Sheol ["abode of the dead" in Hebrew].
>
> —Proverbs 23.14–15

A couple of years before this episode, we had taken Skip to a child psychiatrist. I was perplexed as to why he was so intelligent yet had issues with authority and wasn't a very good student. The psychiatrist told us that divorce is difficult on children. He said it was particularly tough on Skip because he felt his mother had left him, and little boys need to have their mothers around in their formative years.

Those who spare the rod hate their children, but those who love them are diligent to discipline them.
—Proverbs 13:24

Skip was testing boundaries. I just had to hang in there until he was able to work through the fact that his mother had left me, not him. Unfortunately, she never visited Skip and Rene, so I had a hard time convincing them that their mother didn't leave me *and* them.

The Lord disciplines those whom he loves, and scourges every child whom he accepts.
—Hebrews 12:6

Scourge is a strong word, but I got the message. I knew I had to keep letting Skip know where the boundaries were and be there for him when he crossed them. I had tried spanking him a couple of times, but it didn't work for either of us. I hated doing it; it felt wrong. Somehow everything I did felt wrong.

It's a good thing Kim came into our lives when she did. The three of us craved a normal family life. We craved stability. Kim was a structured person by nature. She is Japanese. She is an accountant. Skip and Rene at first resisted the structure that she brought into the house, but after a while they began to appreciate it. They were comforted knowing there would always be food in the refrigerator and toilet paper in the bathroom, knowing their laundry would always be done. They noticed that we rarely argued; there wasn't any angry yelling. Our house was turning into a home. Kim would be the one to visit the principal at Skip's school whenever they wanted to have a parent conference—almost a weekly occurrence. Among his offenses: not doing his homework, reading unrelated books during lectures, telling jokes, doodling, talking, taking class discussions off course, throwing pencils into the ceilings, changing the pages of homework assignments on the blackboard . . . The vice-principal explained to us that Skip wasn't a bad kid; he just needed stimulation. He got bored easily.

Our newly assembled family had settled into a comfortable routine. We decided to take the kids to the Great American Theme Park in Santa Clara for the weekend. This was our first real family vacation together. The kids knew all the rides' names from the park's incessant television advertising before we even got to the park. Skip announced, "The ride I'm hitting is the Demon Roller Coaster."

We paid our admission and rode a few of the more sedate rides together. Then Skip asked if he could go off by himself and ride some of the roller coasters. We agreed to meet at five o'clock at the Carousel Columbia at the front of the park.

We gave him some money for snacks and he went running toward the Demon, quickly disappearing into the crowd.

We were at the appointed meeting place right at five, waiting for Skip. He wasn't there. He was probably trying to stretch his time on the rides. Six o'clock rolled around and still no Skip. I went to park security and told them he hadn't shown up. They told me that an hour was nothing to worry about. Then it was closing time—and still no Skip. We again went to park security. They took a report and said that they would alert all of their security personnel. They did a sweep of the park. We eventually left without him. Kim had a "feeling" that he was okay. He had already proven his survival skills. Even so, the drive home was frightening.

Two days after we'd left the park without him, Skip showed up at home as if nothing had happened. He told us that he had met an eighteen-year-old girl who was an exchange student from China. They had spent several hours together at the park, and then gone to her house. She'd given him money for the bus home. Our talk with Skip was brief; we didn't know how to handle this one.

Since I had started working at thirteen and left home at sixteen, I didn't really know what being a teenager was about. By the time I was supposed to be going through the "difficult teenage years," I was already getting up to do midnight feedings, paying rent, and juggling a full-time job and school. Now I'd put another mother figure in front of him—number three. Sometimes I didn't know what my next move would be with Skip, but then he would come up and put his arm around my shoulders, give me a big hug, and start talking about some book he'd just read. These were the moments that kept me going.

It was November 9, 1984, the day after Reagan had beaten Mondale by a landslide. Skip and I were at McDonald's having lunch and talking about the election. Out of the blue, Skip said, "I read somewhere that a lot of voters don't know who they're going to vote for until they get in the voting booth. In Plato's *Republic* he states that only philosophers should be kings. I think voters should have to take a test before they vote. They probably don't even know what a philosopher is."

I was amazed. "Where did you hear about Plato's *Republic*?"

He looked at me, knowing I would love his answer. "I had detention last week. You're supposed to bring your books so you can do your homework. I forgot my books so I pulled down the works of Plato from the teacher's bookcase for something to read."

I suggested he spend less time in detention and more time in class, but I couldn't resist asking him what else he was reading. He mentioned "another cool book"—*1984* by George Orwell. Had I ever read it? He said it kind of reminded him of school: Big Brother always watching; individual expression forbidden; the thought police. And did I remember "The Book," written by one of Orwell's characters in the novel, a revolutionary named Goldstein? One of the points this Goldstein guy made was about war. "Goldstein says that war is important for consuming the products of human labor; if this work were to be used to increase the standard of living, the control of the party over the people would decrease. War is the economic basis for a hierarchical society." Skip was excited. "Pretty heavy, huh?"

Fall 1986—Southern California

In the summer of 1986, we moved to a small town in Southern California. I had always lived in smaller communities and felt it would be better for the kids to live in a more cosmopolitan environment. The entertainment was limited in Turlock. You had your annual turkey race, cosponsored by the local university; my alma mater, California State University; Stanislaus; and Foster Farms. There were a couple of movie theaters in town and the usual cow tipping and whiskey drinking out in the cornfield. That was about it.

Skip had been working hard helping the family move and set up our new house. One night he asked if he could go see a movie. I dropped him off in front of the theater. As I drove off, I saw out of my rearview mirror that a crowd had gathered around a couple of kids who were fighting. Suddenly one kid pulled a knife and made a slashing motion across the belly of the other kid. Blood was gushing out of his abdomen. No one had come forward to help.

Then I spotted Skip. The kid had dropped his coat when he was slashed. Skip tore open the kid's shirt and pressed his jacket against the gaping wound. The kid had heavy tattoos on his arms and neck. My first thought was, *Not here more than a week and we're already caught in the middle of a gang fight.*

The paramedics arrived in what seemed like seconds. Skip had seen me and pushed through the crowd to the car. A few minutes later, we were at Tommy's Hamburgers on Victory Boulevard eating a couple of their famous chili burgers. My heart was racing like a jackrabbit, but Skip seemed calm as he polished off his second burger.

"Skip, aren't you a little nervous after that?"

"Not really, Dad."

I looked over at him and asked, "How can you not be nervous?"

"I'm just not. I did what I had to do because no one else was going to do anything."

Summer 1987—Southern California

Skip was beginning to fill out and grow taller. In the summer of 1987 he started reading martial arts magazines. He would study them from cover to cover. They were lying around his bedroom and all over the house. There were magazines on judo, kempo, shotokan, tae kwon do, lima lama, White Crane kung fu, jujitsu, aikido, karate —you name it.

One day I came home from work early for lunch and noticed that Skip's bed hadn't been slept in. He was gone. He left a note assuring us that he was okay and not far away. He would call us in a few days. We were worried, but we had gone through this type of thing with him before. At least he'd left a note this time.

A couple of weeks later he finally called. Before I could start asking questions, he launched into a well-rehearsed presentation: "Dad, I apologize for leaving again without telling you or asking your permission. I knew you wouldn't give me permission to do what I did. As you know, I have been interested in martial arts for a while. I didn't want to sign up for a program and take forever to get a belt going one day a week. So I found an opportunity to learn from one of the greatest martial artists in the world, Benny Urquidez. He's letting me live in the attic of his gym. I keep the place clean and he trains me, feeds me, and gives me a place to sleep. If you promise not to get mad I'll tell you where I am." He was living in the attic of the Jet Gym a few blocks away. He invited us to come over the following night.

When we got to the gym, Skip introduced us to Benny. Though not physically big, he was a master of the ring, the man responsible for introducing full-contact karate to the United States. In 1978, *Black Belt* magazine voted him fighter of the year.

Skip led us through the gym to a back hallway and pulled a set of stairs from the ceiling. We climbed up the stairs to the attic. The roof was so low that we couldn't stand up unless we were at the apex. We walked hunched over to Skip's living area. There was a mattress, a blanket, and a protein mix cardboard box turned upside down for a table.

"So what do you think?" Skip cleared a place for us to sit on the mattress. "Benny said I could stay here until the end of summer. I promise to come home then."

I looked around and said, "If this is what you want."

Kim hugged him and added, "But you have to promise to come home a couple of nights a week for dinner."

He stood up and asked if we'd like to see him in the ring. We carefully followed him down the narrow stairs and into the gym. He put on his sparring gear and bowed to his opponent. The kid was much bigger than Skip, but not nearly as muscular. It took Skip a few minutes to dispatch him. Tae kwon do is a dignified martial art, but when Skip had his opponent down on the floor, he said, "Say uncle." Skip let him up, and they bowed and hugged each other before stepping out of the ring. I was amazed at how fiercely they battled in the ring and impressed with the respect they showed each other after their mutual pounding. There was no anger in their strikes and kicks, although I could tell a number of them hurt.

At the end of the summer Skip came home.

We could see our boy becoming a man, but in his soul he still had open wounds that had not yet healed. He still had the hurt of his mother leaving him at a young age. I added to it by marrying multiple times. Kim was earning Skip's trust, but he still had demons to deal with. On March 31, 1989, he joined the army.

On his "Statement for Enlistment, United States Army Enlistment Option, U.S. Army Delayed Enlistment Option Program," Skip was promised the following:

1. U.S. Army Airborne
2. U.S. Army Cash Bonus of $6,500.00
3. An MOS (military occupational specialty) of 31M—Multichannel Communications Systems Operator
4. Term of enlistment for six years

It did not go well for him. Skip wasn't ready for the army, and the army wasn't ready for him. He was a good soldier, but he had issues. He made it though the rigors of basic training and airborne school, but then he took to buying his friends whatever they wanted from his enlistment bonus until the bank wouldn't honor his checks. He committed a number of other offenses, the most serious being getting in a fight with a fellow soldier on July 15, 1990. It started as a friendly wrestling match, but Skip lost his temper and it quickly escalated into an intense fight between two men with knives. The official army report states,

In that you did, at Fort Bragg, North Carolina, on or about 15 July 1990, commit an assault upon Specialist

Joseph XXX by placing to his throat a dangerous weapon, to wit: a knife. This is in violation of Article 128, UCMJ.

Skip's career in the army was over. He was given a Field Grade Article 15 and a general discharge from the army.

He had wanted to be a soldier since he was a kid. Now that dream was shattered.

Skip came back home to live with us. We could tell that something was wrong. When he left for basic training, he weighed 210 pounds. When he came home, he had gained thirty pounds of solid muscle. I walked into his bedroom one day and found a prescription bottle sitting on top of his dresser. It was labeled Halotestin and was full of little mint-green pills. I called our family doctor and he said they were steroids.

When Skip got home, he asked me if I had seen his pills. I told him I had flushed them. He stormed out the front door yelling something, and I didn't see him for hours. When he returned, I asked what he was doing with steroids. He said he really hadn't used them all that much and he wouldn't use them anymore. I believed him.

He started combing the classified ads for jobs. He wasn't interested in flipping burgers or washing dishes. Eventually he got a job selling copy machine toners over the phone. This job lasted for a couple of months. Then he got a job at a local lumber company. At the lumberyard he started hanging out with guys who wore rolled bandanas around their heads, answered "Yo" to most questions, and wore their pants low enough so you could see their Fruit of the Looms. He was seldom home and we had no idea where he was most of the time. One day I saw him walking home from work, so I pulled over and picked him up. I asked him where his car was, and without looking at me he said it had been stolen. I dropped the issue because he seemed really jittery. He asked me to let him off a couple of blocks from home. As I pulled away from the curb, I saw him bang knuckles with one of his lumberyard friends. But it was more than a greeting: it was a transaction. One hand was banging knuckles while a small package was being exchanged in the other hand.

When I got home, Kim and I had a long conversation about Skip. I had overheard him referring to crack on the phone with these same "friends," but pretended to myself that I hadn't. We came to the conclusion that this was just a phase he was going through and his way of dealing with the army fiasco. We decided to talk to him together when he got home. But he didn't come home that evening. He did call and say that he was spending the night at a friend's house, but he was so out of it that I couldn't understand what he was saying. I did hear him say "I love you" at the end of our conversation. No matter what was going on, Skip always told us that he loved us.

The next day, I came home from work hoping that Skip would be around so I could talk to him about what had happened the day before. I made a PB and J and carried it over to my recliner in the living room. I couldn't find the remote for the television. As I was looking around for it,

I noticed there was just a dusty outline where the television used to sit. The stereo was also gone. I ran into the bedroom and the television there was gone, too. Whoever did this was in a hurry because the electrical socket in the bedroom still had the television plug in it with about a foot of torn wire hanging from it.

Just as I started to dial Kim, the phone rang. It was the Los Angeles Police Department. They had Skip in custody. He had turned himself in and confessed that he had burglarized the house while we were at work. As I hung up the phone, I felt like someone had just head-butted me in the stomach. My son stole from me. *Was he trying to get back at me for splitting with his mom? Was this a gang initiation? Was he on drugs? What was I supposed to do now?*

I went down to the police station and picked him up. We didn't talk much on the way home. I asked about his car. He confessed he needed money and had sold it. He sold his car that we had just bought a couple of months earlier for two thousand dollars . . . for two hundred dollars. Now he'd sold our TVs. Kim and I talked about it and decided not to press charges. All Skip could say, over and over, was "I didn't mean to hurt you guys." He was sweating profusely and stumbling over his words. Over the next couple of days, he slept all day and was gone a lot at night. Even more worried now, I wondered, *Would counseling help? What if I just go with the flow?* He'd been through a lot of stuff in his life. I didn't want to crowd his space.

A couple of days later, I was out front talking to my gardener about repairing one of my sprinklers when Charlie, my neighbor from across the street, came up to me. "Sorry to hear about your financial difficulties," he said. "Hope you get to stay here in the neighborhood."

"What are you talking about, Charlie?"

"Skip was making the rounds yesterday telling the neighbors about your situation. You know, you and Kim both losing your jobs at the same time. Must be scary. I kicked in five bucks. Widow Betty across the street kicked in another five."

I could not believe what I was hearing. "Charlie, you mean that Skip collected money from all the neighbors by telling you that Kim and I lost our jobs?" I opened my wallet and gave him a five-dollar bill. Then I went around to all the neighbors and paid them back, too.

I stayed up to wait for Skip. He finally came home at two o'clock in the morning. He was in a really good mood. He was talking so rapidly that I could only catch every third or fourth word. He was high, only he didn't smell of marijuana. I told him things weren't working out. I had given him a number of chances to straighten up, but at this point I was only enabling his behavior. I told him he had to go, and to stay away until he could prove to me that he had kicked his drug habit. Tough love was our last chance. He stood up with tears in his eyes, hugged his mom and me, laid his house key on the coffee table, and walked out the front door. After the door closed, Kim and I embraced and cried. Our son had just left our lives. We didn't know if he would make it back.

Chapter 4

Skip Finds an Angel

It was a warm December day in Pasadena, and Diana Ramirez was on her lunch break, driving aimlessly down Colorado Boulevard in her red Mazda RX-7 looking for a place to eat. She only had an hour before she had to be back at her station in women's undergarments at the Macy's in Pasadena. As she sped past the little shops and eateries in this fashionable part of Pasadena, she spotted a guy jogging along the road. She thought to herself, *Nice butt, big shoulders, powerful thighs, very nice package.* Just then he turned and ran into the Union Street drug rehab building. She had a friend who had been in drug rehab and she had gone with her to meetings there for emotional support.

Diana's friend Rebecca called her up at work the following day and asked if she would go with her to rehab to celebrate her fifth year of sobriety. Diana said she would try to find someone to cover her shift. A few minutes after the meeting began, she slid into an empty chair that Rebecca had saved for her. Someone had brought a "birthday cake" to celebrate Rebecca's five years of sobriety. Diana noticed the guy she had seen jogging the day before sitting across from her. Rebecca stood up and gave a short speech about how she became addicted and how she fought her way back with the help of the center. All during her speech Diana and the jogger kept playing eye hockey. Whenever he looked at her she would look away; then she would steal a glance at him and *he* would look away. She liked his smile and his "high and tight military-looking hair cut." He was wearing a white T-shirt with a poster of Bram Stoker's *Dracula*, starring Gary Oldman, Winona Ryder, and Keanu Reeves, emblazoned across the front.

After the meeting, Skip went out on the patio for a cigarette. Diana was trying to decide if she should go up to him when he put out his cigarette in a butt can and came over to her. They introduced themselves and talked awkwardly for a while. He told her he lived at the rehab center, and she told him she had seen him jogging the day before. She invited him out for coffee, but he explained that he had a strict curfew and had to be back in his room by eight o'clock. He walked her back to her car and they talked for as long as they could. When she got home, she saw the message light on her answering machine blinking. It was Darrell, inviting her to the AA dance.

The dance was held at the First Congregational Church a few blocks away from the rehab center. Instead of dancing, they just talked. It turned out they liked the same music: Pink Floyd, Enigma, Mozart, and Bach. They talked about Skip's sobriety, and he told her he hadn't seen his family in a year. Diana had to leave early—her roommates were having a Christmas party. She invited him along. Skip told her that he didn't think the rehab director would give him permission, but the director was the boyfriend of her friend Rebecca and he knew that Diana didn't do drugs or drink, so he allowed Skip to go as long as he was back by midnight. Diana looked at Skip and said, "C'mon, Cinderella."

She took him to her house in the Glendale Hills, where she was living with a gay couple, Bob and Gary. It was a classy little house owned by a friend who was on a concert tour of Asia for a couple of years. Diana was a master at shabby chic. She could turn a discarded dresser found on a curb into what appeared to be a family heirloom. When they arrived, Gary was playing Chopin on the piano, accompanied by a woman playing the violin. Diana liked the way everyone looked at Skip as he entered the room. She watched him as he mingled easily among her friends. She knew she would have to take him back to the center before the clock struck twelve and his pressed black shirt and Levi's turned to rags.

He was heading off to a camp in Castaic for the last phase of his treatment, and wouldn't be allowed to have visitors for the first month. They wrote to each other every day, and when the month was up she came to see him every weekend. The isolation was good for Skip. It allowed him to do a lot of thinking, and it gave him another thirty days without crack, marijuana, or steroids. On his last day, Diana picked him up at the compound. He swung open the door of her car and tossed a small backpack into the backseat. She asked him if he wanted to stop by his barracks so he could pick up his stuff. "That's it," Skip said as he motioned toward the backseat with his thumb.

They found a studio apartment in the back of a garage in Glendale, and Skip got a job at the Jack LaLanne gym in Pasadena, not far from where they were living. They were sitting around one weekend when he announced to Diana that he wanted to drive by his mom and dad's house. They pulled into our cul-de-sac and sat in front of the house for half an hour. Finally Diana said, "Darrell, why don't you just go up to the door and see if your dad is home?" He started crying and said, "I can't." He turned the key in the ignition and drove slowly past the house and onto the freeway home.

Later that week Skip decided to call us. They had just finished dinner when Diana got up and handed Skip the phone: "Call them." He dialed with Diana's arms around his shoulders.

Kim picked up the phone. When she heard his voice, she waved her hand at me, pointed to the phone, and mouthed, "It's Skip." She continued speaking into the phone: "It's good to hear your voice. You sound good. We miss you. We love you." She could hear him crying on the other end of the line.

"Mom, can I talk to Dad?"

She looked at me and repeated his question out loud: "Can you talk to Dad?"

"Not now," I mouthed.

"Skip, I don't think he's ready yet. Can you call back in a couple of days? Leave your number and he may call you."

A couple of days later Skip and Diana called my office. We talked briefly. I told Skip I wasn't ready yet, but soon. I had a lot of things to think about. I wanted to make sure that Skip had changed. I come from a family of drug users, and I've seen how difficult it can be to really turn your life around.

A week later, we called and asked them to meet us for dinner at the Bicycle Club in Burbank the following weekend. Kim and I got there first and were standing outside waiting for them. It had been a year since the day I told Skip to leave the house. They saw us as they drove into the parking lot and waved vigorously. I could see the smile on Skip's face that I loved to see when he was a kid. My heart started to pound hard like the stereos in the low-rider cars that sometimes pull up behind you on the streets of Los Angeles. Without saying a word, he gave me the big bear hug that I had missed for so long. The sweet smell of Old Spice was great. Standing with his arm around Kim, he introduced Diana to us. He looked really good.

At dinner, the conversation was easy. We didn't talk of the incident that had led to our estrangement. It was history. Kim and I could tell that Skip and Diana were in love. While we ate, we listened to them describe the life they had made with each other. Skip had changed jobs a couple of times, but he was working full-time. Diana had put them on a budget and he was starting to clear up the pile of debt he had accumulated during his "dark" period. Later, Diana told us that on the day of the dinner Skip was more nervous than she had ever seen him. He wanted to make a good impression, so they had gone and bought him some new clothes for the occasion.

Skip and Diana came over to our house for Thanksgiving. Skip was solidly back in the family, and Alexis, his little sister, had just been born. Telling us they had an announcement to make, Skip and Diana called us into the living room and had us sit down. They had decided to get married. They didn't want a big wedding. They just wanted Diana's parents and us to go to the courthouse with them. I wanted them to have a real wedding. I couldn't remember the last time someone in the family got married without being in the teens or pregnant. They agreed.

"Dad, I got another tattoo." Skip pulled down the neck of his T-shirt. It was a Japanese character—the symbol for "root," he explained. "Dad, my life is now rooted."

On March 9, 1994, Skip and Diana were married at a restaurant on a hill overlooking the San Fernando Valley. My sister Sheila commented after the ceremony, "Wasn't it great that none of the bridesmaids or the bride were wearing maternity dresses?"

As a parent I had been sporadic about taking the kids to church. Skip was always questioning God, religion, existence. He was on his way home from work one evening when he walked past the First Southern Baptist Church of Glendale at 725 North Central. He stopped, walked up the steps, and knocked on the front door of the church. Barbara Bacon, the wife of Pastor Fred Bacon, the music pastor at the church, opened the door. As she recalled it, Skip said, "I would like to be saved tonight. How do I go about it?" She invited him in. They prayed with him and he accepted the Lord.

Skip went home that night and told Diana that he wanted to start attending church. "Darrell, I'm Catholic. I've never been to a Protestant church." After considerable discussion, she agreed to go with him. On Sunday, August 21, 1994, they were baptized together by immersion. Thus began Skip's tumultuous relationship with God.

Skip was still bouncing around between jobs at fitness clubs and home supply stores. He stayed employed but hated his jobs. He couldn't decide whether he wanted to be a police officer or an emergency medical technician (EMT). That summer he called to tell me he wanted to join the National Guard. I asked him if he remembered my time in the Guard. I reminded him that I had only joined to avoid being sent to Vietnam, but it was a different world back then. He told me that he felt something inside of him that made him want to do something for his country. He couldn't explain it; it was just there. He believed that able-bodied citizens should have to give a couple of years of service to their country, if not in the military then through civil service.

He was reading Evan Thomas's book, *John Paul Jones: Sailor, Hero, Father of the American Navy*. Born in Scotland to a father who labored as a gardener, Jones was widely recognized as the first American naval hero. He enlisted with the British Navy, but he grew disgusted at the cruelty of the slave trade and resigned his commission. He eventually ended up in the newly founded Continental Navy—the precursor of the United States Navy. A lot of people didn't like Jones, according to his biographer, and for good reason; John Adams described him as "leprous of vanity," and meant no compliment when he called him "the most ambitious and intriguing officer in the American Navy." But he was a courageous defender of his adopted country, and his hatred of tyranny made him "willing to fight to the death for freedom from despotism," according to Thomas. "He fought for a world in which men might advance by their merits and drive, and not be pegged by their birth or place."

Skip and I discussed the book with great intensity. Did Jones do what he did for humanity or to satisfy his lust for power and fame? Did it really matter as long as the results were the same? Could he have accomplished the deeds he did for humanity without his ego-driven personality? Skip and I agreed that it didn't really matter. What was important wasn't his motive, but his actions.

That summer, Skip joined the California National Guard. He accepted a one-year active duty assignment that required him and Diana to move to Lompoc, California, where they lived on Vandenberg Air Force Base. Skip's main assignment while he was stationed at Vandenberg was called Operation Grizzly. This required him to spend a substantial amount of time patrolling the Mexican border. He finally admitted to himself that even if the Guard were necessary for our defense system, it wasn't for him. When his year was up, he decided not to stay on active duty with the Guard. He and Diana moved in with us for a few months until they both could find jobs.

Shortly after they moved into a place of their own, Skip started a Bible studies group, inviting people at work, old friends, and members of his church. They met weekly, and soon it grew by word of mouth to about twenty people. Skip would pick a topic that he felt everyone needed to hear about. He would then spend hours after work each day developing lesson outlines and notes.

When his friend Fred Bacon was diagnosed with cancer, Skip filled in for him as pastor when Fred was too ill to stand in the pulpit. During his final days, Skip and Diana went to visit him at the hospital. Fred was a strong man and it bothered Skip to see him lying in bed near death. "Darrell, I am pretty close to traveling down a road I have not been down before." Skip said, "If any man is ready, you are," and squeezed his hand. The next time he was with Fred was as one of his pallbearers.

Skip was getting tired of drifting from job to job and wanted to start building a professional career. While working these stopgap jobs, he enrolled in the EMT training program at Pasadena City College and got hired by an ambulance company in Compton called American Medical. He quickly got used to hearing shots when he responded to accidents. He saw so many gunshot wounds that he was soon able to identify the caliber of weapon.

Michael Smythe, a clerk at the Archives Bookshop in Pasadena, met Skip in 1999 when he came into the store. Archives sells only religious and philosophy books. The minute you open the heavy glass doors, you know you're in a highly specialized bookstore; you can smell the dusty pages of the antiquarian books. The floor-to-ceiling shelves are labeled Bibles, Biblical Studies, Theology, Philosophy, Church History, Biography, Ministry, and Mission.

Michael has a vivid memory of the day that he met Skip. They were standing in the theology aisle, and Michael remembers thinking at first that it was he who was showing Skip something that might interest him. Suddenly Skip launched into a full-scale lecture involving Karl Barth, the double predestination of John Calvin, "the freedom of God to be God," and Soren Kierkegaard's "teleological suspension of the ethical." This is when Michael resorted to the eschatological and relational themes in Jürgen Moltmann's theology.

Michael realized, as he delicately put it, that he was dealing with someone more intelligent than his bullying manner of argument made him seem. Skip was "big, strong, aggressive, and at the same time equally accessible and vulnerable." The debate raged for several minutes, at which point the combatants withdrew from the field of philosophical combat and amicably parted company. They both knew they had made a new friend.

Skip was with American Medical for about three years. Almost every day was filled with danger and excitement. The one thing he couldn't stand was responding to calls that involved abused children. There was the baby who had been beaten to death by his mother's drunken boyfriend, and then the kid with cigarette and rope burns over most of his lifeless body. One time he had to fish a newborn out of a toilet because the mother was too high to know she had even given birth.

Skip called me to talk about the idea of reapplying for the police department or the army. I asked if he would consider a third option: coming to work for my company. I promised I would pay him three times whatever he would be paid in the army. He didn't have to think about it long. "Dad, I love you and it would be fun working with you, but can you imagine me sitting behind a desk? It would drive me crazy!" I knew he was right. He wasn't cut out to be a desk jockey. But I was worried, like any parent, especially about the army:

was he sure that he wanted to pursue such a dangerous job in an uncertain world? "Dad, I'm not afraid of becoming involved in war as much as I would be afraid of having an uneasy conscience about living in security while other men are dying for principles in which I very much believe." It was a quote, he told me, but he couldn't remember from where. It was Reinhold Neibuhr.

He knew that the issues he had when he was in the army the first time would cause him problems, especially the question on the application that asked: "Have you ever used drugs before?" He was afraid that if he answered the question honestly he would automatically be disqualified. Despite his fears, he started the process of applying for the police department and the army at the same time. The one that came through first would be the direction he would go. This was in May 2001.

He signed his army contract on July 2. He was officially promised the following:

- Military Occupation—11B10—Infantry
- Signing Bonus—$5,000
- Initial Duty Station—Fort Lewis, Washington

That summer Diana and Skip loaded up their car and drove to Fort Lewis.

Chapter 5

A Just War?

Skip was initially assigned to Company B, First Battalion, 5th Infantry Regiment, of the 1st Brigade in the 25th Infantry Division of the United States Army. Based on his prior service he was an E-4 when he got to Fort Lewis. When his mom asked what "E-4" meant, he said "Not-a-sergeant-yet." There was no housing available when they got there, so they had to live off base.

Diana remembers the day that Skip stumbled upon what would become the cornerstone of his library. They were in Half Price Books, a used bookstore in Tacoma that he liked to frequent. Skip said, "I'll find you in a while," kissed the top of her head, and headed straight for the philosophy section. They weren't there five minutes when he came up to her with that look of "I found something I really want." He led her over to the treasure he'd found: a set of *Great Books of the Western World*. He pulled a couple of volumes down. As he rubbed his hand over the spine of volume 23, *Machiavelli and Hobbes*, he said, "This set of books is just a hundred dollars. I've always wanted it." He stood there holding the two volumes in his hands. "So get them," Diana said. He pulled three more volumes down from the top shelf and said to Diana, in a state of high excitement, "Hold these, so no one else can try to buy the set." As he placed the last volume in a shopping cart, he opened it and sniffed the page. Part of Skip's book-buying ritual was to open the potential purchase and smell it. He loved the way books smelled. He grabbed the cart and rapidly pushed it to the checkout counter. When they'd loaded his new acquisition into the car, Skip said to Diana, "You drive," and settled into the passenger seat to explore his goldmine.

Great Books of the Western World was originally published in the United States in 1952 by Encyclopædia Britannica. In fifty-four volumes, *Great Books* covers categories that include drama, economics, ethics, fiction, history, mathematics, natural science, philosophy, poetry, politics, and religion. In 1990 a second edition of *Great Books* was published to include six more volumes covering the twentieth century. This was the edition Skip now owned, and it became his college education, his personal BA.

It was through the *Great Books* that Skip immersed himself in Socrates, Plato, and Aristotle. Of particular interest to him was Plato's allegory of the cave in *The Republic*. In this story, prisoners have been chained in a cave since childhood. Their arms, legs, and heads are all chained in one direction so that the only thing they can see is the wall they face. Behind the prisoners is an enormous fire, and between the fire and the prisoners is a raised walkway. Various shapes are paraded on this walkway that cast shadows on the wall. Behind the cave is a road with the sounds of busy traffic. Thinking these sounds are coming from the shadows they see day in and day out, the prisoners engage in a game of naming the shadows.

These named shadows are their only reality. Their rank in the cave is based on how fast they can recall the names of the shapes. One of the prisoners is able to break his bonds and walk out of the cave. At first he's disoriented by the sunlight. He looks up at the sun, the thing that creates the shapes he sees. Once enlightened, the prisoner goes back into the cave to free his fellow prisoners—but they don't want to be freed. Returning to the cave puts the freed prisoner in the position of having to readjust again, staggering around in the dark until he regains his eyesight. His confusion persuades the chained prisoners that he's been ruined by his brief episode of freedom.

Skip's take on Plato's allegory was that reality and truth are based on perception. Mine was that people are frightened of things outside their comfort zone. We talked about it endlessly.

Capt. Gene Agustin was Skip's first company commander. He remembers the day Skip first came into his office. "I knew he was different. He was bigger and more fit than most of the men in my unit." What really blew the captain away was that his tattooed, tough-looking new recruit's favorite subject was philosophy.

On September 11, 2001, at 8:46 a.m. (EST), suicide hijackers crashed American Airlines Flight 11 into the North Tower of the World Trade Center in New York City. Seventeen minutes later, at 9:03 a.m., a second team of hijackers crashed United Airlines Flight 175 into the South Tower, which collapsed and disintegrated at 9:59 a.m. At 10:28 a.m., the North Tower collapsed.

I tried to call Skip at Fort Lewis. I knew that this inconceivable event was totally going to change what it meant to be in the army. When I dialed the phone I kept getting "all circuits are busy." Finally I got through. Diana answered the phone. She told me that Skip was out in the field on a training exercise in Yakima and wouldn't be back for a few days.

When he got home he gave me a call. The first words out of his mouth were, "We're going to war. I don't know with whom but we are going to war. There is no way that someone is coming into the United States, killing thousands of people, and the president is not going to bring in the army."

We had our typical small talk about Mom and his little sister Alexis and little brother Jordan, but we didn't have our hearts in it. We both knew that terrorists had killed thousands of innocent people and invaded our sovereign space, as well as our sovereign souls. As Skip put it, Americans now woke up each morning with what felt like a chunk of cement in their stomach—the sensation of fear. Now we knew there were people who hated us and wanted to kill us. We knew Bush was going to take our country to war. We has been attacked, so someone had to pay.

Six days after the events of September 11, President George W. Bush identified Osama bin Laden as the prime suspect in the attacks. The stage was set. On October 7, the United States and Great Britain started bombing Afghanistan.

Skip reminded me that the terrorist attack on the World Trade Center wasn't the only time terrorists had tried to get at the West through terrorist acts. He had compiled a list of other attacks that had occurred before 9/11: the bombing of the Marine barracks in Beirut on October 23, 1983; the TWA hijacking on June 14, 1985; the Pan Am 103 bombing on December 21, 1988; the World Trade Center bombing on February 26, 1993; the attack on the USS *Cole* on October 12, 2000. Whether or not the war about to be waged was just, it was virtually certain that the West would keep getting hit by radical Islamic terrorists. The "war on terror" we now faced was harder to evaluate than a war that had a beginning, middle, and end. As Skip put it, we had to "draw a line in the sand somewhere before we didn't have any more sand. I would rather establish a battlefield in Iraq than in the streets of Los Angeles. I would rather take the battle to them."

Chapter 6

Preparing for War

When Skip got to Fort Lewis, the army was going through a major transition from its classic light-infantry organization to a more mobile quick-reaction organization with built-in flexibility for urban combat. In 1999, Gen. Eric Shinseki, the army chief of staff, came to the conclusion that the United States Army could not meet the challenges of the post-Cold War era. Armored and mechanized infantry units were too heavy and depended too much on maintenance (mechanics, fuel trucks, and ammunition handlers) to be rapidly deployed to hot spots around the world. The army units such as Airborne that had been rapidly deployable in the past lacked the firepower to be effective in the new challenges of urban warfare.

The answer was the Stryker, a lightning-fast, eight-wheeled vehicle that could transport eleven soldiers (including a squad leader, vehicle commander, driver, and eight men) through sand, swamps, and tight city streets. It weighed nineteen tons but could cruise at sustained speeds of sixty miles per hour. It had the latest battle-field communications technology to keep in touch with dismounted soldiers, other Strykers, helicopter support teams, and their forward operating base (FOB). Skip would say it was designed to deliver maximum lethality and rapidity to any battle situation.

The decision to transform the army into a quick-reaction fighting force using Strykers was made before they were actually available. The 3rd Brigade of the 2nd Infantry Division (3–2) at Fort Lewis was the first brigade to make the transformation, followed by Skip's unit, the 1st Brigade of the 5th Infantry Division (1–5), which started training light armored vehicles (LAVs) borrowed from the Canadian Army.

Skip was now part of a Stryker battalion that could deploy anywhere in the world within ninety-six hours. Their job was to protect the soldiers inside from small-arms fire and from rocket-propelled grenades (RPGs) and allow them to engage the enemy at close range. As with any new device, Strykers did have their negative points. It was quickly determined that improvised explosive devices (IEDs) could rip the undercarriages of Strykers apart like cans of tuna. And the Strykers weren't cheap. They appeared to be a work-in-progress. A number of soldiers would end up dying in them because of their initial design faults. General Dynamics, their manufacturer, finally got most of the bugs worked out, but a twenty-dollar homemade IED could still stop a Stryker and kill all the soldiers inside.

One question I had was: why not take some Strykers and test them with real explosives, in every dangerous situation conceivable, without soldiers inside, rather than wait to secure the vulnerability data from incidents in real combat situations? I'm sure this was in part because General Dynamics was a big company and it was more cost-effective to perform these tests in the field. Strykers cost an estimated $1.5 million each. Still, all the soldiers I talked to swore by them—and these were the guys who had bullets flying at them.

Skip always seemed to gravitate to other soldiers who were passionate about philosophy. For Skip there was a thin line, if any, between theology and philosophy. One day in late 2002, he dropped by the office of Capt. Michael Klein, chaplain for his brigade, for a chat and to borrow a book from his library. Skip appreciated Capt. Klein's willingness to talk philosophy and loan books to him.

Skip had been studying the writings of the early followers of the Christian church. The last couple of books he borrowed from Capt. Klein were volumes from *The Ante-Nicene Fathers*. Capt. Klein's set had been a gift from his parents when he completed seminary. Klein told me, "This set only occupied my shelves and never made it out of the bookcase except when Griff [Skip's army nickname] would borrow it. I could not in good conscience keep the set. I was compelled to be a good steward of knowledge and pass the set on to your son."

On March 18, 2003, Skip called me to discuss the ultimatum that Bush had given to Saddam: leave within forty-eight hours or face "military conflict commenced at a time of our choosing." "Dad, you know he's not going to leave. Why should he? Where would he go? He's been through a U.S. attack once already."

He called me again as soon as the news hit the airwaves. "We did it," he said. We had launched a preemptive attack against another legitimate country. We had started the war.

Skip and I talked for a long time: Should we have invaded Iraq when we did? Should we have applied more reason to the situation (or at least gathered more evidence) before we started shooting?

Two days later, on March 20, the "coalition of the willing" (U.S.—300,000; UK—45,000; Australia—2,000; Poland—200; Romania—278) launched its bombing campaign in Baghdad against Saddam's palaces and ministries.

Once Skip got into the habit of writing in his journal, he became very disciplined about it. He had an impressive knowledge of the political and historical complexities of the situation in the Middle East, and of the perils that awaited us:

> *One could go on indefinitely concerning the various intrigues and nuances of Arab loyalties and trajectories pertaining to how they relate to each other individually and collectively. On the collective level, we must know whether or not the Muslim world is driven by Arab nationalism atomized into their individual boundaries or whether or not pan-Islamic aspirations invisibly and potentially could unite them all together into one far-reaching religious/geo-strategic hegemony. One must take into consideration that in the religion of Islam, Muslims look for G-d in the very history of their affairs, individually and collectively. Their sacred scripture, the Quran, gives them an historical mission. Their chief duty in the beginning of Islam was to create a just community in which all members,*

even the most weak and vulnerable, were treated with absolute respect. The experience of building such a society and living in it would give them intimations of the divine, because they would be living in accordance with G-d's will. A Muslim must redeem history, and that means that state affairs are not a distraction from spirituality but the stuff of religion itself. The political well-being of the Muslim community, however it is interpreted right now, is a matter of extreme importance. Where is the seat of Islam? The caliphate resided in various parts of the Middle East beginning first with the caliphate of Abu-Bakr who united all the tribes of Arabia in 632–4 A.D. Now, the Muslim world is fragmented with no seat of spiritual or political consolidated power. Like any religious ideal, it was almost impossibly difficult to implement in the flawed and tragic conditions of history. After each failure in their collective history of civil wars, assassinations, and infighting, Muslims had to get up and begin again. Muslims have developed their own rituals, mysticism, philosophy, doctrines, sacred texts with commentary, laws, and shrines like anyone else. But all these religious pursuits sprang directly from the Muslims' frequently anguished contemplation of the current political affairs of Islamic society.

Has Al Qaeda responded to a perceived threat to Islam? Do they know something about the West that Western societies know nothing of, or is Islam breathing its last breath before the secular world crushes it like all other religions? Christianity with its "mega-churches,"

Zionism, and faddish adherence to the teachings of Buddha; religion has finally seen its demise on its own. According to the center of gravity in Islam, if state institutions do not measure up to the Quranic ideal, if their political leaders are cruel or exploitative, or if the Dar al-Islam is humiliated by perceived irreligious enemies, a Muslim could feel that his or her faith in life's ultimate purpose and value is in jeopardy. Therefore, every effort must be expended, including jihad, to put Islamic history back on track, or the entire religious enterprise will fail, and life will be drained of meaning, possibly invalidating their religion. Politics is, therefore, what Christians would call a sacrament: it is the arena in which Muslims experience their god and which enables the divine to function effectively in the world. Consequently, the historical trials and tribulations of the Muslim world—political assassination, repeated bouts of civil war, invasion, colonialism, and the rise and fall of ruling dynasties—are not divorced from the interior religious quest, but are the essence of the Islamic vision.

The Muslim psyche is immersed in the underlying tendency to meditate upon current events of any given time and upon past history as a Christian would contemplate an icon. Today the term "Islamic Fascism" is being used in an attempt to quantify the global war on terror. Whether or not the Muslim world embodies this label one cannot say, but we must consider the fact that an account of merely the external history of the Muslim people cannot be of mere secondary interest, since one of the chief characteristics of Islam is and always has been its sacralization of history. We cannot think in either/or terms when attempting to appease the combatants in the ongoing civil war that started the day we invaded Iraq; we just didn't know it yet. Sunni and Shia alike see their god Allah as playing out his will in history.

The brass ring can only be obtained by figuring out how to make all of the shifting influences coalesce into one unified agenda that will satisfy all the players in this game. We must still remember that when all is said and done, whether we win or lose, we must still potentially have to explain to the world why we invaded the country of Iraq in the first place.

Now that we were actually at war, Skip was thinking a lot about the realities of combat—what it would be like on the ground in Iraq. He was troubled by the prospect of civilian casualties. From his journal:

War efforts should be directed only toward combatants, and not noncombatants caught in circumstances they did not create. The prohibited acts include bombing civilian residential areas that include no military target and committing acts of terrorism or reprisal against civilians. An attack or action must be intended to help in the military defeat of the enemy, it must be an attack on a military objective, and the harm caused to civilians must not be excessive in relation to the real military advantage anticipated.

> *Total trust in diplomacy alone to thwart the ideologues who worship tyranny is akin to the defense of justice without power which is nothing less than impotence. However, total trust in preemption without diplomacy is akin to the exercise of power without justice, which is nothing less than tyranny. But what do we make of the concept that "war is the continuation of diplomacy by other means?" (Clausewitz)*

In the summer of 2003, Skip decided to take some time off from the daily rigors of training for war and visit his mom and me in Southern California. He and Diana drove down from Fort Lewis, nonstop.

He brought a couple of his guns with him, so we decided to go to a target range a few blocks from the house. Kim and Diana had never been to a shooting range before. Kim had never even seen a gun up close that wasn't under glass until she saw the Colt 45 that Skip had brought home from Fort Lewis. When we walked into the shooting area, it felt like being in a bunker. The range was all cement, including the floor, walls, and ceiling, with no windows. We put on headsets to protect our hearing and rented two lanes. Each lane had a trolley system that enabled us to adjust the distance from our target. Kim is about a hundred pounds and four feet eleven. The safety glasses and ear protectors were too big for her.

Skip had loaded seven brass-tipped .45 shells into a clip and shoved the clip into the handle until it clicked. He took off the safety and pulled back the top of the gun, loading a shell into the chamber. "It's live and deadly," he said as he showed Kim how to hold it. The 45 looked huge in her hands. (It actually looks big in everyone's hands.) Skip showed her how to hold the chunk of steel in both hands and squeeze off each shot. Kim aimed and squeezed off the first clip. Bits of concrete went flying.

Skip took the gun, dropped out the clip, and put in a new one. "This time open your eyes and aim the way I showed you." She was a natural. Every one of her shot patterns after that first clip was tighter than the rest of ours, including Skip's. Guns were a big part of his life, so having them in our hands and firing them somehow made us feel closer to him. I felt a weird connection to the weapon when I fired it. It became part of me. Holding a gun in your hands makes you feel a little taller, a little less vulnerable in the world. Guns are seductive.

After a couple hours of shooting, Skip and I grabbed brooms and swept up all the spent shell casings. He asked me if I knew how to clean my new gun, reminding me that it should be cleaned after each use. It was as if it was now part of the family. "If you don't treat her right, you might not be able to depend on her when you need to," he joked.

Later that summer, Skip was in Yakima, Washington, a huge military reserve a couple of hundred miles east of Fort Lewis. The temperatures were in the triple digits. His unit had been practicing field maneuvers, acting as the enemy for the 3–2 brigade. His platoon leader made the unilateral decision to take the platoon down to the Columbia River so the men could take a swim and cool off. To get to the river they had to go down a treacherous switchback road that descends about a thousand feet. Skip was driving one of the LAVs for the platoon. This was supposed to be one of those "below-the-radar, better-to-ask-for-forgiveness-than-ask-for-permission" type of excursions.

After the lieutenant felt the men had had enough cooling-off time, he told Skip to turn the LAV around for the climb back up the road. Skip took the LAV into the river to turn it around in the water and pull it back around to climb up the cliff. As he was in the river the LAV sunk into three feet of mud. LAVs are meant to float, but Skip had forgotten to put in the water plugs so it quickly filled with water. The platoon leader panicked and made the decision to bring another LAV down the bad road to pull Skip's LAV out of the river. As the second LAV started down, it lost its footing and rolled seven times, about two hundred feet, down the cliff. Fortunately no one was hurt.

Col. Todd McCaffrey, the battalion commander, called the lieutenant and Skip on the carpet. He was furious that the lieutenant had put the lives of soldiers in danger. "What the hell were you thinking?" There were other issues: damage to military equipment; trying to cover up the mistake; errors in judgment; the fact that they had strayed onto Indian reservation land. The platoon leader was severely reprimanded and Skip got a counseling statement put in his military file. "Griff was very dialed in, very aggressive on the battlefield," Col. McCaffrey told me. "But sometimes he reacted before he thought."

The soldiers of the 1–5 Infantry knew they were going to Iraq soon because the 3rd Brigade was on its way there. Their "train up" for Iraq included training at Yakima; the Military Operations Urban Training (MOUT) site at Fort Lewis, the army's largest urban combat training center; practical exercises and evaluation at the National Training Center (NTC) at Fort Irwin, California; and training and evaluation at the Joint Readiness Training Center at Fort Polk, Louisiana, in March of 2004, just months before Skip was deployed to Iraq.

There was normally a certain amount of horseplay and kidding around during train ups, but not this time. Skip's unit knew it was training for deadly assignments that were only a few months away. The training allowed the soldiers to get familiar with desert terrain—operating in Iraqi and Afghan villages, or at least in lots of sand—and to get a sense of what it would be like to fight as coordinated units in a hostile environment. Skip said: "The training was as good as you can get, but you knew the guys with rags on their heads [the simulated enemy] were guys that normally worked at the local 7-Eleven and they didn't want to kill you."

An e-mail from Skip before he went to the National Training Center at Fort Irwin, California:

From: Darrell Griffin, Jr.
Sent: Sunday, January 28, 2004
To: Darrell (DAD) Griffin
Subject: Trainup

We are getting ready to go to the NTC trainup for desert warfare. Here are some of my thoughts I have entered into my journals:

A military code of morals develops strength of character, prevents the masculine type from becoming soft and effeminate and imparts to cruel instincts a dialectical character of violent nobility.

There can be no perfect, ideal state, for every state means rule of one set of men over others.

From the moral point of view power ought to be regarded as a duty and burden and not as a right and a privilege.

"Nations may fight for 'liberty' and 'democracy' but they do not do so until their vital interests are imperiled."
- Niebhur

I called Skip to discuss his e-mail. We had both arrived at the same conclusion: Man is by nature a cruel animal whose cruelty is kept in check (not always as evidenced by history) by the need to function effectively and efficiently in a group (society). A military code of morals dictates how the military should conduct itself collectively and individually. The code legitimizes this cruel nature and imparts to it a certain sense of nobility. The desire for nobility, as evidenced by a military code of morals, evolves our cruel instincts into something more than their basic crude roots in our human nature. We talked of the need for a strong, disciplined army, but also strong and disciplined leaders in our government. We both agreed that we have a strong and disciplined army, but neither of us felt that way about our government.

The 3rd Brigade of the 2nd Infantry Division stationed at Fort Lewis was about ready to come home from Iraq and be replaced by the 1st Brigade of the 25th Infantry Division, Skip's unit. Skip asked his mom and me if we could come up and visit him before he shipped out in October 2004. He suggested I make a log of our visit so that he could read it in Iraq whenever he needed to be reminded about what normal life was like. Here's a summary of the emails that I sent to Skip:

8/22/04
Tonight I had a conversation with you. You said that your "A," "B," "C" duffel bags are packed and ready to send to Iraq... Diana is having a tough time dealing with the whole idea of your going to Iraq. I was thinking that I don't have a hard time with you going to Iraq. I have a hard time thinking of you going to Iraq as a soldier. If you had to go to Iraq, I would probably prefer you go as a reporter.

8/28/04
It is 8:00 p.m. West Coast time and I am having a hard time thinking about my son going into the most dangerous place on Earth – Iraq. I have never done anything to honor the family name, but you will. You tell me that I have done an incredible honor to the family by getting a good education and a good job and finally taking the Griffins off welfare. All this pales in comparison to what you are now doing.

I love you more than you will ever know. I have always known that you are destined for more than I could possibly achieve. You were born for greatness that I could only dream about. We both love America, but you are man enough to prove it.

9/10/04–9/12/04

It was a hard trip to make, but I would have gotten to Fort Lewis even if I had to crawl to get there. After dinner, you broke out a couple of bottles of wine and we started drinking and discussing philosophy. The main topic was Descartes and his proof of God's existence. I told you a lot of Descartes' thoughts were based on the 11th-century philosopher St. Anselm. I told you that I had only read a little of Anselm, so you got up and went to your library and got Descartes Selections by Ralph Eaton and St. Anselm's "Proslogium/ Monologium/ Cur Desu Homo/ Gaunilo's In Behalf of the Fool."

You traded these books to me for "Remembering Heraclitus" by Richard Geldard. There are few philosophy books I have ever mentioned that you didn't have an intimate understanding of and probably owned.... When I got up the next morning my head felt like there was a freight train going through it and it derailed.... I was also looking for a digital camera so that you could take lots of pictures for a proposed book that chronicles the thoughts of a father and a son when the son is in a combat zone.... We also rented two films. One was Hidalgo and the other one was South Park's "Passion of the Jews."

We then went out to look at your Stryker vehicles. The gates were not locked so we were able to take some pictures of all of us in front of the Strykers. You told me that you were going to use 3rd Brigade's Strykers that were already in Iraq. 3rd Brigade was returning in 2 weeks. After we visited the Strykers, we went to the place where you normally worked.

It was a little eerie since everything was already packed up in boxes and much if it already sent to Iraq. We visited some of your men in their barracks. We were surprised how young they were.

After this we went into town to the Half Price bookstore. I bought two books: "The Portable Nietzsche," edited and translated by Walter Kaufmann, and "Moral Grandeur and Spiritual Audacity," by Abraham Joshua Heschel, a collection of essays edited by his daughter. You bought "Hammer of the Gods," by Nietzsche (Apocalyptic Texts for the Criminally Insane), compiled, translated and edited by Stephen Metcalf.

9/19/04

I talked to you tonight on the phone. We discussed a little about your thoughts. You said that you feel the war cannot be won. I told you that I heard that a group of Republican senators have just talked to Bush to tell him that our strategy is all wrong. I told you that they told Bush that we need to get the insurgents in line NOW or we will lose the war. As an afterthought, I feel, and higher up leaders in the U.S. feel, that we cannot lose the war in Iraq as it will be a loss to terrorism. There is no option but to win the war in Iraq.

We agreed to talk again in a couple of days. You seemed calm, but as your dad I know that you are scared. Not scared in a wimpy way, but as a tall strong soldier with any sense would be scared.

10/05/04

We had a great conversation. I asked you about the new young guy in your squad. You said that you were going to keep close watch over him until he learns the ropes. You also said that you feel really confident going into combat with your group. As a dad, I liked hearing this from you.

10/7/04

We have been talking every day since your mom and I got back from visiting with you and Diana. I think we called you at about 7:30 a.m. and you were to have Diana take you to formation at 9:00 a.m.... A couple of nights ago I asked you how you were feeling and you said that you had switched to survivor mode. You apologized for this feeling, stating that you felt it was selfish. I could see why you were in survivor mode and it was not at all selfish.

Chapter 7

Iraq

Skip's unit took off from McChord Air Force Base, a few miles from Fort Lewis. From there they flew to Kuwait City via Germany. A lot of the soldiers had never been out of the United States before, including Skip. Curtis Nasatka, one of Skip's buddies in his unit, told me that before they got onto the plane, the platoon leaders lined them up and dropped Ambien pills on their tongues. He said it was like a scene out of a video by The Mamas and the Papas, only it was Ambien instead of acid.

Skip was very conflicted about why we were going to war with Iraq. Two passages from his journal:

> *"The potential for hypocrisy in war"*
>
> *The great ones who have written anything of lasting substance through the ages had one powerful similarity that must be seen and embraced. These great ones were not ignorant of the times in which they lived. St. Augustine wrote in the 3rd century AD about how the mighty Roman Empire squandered its wealth and power by sinking into the depths of decadence. These writings, known as "The City of G-d," would become a classic of not only Christian but Western literature as well.*

Alexis de Tocqueville wrote his classic Democracy in America in 1835 AD which served to draw attention to the dangers of the majority rule, which he thought could be as tyrannical as the rule of the aristocracy. These two men of the past are part of a long tradition of others who dared to critically view the events and experiences of their time. I am nothing compared to these men but I share a like-minded passion. I am not blind to what happens around me. I am not afraid to see things as they are, and thus, I write about the times and events in which I live. Because of this passion, I must question the motives of our government concerning its initiation of hostilities with the nation of Iraq. I must state emphatically that I am not on any one side politically or intellectually when it comes to how I view this war in Iraq. I merely seek the truth concerning motives, reasons, and justifications utilized to substantiate our initiation of hostilities.

"For what reason the call to war?"

When our nation was attacked on Sept. 11, 2001, our government immediately sent forces to Afghanistan to punish those who were behind these attacks. Soon after the initiation of military action in Afghanistan, our government began to speak about a possible connection between the elements that were behind the World Trade Center attacks and the nation of Iraq. Our government made the allegation that Iraq had somehow aided terrorist elements in Afghanistan so that they could successfully carry out these attacks. To this day, no evidence has been given to substantiate this lofty claim. Not long after this our government began to make another allegation concerning Iraq—that it had a vast amount of "weapons of mass destruction" that were being liberally supplied to those who had attacked our nation. Incidentally, the phrase "weapons of mass destruction" has become the new mantra for weapons that can kill a tremendous amount of people at one time. Not long after this second accusation concerning Iraq, our government began to speak of the liberation of the Iraqi people from the dictator Saddam Hussein as the reason for their desire to invade Iraq. This third reason given for our invasion of Iraq is the current justification for our initiation of hostilities. I have only one question. Which of these three justifications for war with Iraq do we choose? They were not all given at once but over time. Now that the war is under way, our government is accusing Russia of selling night vision, GPS [global positioning system], and jamming equipment to the insurgents, thus potentially endangering Coalition forces. This is the hypocrisy: we sold chemical weapons to the Iraqi government during the early to mid-1980s, which in turn were used on the Kurdish people located in the northern region of Iraq. What gives us the right to chasten Russia for selling these devices to Iraq when we sold deadly chemical weapons to Iraq? It was convenient for the United States to sell these weapons to Iraq then, but it is not convenient for us concerning the sale of these tactical technologies to Iraq. What an awesome display of hypocrisy! One might say, "That was then, this is now." I would say that past sins do not extenuate

*present responsibility. I am afraid of what will happen
if no weapons of mass destruction are found in Iraq.
We the people have been given no evidence that Iraq has
such weapons in its arsenal. We run the risk of turning
the world community against us if no such weapons are
found. We must accept the fact that there are no rules
in warfare. If Russia provided military technologies
to Iraq then so be it. No one is guiltless when it comes to
war. There is no moral high ground to be taken. War
is the result of the failure of reasoned diplomacy on all
sides. Everyone is to blame when we feel the necessity to
kill each other. Am I a pacifist? By no means. There are
times when war is justified. These justifications, however,
should be clear to all, "all" meaning the majority of the
world community. But what if the majority of the world
community is wrong? Truth does not always rest with
those who are the consensus. At the same time, however,
truth does not necessarily reside with one. How can
we know when war is legitimate? This question opens
up a universe of debate. How can we know as a world
community when war is a justified action? When asking
this question we must ascend into the realm of moral
justification. Whose ways are right? Most people would
agree that defeating the Nazi regime was a morally
justified action. Adolph Hitler was intent on committing racial genocide, the total extermination of an
existing race. Most would agree that suppression of
political expression, religious expression, and freedom
of destiny are counterintuitive to our human nature.
Other political ideologies will disagree, however. Some*

believe in the efficacy of dictatorships, some believe in democracy, or the rule of the intellectual elite. How can we know out of all the diverse systems of government which one benefits humanity the most? All forms of government may be only relative claims concerning the most efficacious methodology with which we govern ourselves as a race.

Skip's unit landed in Kuwait City in the first week of October 2004. From there they were bused to FOB (Forward Operations Base), Camp Victory, Kuwait, and on to Camp Ali Al Salem, known as Gateway to the Theater. (If you are going to Iraq or Afghanistan, you will most likely go through Kuwait.) Twenty-four hours later, they boarded a C-130 military aircraft for a quick ride to Baghdad International Airport (BIAP); from there it was just a few minutes by Chinook helicopters to Camp Taji, Iraq.

The Stryker that Skip would eventually take command of had clearly seen a fair share of action. There was a gash in the armor where it had been hit by an RPG. The floor was warped where it had trapped some of the gases from the exploding round. It was a sobering sight. None of the soldiers in Skip's battalion had seen twisted metal or spots of blood on the Strykers they'd used for field training.

My connection to Iraq began on October 5, 2004. I was assigned to the 25th Infantry Division, 1st Brigade, Stryker Brigade Combat Team (SBCT) out of Fort Lewis, Washington. I arrived in Tal'Afar, Iraq, approximately

three weeks later. Tal'Afar is located in the extreme north
of the country. I was a Rifle Team Leader initially, with
1st Platoon, Apache Company.

Tal'Afar is a Kurdish city in northwestern Iraq in the Ninawa Governorate about thirty miles west of Mosul. It has a population of about 250,000, mostly Sunni Muslims, but also dozens of tribes of different ethnicities and religions. Due to its strategic location, about forty miles from the Syrian border, Tal'Afar was a key base of operations for Al Qaeda and Abu Musab Zarqawi, Osama bin Laden's second in command.

The terrorists were particularly brutal in Tal'Afar. The town consists of densely packed buildings with lots of blind alleys—perfect for ambushes—and high-walled courtyards with big iron gates where it was easy to hide. There was tremendous unemployment in the city—around 80 percent. It was a great recruiting pool for insurgents. In the center of town was a castle that was believed to be an old Ottoman Empire fortress. This castle would eventually become a main combat outpost (COP) for the United States Army. It overlooked the main traffic circle in town. During the third week of October 2004, the two hundred soldiers of Alpha Company convoyed under cover of darkness from Mosul to Tal'Afar. By this time it wasn't safe for soldiers to be in Tal'Afar, so all operations were carried out from FOB Sykes, a few miles outside of town. There wasn't much effort to maintain a visible presence in Tal'Afar until the arrival of Skip's unit. They arrived at FOB Sykes early in the morning.

Right after chow, they saw this big brown wall of sand coming in their direction: welcome to Tal'Afar. It was as if the entire horizon was coming to greet them. Within minutes visibility was cut to nearly zero. They could feel the sand starting to sting their skin and burn their eyes. For the next few hours, all they could do was hide in their Strykers. Some of the new guys were reluctant to be sitting ducks, but they were assured that Sykes was rarely raided and the bad guys didn't like the burning, blowing sand any more than they did. Sykes was considered one of the most dangerous and inaccessible FOBs in all of Iraq. Earlier, the 3–2 had cordoned off the town and swept through it, trying to flush out bands of insurgents that had the run of the town. The army had reestablished control, and the Iraqi government had installed a new police chief. But a number of factors allowed the safety of the town to rapidly deteriorate in just a couple of months, at about the same time the 1–5 arrived. Thousands of insurgents were slipping through the Fallujah cordon during the big push to drive them out of Fallujah, with most of them heading north to Mosul and Tal'Afar.

Most soldiers felt this was poor planning at division level. It was as if no one had thought about where the insurgents would go if they got through the cordon—as if someone had said, "Let's go to Fallujah and kick some insurgent butt." There were only a few hundred American soldiers from the 1–5 Alpha Company and a small element of the 214 Calvary in Tal'Afar when thousands of insurgents started swarming through the city. The fact that Tal'Afar was a natural stopping place for insurgents going back to Syria and most of the army resources had been redirected to other hot spots didn't help matters. Five hundred soldiers were expected to maintain a presence in Tal'Afar under the most extreme conditions. Most of the soldiers of the 1–5 had no idea of what they were about to be put through. These young soldiers—who were chefs, students, construction workers, and kids who'd just gotten out of high school—had to rely on their army training, kick-ass attitudes, and superior equipment: they were far outnumbered by the bad guys. The insurgents in the Tal'Afar area were estimated to be several thousand. Most of the police stations had been blown up, and the few hundred remaining police were afraid to venture outside of the castle in central Tal'Afar.

Halloween was the first holiday that Skip and his buddies celebrated in Tal'Afar. Technically, soldiers are not allowed to drink alcohol while on duty in Iraq, but they pooled their money and were able to secure a few six-packs of 3 Horses beer, which tastes like beer but has no real alcohol in it. Once a soldier was in Iraq for a few weeks, though, he learned how to get alcohol if he wanted it. Soldiers are smart and they quickly adapt. The wife of one of Skip's battalion mates started sending him lots of Listerine mouthwash. She would empty the Listerine out of the bottles, fill them with Jameson Irish Whiskey, and then reseal the bottles. This guy always had an ample supply, but he never had the time to get buzzed. If soldiers wanted to stay alive in Iraq, they didn't have more than a taste of their alcohol stash. The soldiers in the field would regulate each other when it came to drinking alcohol. No one wanted a drunken soldier watching his back.

An e-mail from Skip:

From: Darrell Griffin, Jr.
Sent: Thursday, November II, 2004
To: Darrell (DAD) Griffin
Subject: your son

Dearest Mom and Dad,
I have been so busy lately and am sorry that I have not been writing as often. I went on my first combat patrol on foot today through the heart of downtown Tal'Afar. There were people everywhere and you just don't know where the next bullet is going to come from. The insurgents from Fallujah are expected to come here to Tal'Afar so we have made our dominance known throughout the city just waiting for someone to pick a fight with us. The city is predominantly Shia Muslim so the people are very jittery about our presence there. We do not know whose side the people will take when given the opportunity. Many police uniforms have been stolen from Mosul so we had to be skeptical when linking up with Iraqi police today. It will be like this for awhile until we can somewhat identify who's who. Last night we were over watching a checkpoint when gunfire erupted about 400 meters from where we were positioned. Another Stryker that went to investigate received small arms fire so we went down to plus them up in order to pull back due to limited night visibility. Yes we do have night vision but it depends on ambient or available light that our [night vision goggles] have available. We are tasked to hold Tal'Afar at all costs; that is our company mission as of right now. We are expecting insurgent forces to make an incursion into this city and have been receiving strong indicators that it has begun. Well, that's

the [news] from my corner of the pie. I love you guys dearly and have not been receiving your packages as of yet. But mail tends to be sporadic so I will continue to be on the lookout for it. I am going to call you guys right now. I love you.

Your faithful son,

Skipper

I could always tell how Skip was feeling based on his e-mail "signature." Skipper is what we called him when he was a kid. As he got older we called him Skip. When he sent this e-mail, he was feeling vulnerable. He wanted reassurances from his dad that everything was going to be okay. I cried because I couldn't give him these reassurances.

Along with Skip's e-mail were the first of several hundred pictures he would send me. We agreed to classify all pictures

as "Red" and "Regular" pictures. We did this so we would know which pictures we should share with Diana and Kim. I noticed on the side of his helmet were the words: "*Post Tenebras Lux*"—"After darkness, light." Skip always had room for humor in his life, even in a combat situation. On the front of his helmet were the words: "This side towards enemy."

From: Darrell Griffin, Sr.
Sent: Thursday, November 11, 2004
To: Darrell Griffin, Jr.
Subject: RE: your son

Son keep safe. We have been writing every day and sending the letters once a week. I hope you start getting them soon. We have also sent two packages to you so far. It appears that the Coalition kicked butt in Fallujah but as you said a big percentage of the bad guys ran to fight another day.

Carie from my office wants to know if any of your guys don't have people writing them or sending them packages. If you have guys like this she would like to know about them and write to them and send them packages.

We love you son.

Most missions were either at the company level or at the platoon level. For the first couple months of Skip's deployment to Iraq, Capt. Christopher Bachl was his company commander. Skip reported directly to SSG Benny Salas, his squad leader. He and Curtis Nasatka were the Alpha and Bravo team leaders for Salas. The soldiers got used to taking small-arms fire and moving as fast as possible in their

Strykers to avoid IEDs. There was rarely a day when they would leave FOB Sykes that they didn't take fire from the enemy. Sometimes to deal with the stress they resorted to gallows humor. They would take bets on what would hit them first as they went out for the day: IED, RPG, or small-arms fire. This was part of the daily routine that never became routine for them.

One of their first missions was to secure a particular police station. According to Nasatka, "The pucker factor on this first assignment was off the charts." (I had heard this phrase used before, and asked Skip what it meant: "When you are in a situation where you are facing potential death the adrenalin throws your body into defense mode. One of the defense mode characteristics is that your sphincter tightens up so tight that you almost can't walk.")

Skip did his normal comprehensive pre-combat inspection (PCI). As Nasatka put it, "Griff was the guy that made sure you reloaded in a firefight." It was a platoon-level mission so there were four squads. Skip said a prayer ("Strength and Honor") before the driver cranked up the diesel on the Stryker and did his usual salute with his arm across his chest; then they rolled out under the cover of darkness. This would be his trademark whenever he got in a Stryker for a combat mission. No one ever thought it was corny. The attitude was always, "Everything helps."

They rolled out of the FOB with the usual small-arms fire pinging off their Stryker, but they didn't take any RPG rounds or encounter any IEDs before they got to the police station. They were a little spooked because it appeared to be abandoned. What if it was booby-trapped? Skip, as always, had written out the plan of attack in his battle-planning book and gone over it with Nasatka.

They hit the police station hard, hearts beating at stroke levels, kicking in the doors and spreading out to the various rooms, ready to drop anything that moved or made a shadow. The police were gone. The squad assumed that they were all crooked and had only signed up to earn a few dollars before they took off with whatever wasn't nailed down; but they may have just been scared, lying dead in an alley somewhere or buried. After completely shaking down the station, everyone breathed a sigh of relief. They then started inspecting the desk drawers, closets, and cabinets for any usable intel.

Nasatka looked over his shoulder as he was breaching a closet that was secured with a large padlock. He saw one of the soldiers carrying a rolled carpet on his shoulder out to the Stryker. As the lock fell off under the pressure of the sledgehammer Nasatka was using, he saw a huge burlap sack hanging in the closet. Knowing these guys like to booby-trap everything, he carefully opened the sack. It was full of cans of Carlsberg beer. He appropriated the sack of beer from the closet and showed it to Skip. Maybe it wasn't very soldierly, or maybe it was totally soldierly, but he and Skip planned to destroy the contraband by drinking it. They stationed their team members where they could properly cover the building and the command element of the third squad relaxed and de-puckered.

They sat on the front porch like sheriffs and, as Nasatka put it, got "twisted"—or as twisted as they could get on a beer apiece. For that brief instant they felt like "the lords of creation." The sack also contained bottles of gin, but they left those alone for obvious reasons. Skip sat there on the porch with his shotgun over his shoulder and they all sat on folding chairs. It was just like a Wild West cowboy scene. Skip talked about (lectured, according to Nasatka) "modern socialism, Kierkegaard and the origins of existentialism, and touched on Heidegger, Sartre, Marcel and the notion of Being." It was surreal for Nasatka, listening to a lecture on philosophy with a teacher who had a shotgun thrown over his shoulder.

They must have talked often, as Nasatka seemed well informed about the subjects of their conversations. He told me that these conversations helped him and everyone else who would listen deal with the stress of knowing that the next "pop" you heard could be the one that introduces you to Skip's dead ancient teachers. Kierkegaard was important to the soldiers because he stressed the importance of faith—a necessary thing to have when you're going into combat. For Kierkegaard, the "leap of faith" wasn't a rational decision; it transcended rationality.

They spent the night at the police station, returning to the FOB early in the morning. This was their first real mission as a squad. They would eventually become the "go-to squad." They went back to the police station several times and got to know the people who worked in the bank next door. The people in the neighborhood liked seeing them there. Eventually the police station was re-staffed with Iraqi police (IP) officers. Few future missions would be this easy.

A few weeks later they were assigned the task of helping the IP secure another police station. When they got there they found a fifty-five-gallon drum of TNT in the middle of the floor. They turned it over to the IP and left to go to another police station to help secure it. When they got in position at the second police station about twenty minutes later, they heard and saw the first police station blow up. The insurgents had rolled into town, killing the police officers or scaring them off and destroying the stations with TNT. The U.S.-trained Iraqi cops didn't have the firepower or manpower to fight effectively against the RPGs, machine guns, and explosives used by the insurgents.

They rarely left FOB Sykes for missions in Tal'Afar without taking fire from the enemy, and it was increasing in frequency and intensity. A couple of weeks after the initial visit to the police station, they were on dismounted patrol not far from the police station when they started taking sporadic small-arms fire. Then the small-arms fire became sustained. The way buildings are constructed in Tal'Afar makes it difficult to see where gunfire is coming from. Often they had to see where the rounds were hitting and trace their trajectory back to their source. It was the middle of the day and the platoon moved from block to block in an eight-hour firefight. No Americans were hit. They couldn't find any bodies of the enemy even though they were sure that they had hit some of them.

It was almost guaranteed that they would take hits when they patrolled the traffic circle in the center of town, just below the castle. After a while, they started getting hit with rockets. According to Nasatka, they developed a "Spidey sense" about areas as they rolled into them. Something would tell them to look harder. He said they started getting in touch with new parts of themselves. "It was almost creepy, in a good, powerful way."

Skip was briefly transferred from the First Platoon, third squad, as a team leader under the supervision of SSG Salas to First Squad under the supervision of SSG Robert Hansen. According to Capt. Christopher Bachl, Skip moved around a lot between units: "Here's the deal when you have a guy like Griff, a strong-willed man with talents a lot of people don't see: once you talk to the guy you realize he is well-read, better than most. In the regular infantry, this is not necessarily a plus. But when you go into an Iraq-type of environment, this is not only one of the types of guys you want but you want him to lead because he understands what is going on."

It was November 14, 2004. Skip's platoon was in the traffic circle getting ready to move because they'd gotten a call that someone was having a problem with a checkpoint somewhere else in town. Suddenly a gunman stopped in the middle of the street and fired an RPG at Sgt. Hansen's Stryker. It hit underneath the vehicle but didn't cause very much damage. Hansen made the call to dismount so they could go after the shooter. As they were dismounting, a number of insurgents on rooftops started spraying them with AK-47s. A second RPG hit a wall directly behind Hansen. The blast knocked him to the ground, peppering him with shrapnel and concrete. Dazed and disoriented, he stumbled into Skip's Stryker. His head and arm were bleeding. He tried to get up a few times but Skip wouldn't let him go until he determined that the injuries weren't life-threatening. They decided to pull out of the crossfire. Skip's Stryker was the last to leave. Skip, armed with a squad automatic weapon (SAW), and a couple of other soldiers were in the hatches of their vehicles laying waste to anything that moved to allow them to get out of the kill zone.

A few days later, they went back to the same area. One of the merchants recognized Hansen and ran up to him and gave him the spent RPG round that had almost ended his life. Hansen was a little suspicious of how this guy knew it was him. No one remembers seeing any civilians around at the time of the engagement. That was one of the most frustrating things about the war: you never knew who was your enemy and who was your friend.

A couple of weeks later, they raided a house and nabbed a "high-value target" they'd been looking for. As they were searching the house, they came across some videotapes and a VCR. They also found a couple of Glocks (.45-caliber handguns), AK-47s, and lots of ammo. They put the video into the VCR to see what was on it. At first it just looked like a bunch of hooded Iraqis standing around. Then the video camera panned down to what looked like a U.S. Marine lying in front of them, hog-tied like a farm animal. The tape was choppy and grainy and out of sequence. One of the assassins pulled a big knife out of his waist and kneeled on top of the marine. The next choppy scene was the thug sawing off the marine's head. The video jumped to the next scene where his severed head was placed on his back.

The guy they had taken into custody wasn't the one doing the beheading in the video, but he was clearly cheering on the hideous act.

Three days later, one of the soldiers from the 1–5 was detailed to guard this same guy. The soldier was one of the unit members who had seen the tape at the insurgent's house and remembered the guy's face. As he looked at the guy, he didn't see an actual person sitting there in the cell; all he could see was his menacing face on the TV screen as the marine was being slaughtered like a pig. All he wanted to do was cut this guy, make him feel the pain that the hog-tied marine in the video must have felt. The soldier kicked him to the ground, took out his pocketknife, and slashed the guy's face. This was this soldier's last act in the army. He was immediately discharged for crimes against prisoners of war. The incident was never recorded anywhere.

Skip was about to be promoted to E-6 SSG, staff sergeant. He thought of himself as a career soldier and this was an important promotion for him. In the army there seems to be an unwritten rule of "move up or move out." He told me that achieving SSG made him feel like he'd balanced the score after getting kicked out of the army during his first enlistment. We agreed there is no scorecard, but it still felt good.

From: Darrell Griffin, Jr.
Sent: Thursday, November 18, 2004
To: Darrell (DAD) Griffin
Subject: hello from Iraq

Dearest Mom and Dad,

How are you guys? Hopefully all is going well with you. Well, I get promoted to the rank of Staff Sergeant on Dec. 1st. I will be in charge of 8 guys consisting of 2 fire teams of 4, a Stryker driver and a vehicle commander. I am extremely nervous about this promotion because these men will rely on me to make sound tactical decisions on the ground, and because of this their lives will be in my hands. I talked to Diana about 20 min. ago and we realized that this will be our first Thanksgiving apart from each other. Here in Iraq Ramadan has just ended. They celebrate a type of Christmas after Ramadan with food and festivities. I was on the roof of a man's house watching down an alley for foot traffic and I tried to tell him that everything was going to be fine and that I did not want to hurt him. He brought his family outside into the courtyard and he told me, 'This is my life...no good right now...bombs...American' and other things in broken English. This is his Christmas right now; a holiday filled with the reality of war and a broken country. He has no power at night to light his home or to provide heat. He has many children and a wife who seems to go on as if nothing is happening. It started to rain heavily that night when we were on the roof and I saw a little opening in the wall of this house. The family had a lantern of some sort that lit the little room they were huddled in and it looked so cozy and warm but there was something else there that I understood but would not dare profane with words. There are some things that war cannot take away from human beings and I saw it that night freezing and wet on that rooftop, guarding this alley while the family slept on. May we also embrace this unspoken presence that binds a family together, no matter what the circumstances present to us. This Unexplainable is what binds Diana and I together, it's what binds us together as Son, Father, Mother, sister and brother as well as friend. I guess we have a word for it and that is love but words are so meaningless when you see this Unexplainable through a little window in a lonely dark little town called Tal'Afar, in a world far different from ours. I love you.

Skipper

We would later talk about this e-mail. It struck me how there are basic things in life that all men want. The Iraqi with his broken country; the homeless guy with the three-legged Collie who stands at my highway off-ramp, holding a sign that says "Vet, will work for food"; and me—we all want to be wanted, to be needed, to be free.

Within a few weeks of getting settled into FOB Sykes (around Thanksgiving 2004), Alpha Company started working out of the ancient castle in the center of town. Over the years it had been used variously as a police station, a municipal building, and as the city's mayoral head-quarters. The castle gave Skip's unit a strategic position in the city.

Once the insurgents found that Alpha Company had taken over the castle, they started mortaring it almost daily. As the weeks wore on, they got more accurate with their attacks. They would lob their mortars at precisely the

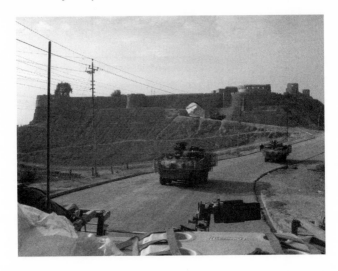

times when platoons were rotating in and out of the castle.
They would watch as the new platoon entered the castle, wait
fifteen minutes, and start their barrage. This way, if they
were lucky, they could hit the incoming and the outgoing
platoons at the same time.

On Thanksgiving Day, Skip's platoon was sent to the
traffic circle to pick up the body of another local citi-
zen who had been considered by Al Qaeda too friendly
to the Americans. You could never tell who was on our
side and who wasn't. It was Skip's opinion that some of
these killings were by insurgents trying to impress their
disdain for Americans on Tal'Afar civilians. But it was
also a time for people to settle scores and kill just for the
pleasure of it. This particular body, of an Iraqi policeman,
was body-bagged and delivered to the local hospital. End
of story.

From: Darrell Griffin, Jr.
Sent: Sunday, December 19, 2004
To: Darrell (DAD) Griffin
Subject: Your son

Dear Mom and Dad,

Things are hectic here right now. We are defending an old castle that seems to be a magnet for heavy small-arms fire. Rounds strike our part of the castle daily and we return heavy fire in the direction that it came from. The insurgents here in Tal'Afar know that within these castle walls stands the last police station in this city, and they are trying desperately to destroy it. We are in firefights daily at this castle and it seems so dream-like when you hear the snapping of rounds as they break the sound barrier above your head. 60 people were killed in Mosul by a car bomb that targeted a military convoy that's all I know for right now. Things are getting thick over here so keep us in prayer ok? It was expected due to the close proximity in time concerning Iraq's elections, which I think will be a total failure. If we start guarding polling stations that will not be good.

Well I must go for now. I will try my best to keep you updated on the situation here. I love you guys so much!

Lil' Skip

I could tell that Skip was feeling particularly vulnerable. Things had to be pretty tough for him to refer to himself as Lil' Skip.

Lt. Lewis Seau became leader of the Second Platoon, Alpha Company, in late December 2004. He was at the castle being debriefed by the outgoing platoon leader, Lt. Stonestreet, about the squad leaders that he would be taking command of, effective immediately. Stonestreet had just gotten to Skip's name when Seau heard a number of shots from what sounded like a high-powered rifle. It startled him, because he had just arrived in the battle zone fresh from officers' school. An elderly Iraqi man came running into the castle screaming and waving his arms crazily. At the same time, in ran Skip yelling, "I'm sorry, I didn't mean to do it." Skip had a wad of money in his hands and tried to give it to the Iraqi. An interpreter was there with Stonestreet and Seau, and after the old man and Skip calmed down he managed to sort things out.

Apparently Skip had been testing his new sniper rifle by firing into a *wadi* (a dry riverbed) next to the castle and accidentally shot the guy's donkey. It was worth about ten U.S. dollars and Skip gave him about a hundred dollars. After Skip handed the old man the money, the old man told the interpreter that he wished he had more donkeys. The man was Skip's good friend after this. He had always hung around the castle, but now every time he saw Skip or Seau there was "that friendly nod."

This was Seau's view of the event. What really happened was that Skip was having a marksman contest firing into the *wadi* with his squad. Specialist Matthew Briggs, one of Skip's friends in Iraq, was a big hunting fan and fellow gun nut. At the time of the mishap, Briggs was explaining to Skip how he never liked the round (5.56 millimeter) that the M-4 used. He said he used the same size round to shoot woodchucks back home. "People are like deer, you need a big round to take them down." The rifle that Skip was known for carrying was the M-14, which shoots a 556 round, better takedown. When Skip got back from paying off the old man, Briggs pointed to the dead donkey and said, "See what I mean? The M-4 gives the bad guy an opportunity to respond. With the M-14 his next response is asking Allah when does he get his virgins."

The push for Fallujah was on. The brass (senior officers) in the army was concerned that Mosul was taking on too many insurgents, so they diverted the 1–5 from Fallujah back to Mosul after a few days. What seemed like a really bad judgment call on the part of the brass was to divert all of Alpha Company except the Second Platoon to Mosul, leaving them in Tal'Afar by themselves. This was a total of about forty men to maintain a city that was being overrun by insurgents. These guys were scared, but they maintained a high presence (as high as they could with forty men in a city of over two hundred thousand). They were running from police station to police station, just trying to keep a presence in the city. It was a long seventy-two hours before the rest of Alpha Company returned to Tal'Afar. Now they again had a couple of hundred men to maintain a presence in Tal'Afar, rather than the forty men in the Second Platoon.

It was common for soldiers to have conversation pits where they could gather after missions. The pit was a hole dug in the ground surrounded by rocks or bricks. Soldiers would normally build these pits away from the major paths of officers. They would often personalize them with a sign pointing toward home—"3,457 miles to Fort Lewis"—or a faded picture of Osama with a bullet hole between his eyes. The pits were informal and you knew a pit was starting when you saw soldiers dragging chairs or boxes to sit on over to the pit area. Soldiers have to unwind. Imagine being out in neighborhoods where the next corner can have a sniper waiting, or an IED buried in the ground, or an RPG ready to drill in the side of your Stryker. And when you dismount, you're weighted down with a hundred pounds of body armor, ammo, web gear, and other stuff that soldiers call their "kits." No one was formally invited to these pit sessions, but everyone knew who was supposed to be there and who wasn't. It was like high school: if you had to ask whether you belonged to the cool crowd, you clearly didn't.

Here is how Matthew Briggs remembered Griff's pit gatherings:

The pit was in Tal'Afar. Several of these pits were around. Some of these pits had an unwritten "NCO's only" code. Joes [soldiers] might come by to say hi. There was also a fire pit in Mosul. This pit was located just outside the company command post. The squad leaders lived on this row of rooms. There was a lot of traffic to the cp [command post], and the leaders would sit out and talk. The row of rooms was an area we avoided a lot because if someone saw you then they might send you out on an errand or detail like picking up trash or digging a ditch.

Griff did not sleep much by this point in the tour. Some of us slept all the time, others not much at all. It gets increasingly more difficult to ramp down after months of living life on high alert. He would sit and talk with anyone; we talked religion a good bit. I was raised a Southern Baptist and know the Bible better than most. Griff and I talked about all beliefs of each religion, denomination, and believer. I remember we talked angels when we stayed on Singar Mountain. It was Christmas or Christmas Eve. There was a small cult or religion that lived in the mountains [in Iraq] for a long time. They had built a small shrine on the mountaintop, located inside the perimeter of the retransmission post. We were sitting in the Stryker and Sgt. Griffin told me what the shrine was and then some people walked up and entered it. We tried to talk to them, but we had no terp [interpreter] so failed. We talked about the powers the angels have and what they do within the kingdom of God.

I liked to talk to Griff about God. He was very well educated and carried a bible 99 percent of the time. So we could just look it up if we got fuzzy. We talked and debated all the time. It was how we killed the time. We would spend days in the Stryker, one man running the remote weapon system, and the rest of us just talked about everything. We talked at the castle, at the flour mill in Mosul, the chow hall, in the Stryker, a fire pit. Go to the range, talk ballistics. Go to the castle, talk about the crusades, talk religion.

Everyone knew about Skip's pit conversations. They were allowed by most senior officers and often encouraged. This was the new army, the thinking army.

Alpha Company had been in Tal'Afar for about a month, and insurgents were increasing the intensity and frequency

of attacks on them and on the civilians of Tal'Afar. Skip and his vehicle commander, Sgt. Gary Robinson, felt the situation in Tal'Afar was rapidly getting worse:

IEDs posed a tremendous threat to us in addition to an elusive, dismounted enemy that would engage you and then vanish. We renamed MSR [main supply route] Santa Fe the "Gauntlet." This is an MSR that spans the entire length from east to west of the entire city of Tal'Afar. Every time we would utilize this road we would be struck by IEDs, some small and some extremely powerful. At one point, Sergeant Robinson and I had contemplated exchanging death letters with each other to give to our wives should one of us die while traveling on this road.

The 214 Calvary and Alpha Company knew they didn't have the resources to take back the city, but orders saying "defend Tal'Afar at all costs" trickled down to the squads and they took it seriously. Although they were small in number, they made sure that the insurgents were aware of their presence and that they were tough. It bothered Skip that he had to project this "tough guy" image but he and his comrades knew the insurgents would pounce on any sign of weakness. They did daily "presence patrols." When they patrolled the streets they would make sure that they were always visible out of their Stryker hatches. It was important that the Iraqis saw people, not just tanks.

Skip's squad quickly became a well-oiled machine. Briggs spent every day in the left rear hatch of the Stryker with Skip in the front hatch. They spent so much time in the hatches that they learned to communicate through body language alone. This was critical because they often would be caught in deadly situations where communication had to be automatic; there was no time to think. There were so few members of Alpha Company patrolling the streets that, as Skip put it, "each man had to project balls as big as ten men." As they rolled down the streets, a lot of people would flash "V" for victory signs or yell "Thank you!" in English. But there was the occasional Iraqi (normally a combat-age male) who would look straight at Skip's Stryker, take his fist with his thumb extended and drag it across his neck. This was a way of saying, "I will cut your throat when I get the opportunity."

> *During one combat patrol we started to notice that all of the houses we went into had no AK-47s that most families have for personal protection or for other reasons. I asked what sect each family belonged to and they all answered that they were Sunni. Iraqi army soldiers had come through this particular neighborhood and disarmed all Sunni families, leaving them defenseless. They would also come through this neighborhood at night and shoot wildly into the homes as a terror tactic that would scare these families into leaving, or reduce them to a terrified existence. This is the Iraqi military that we are hanging all of our hopes on. What will they do once we leave? Will there be sectarian cleansing? There will not even be a civil war because the full weight of Shia/Iranian influence will crush any Sunni elements that dare to stay in the country.*

There was little if any discussion about what would happen after the United States withdrew from Iraq. There was the assumption, at least on the part of the American public, that we would eventually withdraw our troops. Given the imbalance of Sunni and Shia and their history of living together in Iraq, and the history of the conflicts of Sunni and Shia Muslims throughout the world, we clearly didn't have any idea of what life in Iraq would be like after what Skip called A.L.L. (After Liberators Leave).

How do we impose a Democracy on a country with factions that have historically been at odds with one another? Will the Kurds forego their desire for an independent state? If not, then will the new Iraq be forced to intervene militarily in the north in the future? Will the other factions be used as proxy forces for Syria and Iran by intrigue and insurgent war like they are doing right now? Now that Iran is accelerating its nuclear program, how will this shape the region when they do obtain nuclear weapons as pertaining to the Shia in Iraq? Will this create a Shia-dominated hegemony? The strategic future must be placated for a pragmatic success in Iraq and the region. For the present, U.S. forces are filling the power vacuum in Iraq. This is classical irony in that while civil war surrounds us we are filling the power vacuum. Who are our true friends in Iraq, even an ad hoc, pragmatic friend? Even this will prove illusory once we leave. Who do we side with if Democracy is not a viable option? If we side with the Sunni, then the Shia will stab us in the back, and if we side with the Shia the Sunni will do the same. If we side with both, then both will stab us in the front until we leave. We will lose Turkey as an ally if we are too generous with the Kurds. If the only solution is to stay in Iraq for the foreseeable future, the bloodletting could continue and any American sympathies for this war will rapidly diminish, if not totally disappear. We are not only engaged in the war of intrigues but also a war of attrition with the American public at home. This is indirectly a war on two fronts. The ideal conditions that will allow us to leave will be the coming together of all parties under the aegis of a Democratic government. Until this happens we are forced to stay and because forced we do not have freedom to maneuver strategically in Iraq. How do we gain the initiative strategically? If this can be answered then we win. If a representative democracy in Iraq is not an option then we could be forced to choose sides. If democracy means the rule of a given majority then we might be forced to accept Shia rule for the country. The other parties will not accept this so we might also be forced to empower this majority with repressive, military might in order to secure its hold on the country, setting up one repressive regime in place of another.

From: Darrell Griffin, Jr.
Sent: Tuesday, November 30, 2004
To: Darrell (DAD) Griffin
Subject: Your son checkin' in

Dear Mom, Dad, Alex, and Jordan,

Happy late Thanksgiving from Tal'Afar, Iraq. Things are steadily deteriorating here. Another Iraqi police station was blown up yesterday, which leaves one left. The Iraqi police for whatever reason will not stand up to the insurgents and the people in general will not stand up to them either. When the insurgents attack us from rooftops or buildings not their own, we return devastating fire and end up destroying these buildings and homes with people still inside. Until the Iraqi people get tired of this, the devastation will continue. The only place where I have seen an Iraqi army well-equipped and resolved to fight was in the town of Kisik, where a large oil refinery happens to be located. I think our government is only interested in standing up well-equipped armies with good equipment and so forth, at places where we have a vested interest, i.e. oilfields. I have seen it with my own eyes. But in Tal'Afar, which has no economic significance, you see ING [Iraqi National Guard] who have running shoes for boots and can hardly find a matching uniform, body armor, or even vehicles. They are basically cannon fodder. I will keep you posted concerning the situation here in Tal'Afar as it develops. I love you guys and miss you a lot. I miss our country a lot! I feel as if I'm in another universe. G-d be with you and may G-d help this country, and the people who are very beautiful, the Iraqis.

Your loving son, Skipper

Skip called me some time in November: "Dad, this is your son the pirate." He always called us at about two in the morning Los Angeles time, which is early afternoon Iraq

time. In this particular late-night conversation he complained
that he was tired of seeing the ING so ill-equipped. He told
me of a recent time when he'd been working with the ING.
There were ten of them, running in their cheap imitation
Converse running shoes. The totally weird thing was that
they were sharing six guns. In Briggs's words:

The weapons were Glock pistols—the ones the U.S. bought
and issued to Iraqi police. When the police departments fell
in Tal'Afar, 90 percent of the cops walked off the job never
to return. We would be doing house-to-house searches and
we would find these pistols and take them. The Iraqi police
wanted them because in Saddam's time only the special police-
political type had pistols so they were still a sign of power to
the Iraqi. Matter of fact, the sight of a pistol on anyone would
make them scared as all hell. So they would trade anything for
them. Most of the time they came without ammo. Because
they didn't have any way to get them, we could turn around
and trade them more whiskey for bullets since they fired 9mm
same as our sidearm.

The way Skip explained it to me was that this was good
business for the Iraqis and for our troops. He invoked the
term *cēterīs paribus*—literally, "with other things the same."
It was the law of supply and demand. The Americans created
the supply for a pent-up demand. They "stole" guns and
sold them to the Iraqi police for whiskey. Then they sold the
whiskey to U.S. soldiers for a fair price. Briggs told me that
eventually Joes were paying a hundred dollars a bottle for
whiskey. "Wasn't that a violation of army general orders?"

I asked. Skip pointed out that the abolitionists violated laws when slavery was legal. It boiled down to the fact that he got tired of seeing Iraqi police, soldiers, and national guardsmen without weapons. The Iraqis are a proud people, Skip noted, and they would never accept guns as gifts. They needed to feel they had duly paid for the guns. He and Briggs were simply supplying weapons to their allies to combat terrorists. He was frustrated that the U.S. Army hadn't thought far enough ahead to anticipate that insurgents would flood the Tal'Afar region and that only the Iraqis guarding oil fields were sufficiently armed.

In December 2004, Capt. Bachl had some dignitaries visit Skip and his company at Sykes. Although these "dog-and-pony shows" were a pain in the ass, they were necessary to remind the commanders that there are real-life soldiers attached to their grand plans. He selected Second Platoon: like any executive, he wanted to put his best foot forward. Skip always said that in a combat zone planning went out the window when the fighting started.

Second Platoon was out in their battle sector. There was a suspected weapons cache, but they hadn't found it on prior raids. The target was an old garage. There were a number of storage sheds and locked cabinets in the garage. Skip and Capt. Bachl tried negotiating with the owners but they wouldn't budge, so they decided to cut the locks themselves. They didn't find anything. It appeared that their intel was wrong. As they were leaving, Sgt. Anthony Ducre saw something covered with a sheet of plywood. It looked like car parts, maybe transmissions. He picked up one of the parts, examined it, and put it down fast: he knew instantly that it was an Italian land mine. Most of the guys were new and had never seen foreign explosives before. Once they had determined that it was an explosive, they starting looking closer. They popped open the trunk of a car and found it full of AK-47s and RPGs. This place was hot.

Skip told me about the cache find in an e-mail:

From: Darrell Griffin, Jr.
Sent: Monday, December 13, 2004
To: Darrell (DAD) Griffin
Subject: your son checkin' in

Dear Mom and Dad,
My squad was responsible for finding the biggest weapons cache in all of our Brigades [area of operations]. We cordon

& searched an auto-shop and found a fully fabricated IED w/ approx. 25 lbs. of C4 [explosives] attached to it, Anti-tank mines with walkie-talkie triggering devices, 5 [rocket-propelled grenades] rounds and ledgers recording the names of suppliers of these types of materials. The man we detained in this auto-yard is a chief bomb maker in Tal'Afar. Yesterday while at the castle, we took heavy small-arms fire for about an hour. An IED went off at around 9PM to our north from the castle about 400 m. away and hit some guys I know. It hit their Stryker. There were substantial injuries and we were hit again at the castle soon after the IED went off to our north. We received heavy small-arms fire from below (the castle sits on a steep hill) and we returned fire in the general direction. Things are pretty intense here right now. I'm glad however that my squad and I found all those bomb-making explosive materials. An Anti-Tank mine can vaporize any soft-skinned military vehicles and is probably what hit that Stryker. When that Stryker came to a stop, they discovered another IED next to it that did not detonate. Its purpose was to kill troops on the ground once they dismount to execute recovery procedures.

Please keep praying for my squad because we are the only Stryker and only squad that has not been hit with an IED. I had a hard time believing in the miraculous as pertaining to prayer, but it seems as if catastrophe is just out of our reach. We have been doing the killing and not the opposite. Tell your precious friends that I received their care packages and so appreciate their care and concern. I don't have the names with me but they sent me a lot of CDs and candy. The music is beautiful. I received your letter and enjoy so much how you use the narrative as a letter. Please continue to write in this manner. I can't stress enough how I feel and truly believe that your prayers are having a weird effect on me and my men. It is very uncanny how we are so brave and always seem to be just out of reach of things that can kill us or injure us. However, we have had to experience killing others and this is something that will haunt me for the rest of my life. I love you guys so much and truly feel your love for me as your son. I count the days when we can all see each other again and look back on this time, this year. I love you all.

Your son,

Skipper

I was concerned for my son. As a father, I didn't like to know that my son had to kill other people. It's a strange emotion. On the one hand, I was glad that Skip killed rather than let himself be killed. On the other hand, I felt sickened that he had been put into a position of having to kill someone. Who is to blame? How far up the food chain do I have to go? Was it Muhammad's fault for spawning a new religion? Or was it Isaac and Ishmael's fault? Was it radical Islam's fault for perverting the Muslim faith? Was it radical Islam's fault for relentlessly pursuing the United States? Was it Bush's fault for starting a war that put my son in harm's way?

A few days after they found the cache, Skip called to read me an axiom he'd written in his journal: "Technical progress favors war because new weapons have greatly reduced the pain and anguish implied in the act of killing." He told me that when an IED kills someone the perpetrator is either at a considerable distance or not in the area at all. In the same way, when he shoots someone the bullet strikes the victim at a considerable distance from him. When Skip was facing off with an enemy combatant the adrenaline would kick in. If he was lucky and his bullet hit its target, the color red would appear. As it fell a cloud of dust would kick up around the lifeless target. His adrenaline would still be working until he got back and was alone in his quarters. At that point, when he closed his eyes, he said the target began to breathe again, become human; it would look at him and grin.

Most of the soldiers I spoke to about Skip told me that he normally read more after a mission and more intensely after engagement with the enemy. He himself once told me that the books he took with him were as important as his M-4. I replied that if we had to kill each other with clubs and rocks, up close and personal, maybe we would be less inclined to kill each other. He immediately reminded me of the "scorch the earth battles" in the Old Testament. The only thing that has changed is that we're a lot more efficient at it. Now one man can kill a lot more men over a lot shorter period of time. Men have been able to take our scientific learning and convert it to make us more efficient killers.

From: Darrell Griffin, Jr.
Sent: Tuesday, December 21, 2004
To: Darrell (DAD) Griffin
Subject: Skipper checking in

Dearest Mom and Dad,

It's funny how you mentioned me considering my options other than the military because I have been. Yesterday, we fought insurgents in Tal'Afar who were setting fire to the houses of those who are supporting the war effort. I walked in a sniper through my spotting scope, laying in on a target with a black mask and AK-47 running through the area of these burning homes. I got to see him split in half at 600M shot with a .50 cal. sniper rifle called the Barrett. I can sense the combat stress all around me except for my squad because we all have a gallows-type sense of humor that keeps us going. We have our Korean private [Jae Shin] and he goes by the name of Jackie Chan. Actually, the Iraqi kids called him that and it just stuck with him. This is just one example of how we keep each other laughing. Mom, Dad, I really don't want to fight in a war ever again. I have had to kill several people and have seen many people torn to pieces (not on our side) and it is the most horrific and catastrophic spectacle that I have ever seen, aside from having been an EMT. If you could start researching some options for me I would deeply appreciate it. I want nothing more than to enjoy my mother and father and my sister and brother but most of all, my wife. The jump back into the civilian world is scary. Please tell me your thoughts on this because I am being pressured to reenlist and I don't want to. I will do anything to secure a good job so that Diana does not have to work and that I could retire from. If the job facilitates these two things I would work at an ice cream stand if it accomplished these 2 things. Well, I must go for now being that I have been up for over 24Hrs. I love and miss you both.

    Lil' Skip

More than once I tried to offer Skip alternatives to a life in the army, but I never got anywhere. One time he called and asked me how I thought God would treat him on Judgment Day since his job was delivering death to people. Most of the time he felt that this was a just war, but at other times he wasn't sure. For him, following orders wasn't enough of an answer.

Why are we at war with Iraq? We are not fighting against the people of Iraq as much as with those who oppose us for occupying their country. We call them "insurgents" who attack U.S. forces but why do we call them such? Is this a title that presupposes their cause as evil? Are they fighting the cause of right as we think it to be or are they fighting us? What is the cause of "right" as we think it to be? The United States invaded Iraq initially because we believed Iraq to be in possession of WMDs, thus making Iraq out to be a direct threat to the United States. As of the present, there have been no weapons of mass destruction found after occupying the country for some time, subsequent to invasion and occupation. We have had free rein of this country and have found nothing. This tends to invalidate our initial claim for invading the country. How is Iraq a DIRECT threat to the United States any more than other countries who hate us? The next rationalization for invasion was that we wanted to "liberate" the people of Iraq from a brutal dictator. Did the people of Iraq ask us to liberate them or did we insist that they needed this liberation? To apply emotional validation for the invasion, our government showed us images of the Hussein regime gassing "its own people," the Kurds in northern Iraq, and other atrocities. People who live under such brutal circumstances should be freed from this oppression, but how? If the government of a particular country brutalizes its people, do we have the obligation/right to invade that country? We seem to think so. Why then did we not invade China or North Korea? Why not Britain for that matter as they seek to subvert and destabilize the Irish? Why Iraq? Was there a connection between the horrific events of Sept. 11, 2001, and the country of Iraq? I find it interesting that the current administration, under accusation of acting on faulty intelligence, claims that we should not attempt to rewrite the past but focus on rebuilding the country of Iraq. The past is what is on trial! This is a direct attempt to redirect critical inquiry into the past; the past meaning everything from substantiating the initial push into Iraq to the evidence for the claim that Iraq was a direct threat to the United States! Those who want to inquire into this "past" are labeled as unpatriotic, and irresponsible. This is the old ARGUMENTUM AD HOMINUM (attacking the man rather than his argument) which, to any observant philosopher, would indicate that the opponent does not have an argument to substantiate his conclusion or, in this case, his actions, i.e., the actions of said government. As an American, I desire nothing less than the heads of those who killed over three thousand noncombatants on Sept., 11, 2001, but we must make not only the punishment fit the crime but must make the punishment fit those who perpetrated this horrible act. Did these men descend upon the United States from Iraq? Was the Iraqi government under the tyranny of the Hussein regime responsible for Sept. 11th? Our treatment thus far concerning the "war on terror" has been the equivalent of attempting to swat a mosquito with a sledgehammer. No matter where these heinous plans originated, do we proceed with a conventional mindset when responding to what happened to us? Can we win over the "hearts and minds" of those who hate us at the end of a barrel? You do not win someone's heart and mind, you convince them and change their mind by dialogue and diplomacy. When you invade the country perceived to be your enemy, you either strengthen their resolve in hating you or plunge them into the oblivion of the unknown, which is a direct consequence of warfare. War and revolution throw up their share of human wreckage: refugees seek a way out while hegemonic adventurers seek a way in.

Chapter 8

Bloody Days in Tal'Afar

Skip's unit, third squad of the Second Platoon of Alpha
Company, 1–5 Infantry, and a few elements of 214 Cavalry,
were flown by helicopter to Sinjar Mountain, between
Tal'Afar and the Syrian border, where they stayed from
December 24 to 26. Skip volunteered his squad for the
mission. There wasn't much there except for a powerful
retransmission station and a few soldiers to support it. They
had gotten some intel that the insurgents wanted to capture
a few soldiers in order to demoralize the army. They took
a lot of ammo for a show of force, a case of grenades, cases
of automatic weapons and 240 ammo, and some claymore
mines. While sitting around with all that ammo they got
bored, so they had a little fireworks "practicing" with it.
There weren't many soldiers there, the camp was pretty
small, and it was cold. Command didn't forget about the
troops on Sinjar. They flew in Christmas dinner with all
the trimmings.

By the New Year, they were back in Tal'Afar.

It bothered Skip that the media paid so much attention to
the fighting in Iraq and so little to the true casualties of the
war. Soldiers and insurgents are there because they choose
to be there. The citizens of Iraq have no choice:

The Iraqi army and police were not the only casualties in the war for Tal'Afar. Poverty and lack of health services in the city led me to witness one of the saddest spectacles that I had ever seen up to that time. My platoon was conducting a night raid and my squad and I were climbing over some rooftops down into the courtyard of a house that we were instructed to search. Upon clearing the rooms of the house, my team leader, Sergeant Anthony Ducre, and I came into a room where a mother was sitting, holding her infant son in her arms. I noticed that the son had a massive, tumor-like growth on his stomach about the size of a basketball and his eyes were almost completely glazed over and fixed. What broke my heart was that even though it was obvious this little child was dying, the mother had still taken the time to dress her little baby in whatever nice clothes she could find and she was actually combing his hair while holding him as if to calm him, and in doing this, attempting to resign herself to the fact of the impending death of her baby.

When I recovered from the shock of seeing this spectacle of suffering, I immediately felt a sense of perversion for having violated this room, this home which had a sense of holiness and intimacy to it, due to the fact that this family, which had absolutely nothing, was trying its best to cope with this tragedy. I could not help the tears welling up in my eyes and neither could my team leader. I felt so helpless to the point where all I could do was touch this child's face and then slowly stand up and walk out quietly and shut the door. I will never forget this woman and her child for the rest of my life. Hopefully, the memory *of this incident will somehow honor this woman and child in their anonymous suffering.*

In January 2005, Skip and his squad had to go to the traffic circle in Tal'Afar for a particularly gruesome mission. Skip described the scene in his journal:

There were two prominent traffic circles in the city, and one was infamous for attracting beheaded bodies. Our platoon received a call to cordon off this traffic circle due to a dead body being present there. At this time we had started integrating Iraqi police into our operations so that we could teach them some of our TTPs [tactics, techniques, and procedures]. *As we approached the traffic circle with my Stryker in the lead, I immediately noticed the body and called back a SITREP* [situation report] *to my platoon leader, and we circled our vehicles around the traffic circle to establish security. I noticed that the one Iraqi police truck that had come with us had ended up opposite my vehicle on the other side of the traffic circle. As the Iraqi policemen exited their vehicle, I noticed that when they saw the decapitated body one of the policemen began to slap his face repeatedly while beginning to cry. I then realized that he somehow had a close relation to this victim. He then began to approach the body and I screamed and motioned with my hand for him to stop because it appeared that the body was booby-trapped. The body was elevated about four inches off the ground with a blanket between the body and whatever was under it. When this police officer got within*

approximately ten feet of the body it exploded, sending
fragments of torn flesh everywhere, some of it hitting
my vehicle. The police officer was killed instantly. With
no follow-on-attack, we began to pick up the pieces of the
decapitated body due to religious sensitivities, and then
had to pick up the dead police officer's body. His brain
had been blown out of the side of his face and that had
to be retrieved as well. This was a bad day for the Iraqi
police officers who had gone out with us.

Skip called me that evening after his unit got back to FOB Sykes. We discussed what he had just witnessed. He quoted Ernst Kohn Bramstedt, a German historian whose book *Dictatorship and Political Police* he was reading: "Past terror accentuates present propaganda, and present propaganda paves the way for future terror. This is true for democratic as with dictatorial regimes if the term terror is replaced by efficiency." He also quoted Chesterton's axiom, "Man is more awful than men," adding, "If not, mankind is in deep trouble." I asked him what he meant. He answered that he didn't think mankind is meant to be vicious, but man tends to be vicious.

From: Darrell Griffin, Jr.
Sent: Monday, January 03, 2005
To: Darrell (DAD) Griffin
Subject: bad day, Skipper

We heard news that an Iraqi cop's son was beheaded and his body left on the street in Tal'Afar. We took some Iraqi cops to the scene and did in fact see a headless body with the head carefully stacked on top of the chest with the body lying flat on the ground. The police officers (3) went up to the body to identify it while security was maintained for them by us. Before they got within 8 ft. of the body, the body exploded and killed one while injuring severely the others. Body parts went flying everywhere, like a nose, jawbone, top of skull, eyeball, and lower torso. Flesh was completely blown off the bones. We took the torso back to the castle where we have been for awhile and had to unzip the body bag so that other family members could identify the lower half by the shoes he was wearing. Later in the day, the Iraqi police who were family members of the destroyed body began to drink heavily and one of them … started shooting randomly into the crowded traffic circle below the castle. We watched as he killed a 17 yr. old girl, a 7 yr. old girl, and a 28 yr. old male. We could not intervene as this was happening for very complex reasons. This has been one of the most horrific days of my entire 34 yrs. of living on this earth. Flesh flying everywhere, and senseless violence ruled the day today. I am stupefied and stand in tragic awe in the face of this carnage, what could I possibly say? Where was G-d today? One of my soldiers was deeply affected by today's events. These images brought back many painful and macabre memories of what I used to do as an EMT. I had to talk to my squad to see where their heads and hearts were.

Well, I must go for now because I need to sleep. I love you guys and really need your prayers and so do my men. May G-d give us the strength in the face of such senselessness.

Skipper

From: Darrell Griffin, Sr.
Sent: Monday, January 03, 2005
To: Darrell Griffin, Jr.
Subject: RE: bad day, Skipper

Son we love you very much. God gave us minds and we are allowed to doubt. The only explanations that satisfy me when I ask myself where is God today are the following:

1. C. S. Lewis (from the book that you and Diana got me for Christmas) said that early man felt he was on trial before God and modern man feels that God is on trial before him. We now live [in] a society/world where we always question God. This is not a bad thing, but our acceptance of the ability to question God's judgment does add significant complexity to our relationship with him.

2. When I think of my love for Mom and her love for me, I understand my relationship with God. I would not want the love of Mom if I forced her to love me. When her love is given freely to me, it is a gift that is just beneath the gifts [of] our Lord, but far above any imaginable earthly pleasures. Our relationship with God is similar. He loves us so much that he stays out of our (the people of this planet) way and lets us go on our way, be it good or bad. Unfortunately, man has a way of constantly screwing things up and constantly coming back for forgiveness from God.

You are seeing things that no man or woman should ever have to see. You have a strong relationship with God. God will see you through this ordeal.

He has great plans for you, which may not be in the army, or may be in the army. As I have told you on a number of occasions, once you let me know which direction (the army or no-army), I will deploy whatever resources I have to help you in the direction that you and Diana choose.

We love you and as always we pray for you, [your] men, and Diana daily.

Skip's squad was on patrol in Tal'Afar when they got a call to go pick up another body left in the traffic circle. The insurgents like to use the traffic circle to get maximum exposure for their macabre deeds. When Skip and his men pulled up in their Stryker, there was the body, with its head detached and on the back of the victim. They had seen these booby traps too many times to approach the body without proper precautions. They called the explosives detail and stayed in the safety of their Stryker to wait. As they were watching through their digital viewing equipment, a dog approached the body and started sniffing it. They all took bets as to how long it would take for the dog to blow up. After a few minutes, the dog grabbed the head in its mouth and started to drag it off. For some reason it lost interest and walked away. Within a few minutes the explosive ordinance disposal (EOD) unit came and the Second Platoon took off to complete patrol.

Skip was baffled by the relationship between our troops and the Iraqi police, who were not only ill-trained, but often difficult to identify.

My experience with the Iraqi Police in Tal'Afar was very eye-opening to say the least. The police forces that we worked with seemed at times to be a ragtag, motley assortment of "cousins who knew nephews of best friends who knew their brother's uncle." This, it seemed, was the vetting process in place at the time. This would prove to be fatal to our local security when, on 02 April 2005, my platoon with another platoon had been conducting another "presence patrol" in the Al Serai neighborhood on the east side of Tal'Afar. A police detachment had approached our company commander who was on the ground with our 3rd platoon 2nd squad, SSG Iosa Tavae being the squad leader. One police officer stated frantically that an interpreter had been kidnapped and was being held in an alley close to where our patrol was located. SSG Tavae was directed to proceed down an alley close to his position where the interpreter was allegedly located, and as soon as his squad began the approach into the alley an RPK machine gun opened up on his squad and he was hit first along with his Alpha Team Leader Sergeant Cassidy. SSG Tavae was struck in the face and died en route back to FOB Sykes. Sergeant Cassidy received wounds to his abdomen due to a grenade being thrown at the squad after being engaged by the RPK machine gun. Once SSG Tavae's squad broke contact from this alley, I dismounted my squad from our Stryker and informed my men that we would be entering this alley in order to gain contact with those who opened fire on SSG Tavae's squad. As we proceeded down the alley, we were engaged by small-arms fire and had to kick in a door in the alley in order to get out of the kill zone. This door was the entrance to a courtyard and house that we had to enter and clear. Once on the rooftop we attempted to get eyes on any potential insurgents who had opened up on us, and found nothing.

With our experience concerning the police forces in Tal'Afar, one could never tell who the legitimate police were at any given time. I was able to form relationships of convenience, if you will, with some of them however. I knew of one particular policeman named Hayder who would bring us Jordanian whiskey, notwithstanding the high price we paid for it, and we would drink together during the long cold winter nights guarding an ancient castle that dated back to the Crusader era. Ali, another policeman, said that he had served in the Iraqi Special Forces during the midpoint of Saddam's regime, and seemed to be the more resourceful one of the group of police officers that we came to know. Ali had a friend who was beheaded in the city, and was so distraught over this that he began to fire indiscriminately into a crowded marketplace one day as we were about to leave the castle after our twenty-four hour rotation there. My Stryker was facing the marketplace when he did this and we saw a thirteen-year-old girl [seventeen in his email] *struck in the chest, killing her instantly, and a five-year-old boy* [seven-year-old girl in his email] *struck in the face. We wanted to go back up the hill into the castle to stop him but could not because we were afraid that this would initiate a gun battle between us and* the company-size element of Iraqi police guarding the castle. He was detained by his own and was sent to Abu Ghraib prison, where he subsequently escaped and we saw him three weeks later at the castle working again but without a weapon. More police officers were hired but no weapons had been available for them, so we would provide arms to them from weapons that we confiscated during various raids. Sometimes these weapons given would generate whiskey given to us as a show of appreciation, and out of these exchanges of whiskey and guns developed a quasi-trust between us and the police.

This was my introduction to the war in Iraq. My preconceived ideas prior to deploying to the region had to be reevaluated when I "got on the ground," facing an elusive enemy, forming relationships in the most unconventional manner, seeing the Iraqi people caught between U.S. forces and insurgents fighting each other, and seeing my comrades injured and killed. I knew these men, their children, and their wives, which made their deaths even more difficult to deal with. I thought that witnessing the suffering of the Iraqi people would be easy to cope with because I did not know them on a personal level, but I was wrong, because the one thing, the most sacred commonality, is that you are both human. This was Tal'Afar, Iraq.

From: Darrell Griffin, Jr.
Sent: Thursday, January 06, 2005
To: Diana Griffin
Subject: Another bad day, Iraq

My squad was working with 2–14 [214] Cavalry on this day. They use us [infantry] to kick in doors for them while they surround the area with Strykers so that no cars get out of the area that we are working in. Well, we had been working in one objective area, searching houses, when we heard a loud explosion nearby. I thought it might be an IED or RPG. We were told to pull off our current objective in order to provide medevac support for 2–14 Cav. up the street from us. They were in the process of setting up the outer cordon for us so that we could hit the next set of objective houses. An RPG round was fired from an alley at close range and impacted just above the slat armor on one of their Strykers and killed a private pulling air guard out of one of the hatches leaving a gaping hole on the left side of his torso, which I saw. The next day, as we were leaving the castle in Tal'Afar, we received heavy fire from both sides of an alley that we were driving down and rounds were impacting all around us and you could hear them pinging off the armor on our vehicles. There was so much fire that all we could do was duck down and I told my driver to punch through the alley (we were the lead vehicle). I wanted to stop and fight but there were too many Strykers in the kill zone and we did not know where the fire was coming from.

From: Darrell Griffin, Jr.
Sent: Saturday, January 08, 2005
To: Darrell (DAD) Griffin
Subject: Skipper checkin' in

How are you all? Hopefully this e-mail finds you guys doing well. As I write, I can hear the 21 gun salute firing for the soldier that was killed right in front of me. I forgot that the memorial service was today and it made me jump right out of my seat! Well, it was a quiet 24 hr. rotation at the castle in Tal'Afar. That is what we have been doing for awhile. We will go on missions outside of the castle such as raids, cordon/searches, cordon/knocks, and route interdictions. If not on these missions, we guard this old castle along with Iraqi police that are too scared to do their jobs. We called in an air strike yesterday with AH-64 Apaches that decimated a suspected insurgent meeting place. We had the privilege of sitting back and watching the fireworks. I wanted to enter and clear this building to find any valuable intelligence but higher would not let us. There is a growing trend where we get anonymous tips concerning possible locations where insurgents live: we show up and nothing is found, not even people living in the target house. We found out that in Mosul, this same thing is done and Iraqi cops rush into target houses just to get blown up once inside so we have to really scrutinize these so-called anonymous tips because we kick in a lot of doors with me leading my squad into these target establishments. Well, I gotta go for now. I love you guys and truly covet your prayers and do not take them for granted!

The press had been concentrating on Baghdad, Fallujah, and Mosul; Tal'Afar was under their radar. They were skeptical of the intensity of the fighting going on there. Capt. T.J. Siebold had been called by *Time* magazine to see if they could embed a couple of news people and photographers with Siebold's Alpha Company, the only infantry company in Tal'Afar. He was more than happy to show them what real combat was all about. Siebold already had a mission planned where his soldiers, working with about twenty Iraqi police officers, would hand out leaflets about the upcoming elections on Corvette Avenue, the army name for the main street in Tal'Afar. Only twelve of the expected twenty IP showed up for the afternoon mission. Siebold wasn't discouraged; he considered this the first step in developing the IP in Tal'Afar and was happy that even the twelve showed up.

The mission started with a quick loop around the cemetery, before the troops headed down a deserted alley. They had only been out a few minutes when they started taking small-arms fire and RPGs in their direction. The IP, not as well-trained or well-equipped as Siebold's soldiers, started shooting in what Skip called their "spray and pray" technique of returning fire. Whenever they went into this mode, Skip would yell at them to target the rooftops. At least they wouldn't hit any civilians or soldiers. I asked Briggs if he was scared when the firefight hit them in the face. He said, "Yeah, we were scared, but it was like an everyday thing for us. We were so much better trained and better equipped than the bad guys. They could never engage us face-to-face. We were U.S. troops. How would they dare challenge us in a one-on-one fight? Our platoon was wired tight all the way around. We welcomed them, bring it on, any day, any time. 'Do you really want to go to Allah? If so, we are here to send you.'"

From: Darrell Griffin, Jr.
Sent: Monday, January 17, 2005
To: Diana Griffin
Subject: A really close call

2 Time magazine reporters were with us while we were on a patrol in a really bad part of Tal'Afar. We started receiving fire sporadically with single shots. Then all of a sudden we were receiving heavy machine-gun fire from every direction. You could see muzzle flashes from every house and building with more than one story. Sgt. Ducre, my Alpha team leader, was crouching right next to me as we were pulling rear security when several rounds impacted between us at our heads. I was hit by all the flying debris from the wall as the concrete chipped away because of the rounds, and Sgt. Ducre was burned by the back pressure of the rounds because they hit so close to us. We bounded forward as we fired and I watched an RPG round fly right past us down the street and it impacted at the back of one of our Strykers. Luckily, something caught my eye and I saw a man crouching low on a 2 story building raising a weapon at me and I unloaded my whole magazine (30 rounds) at him and he fell to the ground about 20 ft. from us across the street and then Sgt. Ducre finished him off. We then had to fight our way back to the castle and were pinned down several times because we could not get to the Strykers. We had to fight back on foot for about 1 mile. We all made it back safely. I have never been so sure that I was going to die right there on the street that day (yesterday). I had to run across the street to plus up another squad with my guys and I could feel the rounds impacting at my feet and flying past me with the feeling of a rush of air going past me. The Time magazine reporters were scared, real scared. Be on the lookout for me in that magazine! Well, I have to go for now but please

continue to love me and pray for me. I really thought that was it yesterday!

Son, husband, brother
Darrell/Skipper

Skip's squad was resting in their Stryker at the castle on a cold day in January. It was cramped but warm. PFC Vasquez announced that he was going to "take a piss." As he started to climb out of the driver hatch a single shot rang out and ricocheted off the driver hatch. Vasquez jumped back down through the hatch and screamed, "I'm hit. I'm hit, Sergeant!" Skip started patting him down, looking for the wound. There was no blood or torn clothing. Skip said, "You're not hit, now go shut the hatch." Vasquez told Skip he wasn't going back out there. Skip rolled his eyes and crawled out of the Stryker and went around to shut the driver hatch. Just then a couple more rounds cracked the

morning quietness. Skip felt a sting in his leg and dove back into the Stryker. He patted himself down and saw one of the cargo pockets on his pants was torn. He put his finger through the hole. He took out his battle planning book and the folded set of op orders for Operation Virgo. They both had bullet holes where the round hit them. He only had a graze on his leg. The book and folded op orders had deflected the round. Over the last few weeks the insurgents' accuracy had improved.

Tal'Afar is the largest city in western Nineveh Province. In the elections held in January 2005, of about 190,000 registered voters, 32,000 people went to the polls. This was about a 17 percent turnout. Only Fallujah had a lower participation rate. The army had just regained control of the city two months before and the local police were not equipped to maintain order. By election time the insurgents had reestablished themselves with a vengeance in Tal'Afar. They had demonstrated their vigor by exhibiting several beheadings, blowing up all the police stations in town, and leaving the police cowering in the castle. Al Qaeda was determined to take back Tal'Afar and use the city to smuggle men and weapons from Syria into Iraq. Insurgents were crawling all over the city trying to take it back and disrupt the elections.

Skip's squad rolled out about forty-eight hours before the election. They accompanied an engineering element that set up and fortified the polling places. Skip and his men helped the engineers roll out C-wire (razor wire), pound stakes, place sandbags, and string phone wire. American soldiers were not allowed into the polling areas on Election Day, but they helped the Iraqi army build a protective cordon around each voting station.

On Election Day, Skip's squad occupied a house across the street from the school. They wondered if anyone would show up at the polls, given the intimidation of the last couple of weeks. There was a country ban on driving on Election Day within the city limits. In order to get to the polls, people had to walk. On Election Day morning, at sunrise, they began to show up. At first it was only little old ladies, some using walkers, some stooped over, walking ever so slowly. Matthew Briggs recalls an old lady who was slowly shuffling, one foot in front of the other, barely moving. As she crossed an open area to get to the voting station, bullets began to pick up the dust around her. She just kept shuffling, small steps, one foot in front of the other. A number of younger people watched her as she continued across the courtyard. Whenever the shots subsided, a group of the younger people would make a mad dash across the yard, the shots would begin to ring out again, and soon only the old people would be walking across the dusty courtyard. She made it to the voting area. On her way back, she held up her purple finger as a symbol that she had voted. There were sporadic shots fired at the voters throughout the day. Once, a mortar fell on the line that snaked its way into the schoolhouse, killing a couple of voters. Immediately after it hit, people got right back in line to vote. As Briggs put it, they had the look on their faces of "this insurgency be damned, I am going to vote!"

The insurgents targeted the surrounding buildings at about 9:00 a.m. and started firing into the crowd. The cordon had been set up so the voters would go through checkpoints. While they were waiting to vote they would huddle in a fenced playground next to the polling area. The army had neglected to build them any kind of shelter. But even when the mortars started coming in, the voters just kept coming.

According to my interview with Gen. Robert Brown, then a colonel and commander for the 1st Brigade, 25th Infantry Division, Al Qaeda documents were captured that stated they hadn't been able to disrupt the elections in Fallujah because there were too many army brigades there. Gen. Brown described the fights they got into in Mosul and Tal'Afar in the weeks before the election as "pretty amazing." He noticed the fighters were a well-trained enemy for the first six months of the fighting in Tal'Afar and Mosul. After that, they were a little less efficient, less well-trained. They would do stupid things like stand in the middle of a street and fire an RPG. This was an indication that the U.S. Army had been thinning out the fighters' original ranks. Brown said there were a couple of other techniques that helped the army pull off the elections: The army leaked false polling sites to an Iraqi leader known to be working with Al Qaeda. Then army leaders started a "no roll," which stopped all traffic flow a day before the elections. They knew these strategies were working when Al Qaeda took the bait and posted snipers and RPGs near the fake election sites. Twenty-four hours before Election Day, the Iraqi government advertised the correct locations on TV and dropped millions of leaflets throughout Nineveh Province, including Tal'Afar. On the day of the election, Brown's brigade posted recognizable signage at all neighborhood polling places. The symbol was a girl poking her head through a fence. They nicknamed her Lady Liberty.

From: Darrell Griffin, Jr.
Sent: Monday, February 28, 2005
To: Darrell (DAD) Griffin
Subject: Hey Mom and Dad

Dear Mom and Dad,

How are you all doing? I received your package with the camera and was so happy. Everything was intact and not damaged. I like the book 'Servants of Nature' [*A History of Scientific Institutions, Enterprises, and Sensibilities* by Lewis Pyenson and Susan Sheets-Pyenson] that you sent and can't wait to read it.

Well, my Stryker is out of commission because we finally got hit by a large roadside bomb 2 days ago. It was a gas-bomb that develops a fireball around the entire vehicle when detonated. All of our tires were blown out and all the tie rods were destroyed. Not one of my squad members was hurt. The next day, as we were convoying down a road, our other 2nd squad vehicle was hit by the same gas-bomb on the same road that mine was struck. This town is still out of control and I don't know if our many offensives into the El-Sari neighborhood did any good. There are certain people that we are working with to root out pockets of insurgent resistance but their intelligence doesn't seem any better than ours. Almost daily, our Strykers are being hit by powerful IEDs. We are even starting something similar to a football pool as to who will get hit on any given day. An NCO [noncommissioned officer] from a Cavalry unit here was killed the other day by one of these IEDs. Well, I must go for now but I will try to e-mail you guys more than I have been. I love you guys so much and just knowing that I have you guys as my parents keeps me going through these scary days.

Skipper

Skip and I talked about this pool. They were all scared every time they went out. Setting up a pool and joking about death was one of their ways of dealing with the stress. But as the possibility of death stepped closer to Skip and his squad, they began to take a more serious tone. Skip told me that he could see most of the guys' lips moving in prayer as they left the safety of "the wire" (another term for the FOB). He would always put his hand across his chest and say "Strength and Honor" as they were about to leave on a mission. One day he asked the guys if he could read a verse from the Bible before they rolled. These are the verses he most often read:

Psalm 23
1 The Lord is my shepherd; I shall not want. 2 He maketh me to lie down in green pastures: He leadeth me beside the still waters. 3 He restoreth my soul: He leadeth me in the paths of righteousness for His name's sake. 4 Yea, though I walk through the valley of the shadow of death, I will fear no evil: for thou art with me; thy rod and thy staff they comfort me. 5 Thou preparest a table before me in the presence of mine enemies: thou anointest my head with oil; my cup runneth over. 6 Surely goodness and mercy shall follow me all the days of my life: and I will dwell in the house of the Lord forever.

Psalm 91
1 He that dwelleth in the secret place of the most High shall abide under the shadow of the Almighty. 2 I will say of the Lord, He is my refuge and my fortress: my God; in Him will I trust. 3 Surely He shall deliver thee from the snare of the fowler, and from the noisome pestilence. 4 He shall cover thee with His feathers, and under His wings shalt thou trust: His truth shall be thy shield and buckler. 5 Thou shalt not be afraid for the terror by night; nor for the arrow that flieth by

day; 6 Nor for the pestilence that walketh in darkness; nor for the destruction that wasteth at noonday. 7 A thousand shall fall at thy side, and ten thousand at thy right hand; but it shall not come nigh thee. 8 Only with thine eyes shalt thou behold and see the reward of the wicked. 9 Because thou hast made the Lord, which is my refuge, even the most High, thy habitation; 10 There shall no evil befall thee, neither shall any plague come nigh thy dwelling. 11 For He shall give his angels charge over thee, to keep thee in all thy ways. 12 They shall bear thee up in their hands, lest thou dash thy foot against a stone. 13 Thou shalt tread upon the lion and adder: the young lion and the dragon shalt thou trample under feet. 14 Because He hath set His love upon me, therefore will I deliver Him: I will set Him on high, because He hath known my name. 15 He shall call upon me, and I will answer Him: I will be with Him in trouble; I will deliver Him, and honour Him. 16 With long life will I satisfy Him, and show Him my salvation.

It didn't matter if a soldier was Christian, Jewish, Mormon, Muslim, or Buddhist; these words seemed to comfort everyone. The idea that somehow there is a Supreme Being that could redirect a bullet or put a shield around them made them feel less exposed to the death lottery. You reflect and try to get closer to your God if you want to live through a day in the same city as a few thousand people intent upon ending your life.

It's hard to imagine being in any combat situation nonstop for twelve to fifteen months. The army wisely made it policy to let every soldier go home on R&R during the middle of their combat tour. Skip was ready for his turn. He told me that he wanted to come home for a while to be with people who were not trying to kill him or who would explode if you got too close—people who loved him.

From: Darrell Griffin, Jr.
Sent: Friday, March 25, 2005
To: Diana Griffin
Subject: bad day

Today my squad and I were pulling overwatch on a rooftop looking down on 1st squad when heavy, heavy gunfire erupted all around us on the rooftop. One of my soldiers was struck in the arm, hitting a major artery. We returned fire and while doing so I got him to the ground and began first aid to dress the wound and to stop the heavy, squirting bleeding. One of my other soldiers, PFC Williams, was almost struck in the head. I was standing beside him during our earlier contact and was pointing where I wanted him to shoot when rounds impacted about 2 ft. from our head. It was a bad day.

"Stairway to Heaven" by Led Zeppelin was playing on someone's iPod that had been spliced into the Stryker sound system wiring. They were running the gauntlet: Route Santa Fe. It was important to keep a visual presence on Santa Fe because this was the only way to get supplies into Sykes. It was a two-and-a-half-mile stretch of road filled with IEDs and bad guys with AK-47s and RPGs. The music kept them pumped. On this particular day their music was interrupted by several bursts of small-arms fire. Their vehicle driver, Specialist Jason Mitchell, said it sounded like BBs hitting a Pepsi can—"nineteen tons of steel wrapped around you protecting your ass." As the driver, he had the Caterpillar 350 diesel engine running beside him and his radio headphones on at all times. It was his Stryker, and he took his job seriously. Skip told me that if you had a sissy for a vehicle commander and a sissy for a driver, you were dead meat. That day had started as a good day, no IEDs, RPG, just Led Zeppelin and the pinging of small-arms fire on the other side of an inch of steel and hot chow waiting for them when they got back to the FOB.

They got a call to do overwatch for the 214 Calv on the outskirts of Tal'Afar. Skip's squad arrived to find the 214 digging in a *wadi*, looking for a cache. There was a lot of conversation between the Strykers over their radios, when all of a sudden hell opened up with a huge fireball below 1st Sgt. Jason Roach's Stryker. It lifted the entire nineteen-ton Stryker ten feet off the ground and slammed it back down. The blast was so intense that Skip and his squad could feel it before they saw it. The explosion blew one of the tires more than a hundred meters away. Sgt. Chris Gordon was blown out of the rear hatch and onto the top of the vehicle, and he gave out the most bloodcurdling scream Skip had ever heard. PFC Rosenthal ("Rosie"), who was in the other rear hatch, was sucked out of the ramp as it was blown completely off.

Skip grabbed his medic pack but stopped in his tracks when someone squawked over the radio that another IED was ready to go off. They were waiting for this IED to detonate when a third IED exploded under Gordon's vehicle. Dirt and debris were still falling to the ground, the explosion was still echoing in their ears, and small-arms fire was erupting around them as they ran to Gordon's vehicle. They were taking fire from the south and the east. Briggs opened fire with the automatic weapon on top of the Stryker, but it jammed. He had to take one shot, then recycle the gun manually and shoot again. The driver, Specialist Mitchell, popped out of the driver hatch and started laying down cover fire with his M-4. Briggs told Mitchell to move their Stryker to a position that would give their dismounted soldiers some protective cover. There was a gap of about thirty feet where Skip, SPC Gregory Perrault, and Sgt. Anthony Ducre had to run through the rounds, hitting the ground between Roach's vehicle and the evacuation vehicle. Gordon was blown onto the top of his Stryker. He first heard a small ping, he remembered later, and then everything turned white. He felt his body slam against the hot metal of his vehicle. He remembers screaming from the pain, but at the same time thanking God that he felt pain because this meant that he was still alive. He could hear voices telling him that he was going to be okay.

Skip pulled Gordon the rest of the way out of the Stryker and was surprised that his legs stayed attached since there was so little flesh left between them and his body. As Skip stood on the Stryker working on Gordon, he could see the sparks and chunks of metal fly from where the rounds were hitting. He saw what he thought were sandbags but turned out to be someone's lower intestines. Perrault was running a stretcher with another soldier to get Rosenthal to the evacuation Stryker. The guy carrying the front of the stretcher hesitated because the small-arms fire had grown more vicious. Perrault rammed him with the stretcher and yelled at him, "Stop and I'm going over you with this stretcher!"

As soon as Rosenthal was safely on his way to the FOB, the Second Platoon moved north toward a mosque from where they were receiving small-arms fire. Ducre, a soldier as tough as they come, cried after the adrenaline slowed down for a minute. The entire platoon arrived after Lt. Lewis Seau had gotten permission to fire on the mosque. The Strykers were doing gun runs back and forth in front of the mosque with their .50-caliber machine guns, their hatches filled with soldiers firing their M-4s. Lt. Seau had made a call for air support, and shortly after the platoon got there a couple of Apache helicopters showed up firing their mini-cannons and missiles into the mosque. After the choppers unloaded their payloads, Skip yelled, "Let's go!" Briggs told Specialist Matthew Mitchell to drive their vehicle into the front door of the mosque, but it had been bricked up. Mitchell rammed the front door, blasting it open. Skip got out with the rest of the squad, threw in a couple of grenades, and kicked in the doors. By this time the insurgents had run. There were hundreds of shell casings, some still warm from having been ejected from their weapons.

From Skip's journal:

*During our seven months in this old city, we were imme-
diately pulled into the carnage of insurgent warfare.
On certain days when our Stryker platoon would escort
the fledgling Iraqi National Guard to and from their
various checkpoints, insurgents would target their tiny
Nissan trucks with IEDs and they would be blown to pieces.
On one of these many escort missions, an ING truck was
integrated into our Stryker platoon of four vehicles, one
ING truck positioned directly to the front of my Stryker.
An IED struck the ING vehicle with such explosive force
that it tossed the vehicle like a rag doll into a ditch on
the side of the road we were traveling on. What added
to the macabre nature of this particular incident was
that it was dark out, and with the momentary flash of
explosive light I could see the truck and pieces of bodies
mixed into the mess thrown into the ditch on our left.
The rest of the ING convoy began to immediately return
fire wildly in every direction cynically called the "death
blossom." You could hear these rounds ricocheting off of
our Strykers as we frantically tried to make them cease
fire while we established a protective perimeter around
the destroyed vehicle. Since my Stryker was closest to
the targeted vehicle, I knew that I would have to begin
the CASEVAC* [casualty evacuation] process until our
platoon medic could get to us from the rear of our platoon
column. One of the many difficult things I had to do as
a leader was to bring some of my men from my vehicle
to assist the wounded. As we approached the twisted
wreckage, I turned on my gunlight to assess the damage and the casualties. From dark to light appeared a*

dead soldier with his face blown completely off with a groaning Iraqi soldier beneath him in the back of the truck. I then looked at one of my best soldiers, Specialist Gregory Perrault, and told him that I was about to ask him to do something that he was not going to like at all, but that I needed him to do it in order to get to the wounded soldier beneath. I told him to try and pull the dead body off of the truck, and he did so without even hesitating. As the body was pulled off, I saw the groaning Iraqi soldier calling out to Allah with both of his legs gone and blood pouring out of what was left of his legs. I attempted to apply two tourniquets to the stumps but the dismembered ends were too high up on his legs and the tourniquets kept slipping off. We could not stay long because the longer we stayed, the more we risked being engaged by small-arms fire so I had no choice but to pull him into our Stryker and get him back to our FOB. Needless to say, this brave soul died en route.

From: Darrell Griffin, Jr.
Sent: Monday, February 07, 2005
To: Diana Griffin
Subject: A really bad day

Honey, we were escorting an Iraqi National Guard truck convoy to their various checkpoints when a roadside bomb detonated on the right side of the road directly in front of us and hit the ING truck in front of us. The truck was opened up like a sardine can and I saw different body parts flying through the air and blood mist mixed with twisted metal parts. I stopped my Stryker and prepared to receive small-arms fire from anywhere. We waited for about 3 minutes and decided that no small-arms fire would come so we then ran out to assess the casualties. I stepped on half of a head and found its body twisted into the truck. I heard a moaning sound under this headless body and told one of my soldiers, Perrault, to help me pull the dead body off of the one trapped under it. I found a soldier still alive and secured his legs so that we could pull him out. Well, his leg came off but his body stayed. I then applied a tourniquet to stop the bleeding where the leg was severed. We might have saved this one, I don't know yet because he was choppered to Mosul. I had to tell my privates that we had to lift the headless body onto the Stryker to take back to the FOB and this is when things got even more horrifying. This body was pouring out blood from the neck and as we lifted it onto the Stryker blood got all over us: face, shoulders, DCU [Desert Camouflage Uniform] everywhere. It looked like we where the ones hacked to pieces. By the time this was all over, upon returning to the FOB, I was so worn out that I literally passed out on my bed still stained in blood on my hands, arms, and uniform. 2 hrs. later I had to get up to go on a raid in Tal'Afar. I managed to shower and the bottom of the shower was blood stained as I rinsed it all off. This was the most horrible scene I have ever witnessed in my life. It was so hard to tell my soldier, 'I have to ask you to do something that you will never forget; I need you to help me pull this dead body off the soldier still alive' and the other things I had them do. It was so difficult to see my men covered in blood and to lose whatever innocence was left to them. Honey, I am really hurting right now. My heart is broken, I am broken and will never be the man I was before coming here. Please send this to my Dad, it's very important that you do okay? You guys have to know our story and our pain. It helps us deal with this somehow.

Darrell

Lt. Seau put Skip in for a Bronze Star with Valor, but there was talk that the chain of command was planning to downgrade it. Skip wrote to the officer in charge of his division:

This letter is being written to formally request the decline of my Arcom with "V" device. The reason for this request is manifold. First of all, I always thought that a Bronze Star meant something more than merely serving in a combat zone with exceptional service. I was under the impression that one's life was willingly endangered in order to perform a certain act of heroism that went above and beyond the call of duty and not for simply "serving" in some capacity already mandated by duty and position. Everyone in the military performs that general role and that, not even in a combat environment. I risked my life and the life of my team leader in order to rescue a 1SG and his air guards who were horrifically attacked by an IED. My team leader and I took heavy fire from two directions, directed at us, yet we continued to pull out this 1SG. We placed a tourniquet on Sergeant Gordon's mangled leg and saw the fecal matter that was blown out his rectum all over the top of the Stryker he was riding in. I had to drag PFC Rosenthal over debris without even having

*splinted him because once on the ground assisting him,
I took heavy, direct fire once again. I watched as an
Iraqi army truck blew up in front of my Stryker in
Tal'Afar and since I was closest, directed my squad to
assist with CASEVAC, knowing that they would see the
horrific carnage. One soldier's face was blown off and
I had to direct one of my soldiers to pull the dead body
off so that we could get to the live body beneath. I was
directly responsible for saving the remaining soldier's
life by placing a tourniquet on his mangled leg. Here
in Mosul, another convoy of Iraqi soldiers was traveling
to my front when it too was blown up by an IED. Their
immediate command left them dead in the back of a
blown-up truck and I directed my squad to assist me in
policing up the dead. I had to act fast so that we would
be prepared for a follow-on attack should it happen,
so I had both bodies out of the back of their truck in a
demeaning manner for any righteous dead, hearing
their heads impacting the ground as I dragged them
off in haste, and having the wits to still police up all
sensitive items like radios, weapons, and other items
that could have fallen into enemy hands. I killed a man
who murdered an innocent Iraqi soldier and was able
to mitigate any and all potential collateral damage as
I gave chase to the absconding. I came upon an Iraqi
police officer from Ninevah who had been shot while
traveling down Alaskan way, and did not hesitate to
dismount from my vehicle, not knowing if the area
was secure, in order to save his life with critical first
aid, and was covered in his blood but still able to draw*

upon my paramedic skills to make a valiant effort to save him while still commanding my vehicle and squad from below. Someone who receives a Bronze Star for "Service," I wonder if they have seen the horrific face of the war that is happening in the streets of Iraq as I have. I highly doubt that a Brigade Commander or even a Battalion Commander has seen what I have seen or done what I have done. I have gone far above and beyond the call of duty, I have risked my life under the direct fire of a very real enemy, have they? I have faced the enemy under extraordinary circumstances, and have seen the result of their hatred, have they? If this is the reward that I deserve when seeing other Bronze Star awardees and what they HAVE NOT done then I want no award at all. I do not want to dilute the sanctity of the Bronze Star by gazing on those who willingly receive it for "serving." I can only do this by declining the Arcom with "V" device which merely placates my sacrifice. One has said in the far past, "Do not throw your pearls to the swine," and this is what I am doing. I will not, I cannot consider all the things I have done for this Brigade as worthy of less than what I was originally nominated for.

SSG Griffin, Darrell R. USA

In the end, Skip got his Bronze Star with Valor.

I remember him telling me that he did not want his life to end with someone shoveling his entrails from a dusty road in Iraq. He once had a nightmare of a U.S. soldier scooping up what was left of him, mixed with the gritty, ugly sand of an Iraqi street, and dumping him into a Glad brand Tall Kitchen plastic bag—the kind that has the red pull strings at the top.

I had ended one of my e-mails to Skip: "As I always tell you we pray for you every day of our lives. We have been talking about optimism and pessimism. I am the eternal optimist and I always see the glass half full." His reply:

From: Darrell Griffin, Jr.
Sent: Monday, April 11, 2005
To: Darrell (DAD) Griffin
Subject: The Optimist

The optimist is also an idealist who ignores the tragic vicissitudes that terrorize our individual and collective lives. Idealism ushered in the age of reason, where all of man's problems were expected to be solved eventually through reason. The coming century would prove to be the bloodiest ever seen to this day. The pessimist ignores the fact that good does exist in this world in varying degrees. The realist acknowledges that good will always be intertwined with evil as Christ even alluded to when He said, 'let both grow together.' We have the tragic capability of freedom of will which can never offer any guarantees because this will comes from the very abyss of being. Tragic freedom is our legacy.

Well, I can't wait to see you guys. I will not be right for some time when all this is over. I have done some things that will haunt me for a long time to come and pray that God will forgive me for having done them. Let's just say that the enemy can start to appear in the very people that you are here to 'help.' The Iraqi people will not stand up for a better life than what they currently have. We stand up an Iraqi army that will not leave the protective edges of U.S. Infantry firepower and we end up engaging insurgents for them. They are too accustomed to being led by a benign father-figure/dictator that rules for them as opposed to standing up on their own. These Iraqi 'forces' are lazy, undisciplined, and too prone to corruption to be of any effect. We expect them to fend for themselves when all they have to drive around in are beat-up old Nissan trucks with no armor protection whatsoever. We are making no substantive efforts to stand up a real, self-sufficient and self-protecting army. The fault stands at both ends. I love you guys so much and long to see you, God willing.

Chapter 9

Home

Skip got a chance to come home in April 2005 for R&R. He needed it. He told us that he didn't want to go back but realized that if he didn't someone would have to go in his place.

We couldn't wait to see our son. He had wrestled with Satan in the sands of Iraq for the last six months, and we wondered what he would be like. We got to Fort Lewis at about dinnertime. Diana had dinner waiting for us. Skip was ready to see the bottom of a couple of bottles of merlot and talk about our book, *The Great Conversation*. We had never firmly decided on a title because the focus of the "book-to-be" constantly changed. Skip poured a couple of goblets of merlot and handed me one as we settled down in the living room. He went to his study and grabbed his journal. He wanted to read an entry:

Out of the Labyrinth: Essays in Clarification *(Erich Kahler)*
"*The overwhelming preponderance of collectivity with its scientific, technological and economic machinery, the increasing incapacity of individual consciousness to cope with the abstract anarchy of its environment,*

> *and its surrender to the collective consciousness that operates anonymously and dispersedly in our social and intellectual institutions—all this has shifted the center of gravity of our world from existential to functional, instrumental, and mechanical ways of life. At the same time, the hypertrophy of rationalization has produced an overcompensating irrationality, reversing to the bodily concrete or spiraling to the absurd."*

In other words, no one was thinking.

We talked until our wives were cuddled together, sleeping, under a blanket on the couch and the only thing on TV was the late, late news. We tried to watch it, but it was a repeat of the evening news, which had already been repeated on the late news.

We both knew, but neither of us wanted to acknowledge, what Skip was going back to in a few days. The short time we had together made us want to stay up longer. We didn't want the night to end. But after three bottles of merlot (we had only planned to knock out two), we couldn't keep our eyes open. As I rose from my comfortable position in the easy chair, he rose from the couch and we hugged. He whispered in my ear to take care of Diana if anything happened to him. He knew that Kim and I would take care of Diana, but this was his way of telling me that he didn't know if he would be back. He woke up Diana and I woke up Kim. We said good night and they went upstairs to bed.

Our time with Skip was over way too soon. It seemed as if we had just walked through the revolving door at the airport and been greeted by him and Diana. On the plane back to Los Angeles, Kim and I talked of how stressful it is to be the parent of a soldier in combat. It was hard to believe that we were with him at Fort Lewis, drinking, laughing, eating, and enjoying each other's company, and a few days later he would be back in the sands of Iraq. Skip said that it was like stepping from one world into another. Kim cried a little and slept for the rest of the flight home.

Chapter 10

The Second Tour

Skip returned to Iraq in May 2005. While he was home, Alpha Company had been transferred from Tal'Afar back to Mosul to rejoin the First Battalion of the 1st Brigade of the 25th Infantry Division. They rolled into FOB Marez Mosul at about 2:00 a.m., expecting to quietly park their Strykers and find a place to bed down for the night:

Upon arriving in the city, I was overwhelmed by the size and layout of the urban sprawl as compared to Tal'Afar. My first feeling was wishing that I had 1 million pairs of eyes to look at all the potential threats that presented themselves to me. The name of the FOB was Marez on the west side and Diamond Back on the east of an old military/civilian airfield located on a gently sloping hilltop overlooking the entire east side of the Tigris River. The location of this FOB, situated on the top of a gradually sloping hilltop, would plague us constantly because, as an enemy mortar cell, if you could see it you could shoot at it. We were always worrying about the many rounds that would impact on the airfield and other areas west of it where large concentrations of troops were located. Once again, we were tasked to incorporate into our combat operations the Iraqi military and police forces. As compared to the military and police in Tal'Afar, these elements seemed to be more prepared but not equipped enough to fight and win against insurgents.

The main issue on the ground was the same as in Tal'Afar. The military vehicles were not armored so as to protect against IEDs. On some occasions the police officers didn't even have uniforms, and this made for the perfect storm when it came to not being able to identify friend from foe when seeing an individual with an AK-47 standing on the street. Some Iraqi infantry units couldn't even acquire fuel for their vehicles half of the time, as well as foodstuffs. This is what we had to work with. We were telling ourselves and the Iraqi police and military that they had to stand up and take control of their neighborhoods and patrol sectors while not having the equipment to achieve these objectives. It seemed hypocritical on our part to demand something of them that we would not do if not given sufficient tools to do so. It is to their credit, sincerity, and sense of purpose that, in spite of the lack of means to accomplish the end of defending themselves, the Iraqi military and police in Mosul, for the most part, continued with their mission.

My first combat patrol in Mosul came the very morning that I arrived coming back from R&R. This would also be my first firefight in this city as well, on that morning. My Stryker was 3rd in the order of movement when we were engaged by small-arms fire to our left from an open field, and we immediately returned fire while once again not being able to positively identify [PID] the enemy. When not being able to PID the enemy we would "return fire in the known or suspected direction of contact," which basically meant throwing a wall of lead in hopes of hitting or at least suppressing the enemy's fires. A large mansion was located to our twelve o'clock direction of travel about four hundred meters out, and we began receiving fire from there as well, at which time we called in for close air support from our "Warmonger" element consisting of OH-58 Kiowas and AH-64 attack helicopters, which were designated as "Hunter-Killer teams." The mansion was engaged with Hellfire missiles but with little effect due to the way that houses are built in the city with masonry brick and mortar. We entered and cleared the structure with no enemy contact because the insurgents would utilize the "Spider-hole" technique of engagement. They would engage us from one or two structures back with a very narrow field of view and would then flee. We would engage the structure where we thought the fire was coming from, when in reality the small-arms fire was coming from a more in-depth location. To counter this, we adopted the "look-deep" method of scanning, which meant looking two structures back and in between structures in-depth in order to possibly spot those engaging us.

I wrote earlier as to how the Iraqi army and police would return fire when engaged by small-arms fire. What also needs to be covered is how the insurgents would employ different weapon systems in the battle-space. My platoon was tasked to proceed to a known POI [point of impact] for a mortar strike in the city. This particular POI was *unusual at the time because this mortar round fell in the city and was not apparently aimed at our FOB as usual. The grid coordinate given to us led our platoon to a heavily populated neighborhood in the middle of our patrol sector.*

I was once again the lead Stryker and as we came closer to the given grid coordinate, I noticed an alley filled with more people than usual so I turned the platoon toward this crowd to investigate. My squad dismounted and we went into a home where a woman's screams were coming from. As I walked into one of the rooms, I immediately noticed large amounts of blood and skull fragment with hair attached to it all over the room. I then noticed that the window was broken and could see the blast pattern of where the mortar round had landed coming through the window. This was the POI that we had been looking for. The mortar round launched by insurgents had more than likely been targeted for a nearby Iraqi army compound and had fallen short, coming through the window of this home and killing a little girl, whose mother's screams I had heard upon entering. This was simply collateral damage on the part of the insurgents. Needless to say, this was a bad day.

The insurgents that we were fighting had displayed a high degree of guerilla-type combat efficiency. I was again the lead vehicle in our Stryker platoon of four vehicles and we had just come into sector for another combat patrol. I noticed that a car to my twelve o'clock was acting in a suspicious manner by driving errati- cally in and out of traffic, as if trying to get away

from us, and he would then slow down and end up
close to my vehicle, and would then speed up again
while looking back suspiciously. I began to give chase,
wanting to start a fight. I followed this vehicle south
on a minor street to the south. I thought we would lose
him because the car was small and fast as compared to
our large Stryker. He would slow down one last time
as if to allow me to catch up to him (looking back in
hindsight!) and he then turned north. I noticed a car
sitting off to my right as we turned the corner and
thought that he had stopped to let us pass by, which was
not unusual. No sooner had I turned the corner when
I heard the wind-up and revving of a motor and then
everything went black and I felt our Stryker lurch back
and forth, fishtailing wildly as my driver struggled to

regain control of the vehicle. I knew at that moment that I had been baited by a chase car into the SVBIED [suicide vehicle-borne improvised explosive device] *waiting on the corner for us. A large piece of this car lodged itself into the right side of my Stryker, and we were dragging it along so as not to stop if we didn't have to in the kill zone, because one enemy tactic is to follow up with small-arms fire after initiating an attack with a spectacular device in order to take advantage of the initial shock of being blown up. This was cynically labeled "getting your bell rung."*

We limped our way to an Iraqi army compound about six hundred meters to the north. We had to dislodge the piece of vehicle from our slat armor and had to pick pieces of flesh out of the slat armor as well. Upon returning to the attack site, we noticed that there were large chunks of flesh strewn all over the road. This was an extremely macabre scene with spinal cord, skull, and a turned inside-out torso on the road. This man died for four flat tires on this day.

Another indicator as to how well the insurgents became practitioners of guerilla-type warfare was in how they emplaced their IEDs. We like to call this game "IED Chess." When driving down any given road, if you are paying attention, you might notice a fresh patch of dirt on the road that wasn't there the day before or unusual amounts of trash, animal carcasses, and one million other potential roadside oddities that could be potential IEDs. In the event that this occurs, we would stop at least two hundred to three hundred meters away in order to maintain a minimum safe distance. These indicators could possibly be feints to make you stop at the predicted safe distance so that you actually stop where the real IED is located. IEDs could be overtly placed just to make you stop, so that you can be fixed in a small-arms kill ambush from your flanks. IEDs are used in many ways just described for many different reasons, thus showing a high degree of sophistication and foresight in planning on the part of the insurgents. These examples of emplacement are what I mean by the game of "IED Chess." I want to linger on this particular point for a moment because these devices were the primary means that the insurgents would use to inflict damage on Coalition forces. These devices offer the advantage of stand-off capability so that the user will not be forced into direct-fire engagements, thus achieving Economy of Force. These devices also have the potential for terrain denial, because if you can't secure a route you can't travel on it. If you can't travel on it, then surely supply convoys can't travel on it. Psychological impact can be achieved as well due to the spectacular nature of these attacks when filmed by insurgents as the device detonates on its intended target, which, in turn, gets a lot of press coverage because the media feeds off of the spectacular. Suicide Vehicle-Borne IEDs are also an effective tool used in the battle space as well. Like the Kamikazes of WWII, these platforms never miss their mark because they have the ultimate guidance system, a human being. In some cases we would notice that the operator would be handcuffed to the steering wheel just in case he lost his faith. Another car would shadow this

device and, if need be, detonate the car with explosives
by a fail-safe device under his control.

It was July 8, 2005, a hot day, and Skip's squad was on patrol in Mosul. I was always amazed at how closely the climate of Mosul tracked with the climate of Los Angeles. I would key in Mosul and Los Angeles on Yahoo weather so that I could always know what kind of weather Skip was dealing with. It made me feel closer to him.

The platoon was traveling down Tacoma Boulevard (the name of the street given by the soldiers out of Fort Lewis). Picture the "auto row" in any big city. On one side of the road there were auto dealerships and on the other side were hundreds of people milling about. They were going really slowly up the middle of the street. Lt. Seau was concerned because if something came up he couldn't roll to the right or left. Suddenly they noticed a vehicle with its doors open. There was a badly wounded man in the driver's seat. Lt. Seau looked over and saw Skip in the middle of the crowd. He was totally unprotected. Apparently, Skip had seen the vehicle with the wounded driver before Seau saw it. As Skip ran up to the vehicle, Seau noticed another vehicle take off with what looked like gunmen inside. It turned out they were Iraqi policemen. Lt. Seau had everyone start pulling security while Skip administered first aid to the driver.

Once Skip stabilized the Iraqi policeman, they put him in the back of a Stryker and took him to the hospital. Seau felt that Skip had saved this guy's life. It was a normal day's work.

One day Skip walked into 1st Sgt. Jerry McCullough's office. He was a big, muscular, but soft-spoken man nearing retirement. Skip used to be amazed at how McCullough could "smoke" him in the gym. He was a tough first sergeant, too tough for the men under his command to tell him they loved him, but everyone did. Skip's Stryker was in for maintenance and he needed a Stryker to go on a mission. McCullough's Stryker was sitting in the motor pool and begging to roll. Skip asked Sgt. "Mac" if he could borrow it. McCullough agreed, but with certain conditions: "Bring it back with a full tank of gas, don't mess with my M&M's, don't mess with my fly fishing magazines, and don't get it shot up. I don't want any bullet holes in it." (Skip's reputation for somehow finding firefights was legendary.)

The next day, Skip rolled out with his platoon, led by Lt. Seau. One of their guys, Sgt. Peter Ewen, had almost been taken out by a sniper the day before. They were going to search the area to see if they could locate the gunman. Lt. Seau had just finished briefing the platoon Strykers over the radio when Skip yelled "Strength and Honor!" into the radio. Lt. Seau completed the message with "God Bless America and the Outlaws!" (the nickname for the platoon). The other squad leaders were SSG Ogle, SSG Staley, SSG White, and SFC (sergeant first class) Simpson. Skip was in the lead Stryker, with three Strykers behind his (borrowed) vehicle. Part of their routine was to roll past an Iraqi army (IA) outpost. As Skip's Stryker rounded the corner, he saw an old red Opel pull up in front of it. An IP guard walked up to the car as one of the occupants stuck an AK-47 out of his window and shot the guard point-blank, then tossed a grenade out the window. Strykers are relatively quiet when they roll, so the insurgents couldn't hear them coming. They were concentrating on murdering the guard, and didn't know there was a platoon of Strykers bearing down on them.

Skip started firing at the car as it sped away from the IP compound, and pulled in behind it. They had shot out their back window and were firing at Skip's Stryker while he returned fire. Skip hit the driver in the back of the head and the car came to a stop. Killing killers added to Skip's experience, which made killing easier. This bothered Skip for the rest of his career in the army.

Two passengers scrambled out of the Opel and began spraying Skip's Stryker with AK-47s. Skip's unit fired back, wounding one of them; the other one got away. Once all the gunfire stopped, they had to check out the car for booby traps. Skip took some wire from his Stryker and wrapped it around the driver and pulled him from the car; he was afraid the body would explode. They later found a bag of maps rigged to explode if disturbed; two AK-47s; five grenades; and eleven ammo magazines.

They bagged the guy and, according to standard operating procedure, took him to the main hospital in Mosul. Then they tagged the scene, marking the spot where the insurgent went down. Every platoon had an insignia: Skip's was The Outlaws.

When Skip came back that night, Mac was out on a mission. The next morning, Mac went to his Stryker to get his fishing magazines and his bag of M&M's. When he got into his Stryker, he couldn't believe what he saw. There was blood all over the place, hundreds of empty cartridges,

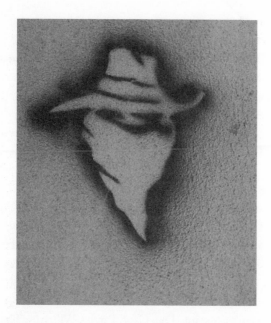

the remote weapons systems sight was all shot up, and his M&M's were gone. Mac called the command post (CP) and told them he wanted Skip at his door *now*. When Skip walked in, Mac gave him a hard look and demanded: "What did you do to my vehicle? Do you remember my instructions?" Skip repeated the instructions back to him. "You better clean up my vehicle now or you'll never see the inside of this FOB again!"

Skip and his squad got it cleaned up fast.

Mac told me some time later: "One thing about Griff is he always produced body counts. He was a warrior. He took pride in the American flag." He said he often saw Skip flying the American flag while on patrol, and thought he was provoking a fight. "Sure enough, I'd wait a couple of minutes after seeing Griff and his flag and I would hear gunfire." When I asked Skip about this, he said that anyone who was going to shoot at him would eventually shoot at him with or without the flag. He was just speeding up the process a little. He also said that he would rather be the one shot at than one of the guys in his battalion. He thought of it as drawing fire.

It was August 21, 2005, and the 1–5 Infantry, 1st Brigade, was on its last few missions before packing up to go home. Sgt. Duane Wells's platoon was out in its sector, an area of Mosul referred to as Palestine. Duane and Skip had been friends since Skip first arrived at Fort Lewis in 2002. Riding with Duane in his Stryker were a couple of soldiers from the replacing unit, the 172nd out of Alaska, and a battalion physician's assistant (PA), Capt. Patrick Williams. The PA normally doesn't go out into the battle space, but Patrick wanted to get familiar with his unit's newly assigned area of operations.

Nearby was Sgt. Nicholas Malich's unit. Malich was in charge of a sniper team from Headquarters Company (HHC) of the 1–5 infantry. They had been driving around an "area of interest" over the last forty-eight-hour period, waiting for a particular insurgent to turn on his cell phone. The CIA had developed a tracking device that could locate and zero in on a cell phone, and they were testing it with a couple of elements of the 1–5, including Malich's team. This was the way it worked: The CIA was fed insurgent phone numbers through various informants who were keyed into this tracking device. When their cell phones were turned on, the devices would lock onto them and pinpoint their location. According to Malich, it was a pretty successful tool. Over the last couple of months they had tracked down and killed over thirty insurgents. Malich's unit had been patrolling the area in pursuit of a signal from the tracking device; the night before they had pulled up to the target house and seen a guy peeking around the corner while talking on his cell phone. When they searched his house they couldn't find the cell phone, and he denied even owning one, though they did find a cell phone charger and other accessories in a freezer. On the second night they were directed back to a field across the street from the same house. As they approached the field they lost the signal.

The next night, they got more CIA intel that there was a potential target in the same area. Malich's unit was unconvinced; they just wanted to do their last couple of patrols and go home, but when they got the "hit" call, Specialist Brownley, the Stryker driver, called out, "Hey, this is the house right here." SFC Joseph Martinez, Malich and Wells's platoon sergeant, directed them to attack. Since they were right at the target house, they didn't have time to plan for the mission. They just pulled their Strykers up to the driveway.

Sgt. Tim Clanin was in charge of the third Stryker. Sgt. Martinez directed Wells and his squad to go through the front door. Clanin's squad was to pull security for the 1–5 out in front of the house. Malich's sniper team was waiting in the Stryker as reinforcements in case more soldiers had to go into the house. Since Malich had been to this particular house, he knew there was a courtyard behind it and suggested to Martinez that the target could escape through the back. Martinez instructed Malich and his team to work their way to the back of the house along the six-foot-high block wall surrounding the courtyard and secure the back door. Wells was adamant: he wasn't going in the front door until Malich had his team in place in the backyard.

As Malich's men went around the back corner of the courtyard, they came face-to-face with their man. He and Malich froze for an instant. It was one of those moments when you know you're probably going to kill this person or he is going to kill you—a real "pucker" moment. In this brief instant, Malich noticed the target didn't have a weapon so he couldn't shoot him—official combat protocol. He instructed Sgt. Miller to grab the suspect. Malich and his squad poured into the courtyard and pounced on the insurgent as he and Miller were struggling. They flex-cuffed him and moved toward the back door. Malich sneaked up to the back window and stole a quick look inside: the room was filled with AK-47s, RPGs, explosives, and other killing tools. His army instinct told him the air was going to explode within seconds. He yelled back to Miller, "Cache! Cache!" Miller lost his cool for a couple of seconds and started kicking the guy on the ground. Malich knew that Wells was about ready to kick in the front door. He didn't have time to get on the radio, so he started yelling as loud as he could, "Stop! Stop!" Just at that moment a grenade bounced down the stairwell by the window.

Wells's squad was in the house when someone yelled "Grenade!" Everyone dove into a different room as it went off. Wells noticed that it was one of those little two-inch-tall plastic grenades that can "ring your bell" but couldn't really hurt you unless you were standing right over it. Within seconds another grenade rolled down the stairs. When it exploded, it put a huge hole in the floor at the bottom of the stairwell. Wells recognized from the savageness of the explosion that it was an anti-tank grenade. Shrapnel was still flying from the exploding hunk of metal and hitting walls when an insurgent at the top of the stairs opened fire with a machine gun. Wells and his men started working their way out of the house to regroup. Sgt. Justin Blair spotted three snipers on the roof firing down into the courtyard.

Malich knew he had to get his men out fast. Before he could even take a step it was like a cloudburst of lead. Bullets and shrapnel were raining down from the second story and the roof, fire coming from everywhere. Malich's guys had made it out of the courtyard and he was right behind them. Before he cleared the back gate, he felt a blow as if he'd just been punched in the back. He was a master in martial arts and knew how to take a punch. As he continued to run he glanced down and saw his arm twisted behind him, dangling as he ran. He tried to bring it around in front of him, but he had lost control of it. His first thought was that he had been hit by RPG shrapnel. He ran out of the gate past Miller and yelled, "I'm hit!" As he made it out of the gate the only cover he could find was a tree, so he ran for it.

Skip's unit, one of the squads under the command of platoon leader Lt. Lewis Seau, was responding to a broken-down truck with a dead driver to check out if it was wired with explosives. As they were completing this assignment, after an EOD team had been called in to take over the situation, they heard a radio transmission over the Apache Company Net call for help from their recon element (Malich and Wells's unit, under the command of Sgt. Joseph Martinez). The helicopters above them led them to where their recon unit was under attack. Their Strykers moved fast to the target area but couldn't get close to the site because of the narrow alleyways, cars, and other barriers. Seau had his squads, including Skip's, dismount and head for the building on foot, while the Stryker drivers were directed to find some way to get the Strykers in there. It was late at night, so visibility was only through their night-vision devices and a few lights from the dimly lit buildings surrounding the target building.

Once Malich got to the tree, he sat down and removed his gear to see how bad the injury was. Blood was spraying from his cheek. "Help, I need a medic over here now, I'm hit bad!" he yelled.

The medic yelled back, "Sorry, man, I can't help you, I'm hit too!"

Malich could see the medic leaning up against the outside wall of the courtyard, also bleeding badly. He yelled at SPC David Shaver, "Get on the radio, I'm hit! I'm in bad shape!" Shaver was on the radio while at the same time firing his weapon at the house. They were trying to keep the insurgents from coming out the back way. Shaver was calling for help over the radio when an insurgent armed with an AK-47 started through the back gate. Shaver dropped him with a burst from his M-4. Malich could see the rest of recon at the front of the house and tried to warn them away, but they couldn't hear his screams over the sounds of the raging firefight. He knew he would bleed to death if he just sat there, so he got to his feet, thinking that he had a better chance running through the wall of lead that had been erected by the insurgents and soldiers. He got up and fell back down. He had lost too much blood. He could feel the life pulsating out of his torn artery and forming a pool of warm blood under him. He knew he was done for, so he turned over on his stomach and started praying that God would take care of his wife and children.

Sgt. Clanin heard Shaver calling for help over the radio and was the first one to reach him. Patrick Williams, the PA in Sgt. Duane Wells's Stryker, also heard Shaver's call for help. He jumped out of the Stryker and ran through the middle of the firefight from the front of the house to the back of the courtyard, where Clanin was attending to Malich. The PA was just a ride-along for the day and didn't have any medical gear with him. Malich was still lying under the tree praying when he opened his eyes and saw the PA standing over him. The PA rolled him over and asked where he was hit as he assessed Malich's situation. "Man, I need morphine, I'm hurting," Malich begged. Normally, Malich would have morphine on him, but since they were getting ready to leave Iraq, the soldiers had given it all back to supply so that they could take a complete inventory of it.

The PA told Malich that he had lost too much blood and it was too dangerous to give it to him now. He saw that Malich had a severed artery and a collapsed lung. He helped Malich sit up against the tree. "Look, man, I don't have any medical gear with me. I'm going to use my pocket knife to cut open your chest so I can reach your artery with my hand and stop its flow."

Malich nodded. "Okay, but first give me some morphine for the pain."

The PA repeated, "I told you why I can't."

Malich clenched his teeth and said, "Go for it." Malich was scared because he had seen *Black Hawk Down*. In the movie, the doc tries to go into a soldier's leg to grab an artery and clamp it shut so he doesn't bleed to death. The soldier dies.

Malich thought the pain couldn't get any worse until the PA stuck his hand into his chest and grabbed the gushing artery with his fingers to clamp it off. "I got it, I got it," he said.

At about this time Sgt. Miller made it over to Malich. He and Malich were like brothers. "Hey, man, it's not that bad," Miller comforted him. "You're going to be fine."

Just then the PA moved his hand a bit inside his chest to remind him that it was bad. The PA turned to Sgt. Clanin: "Get on the horn. Tell them if we don't have him in the 'cash' [combat support hospital] in fifteen minutes. . . ." He looked at Malich and realized that the wounded soldier was hanging on his every word. The PA looked back at Clanin and said, "Just tell them he's going to be in big trouble."

Malich started yelling at Clanin and Miller: "You guys are liars! You know I'm dying here, you guys get me out of here!" At this point Sgt. Martinez appeared out back in his Stryker and loaded Malich into it, along with the wounded medic, and sped off to FOB Diamond Back. Inside, Malich was lying on a bench with the PA's hand still in his chest.

Sgt. Wells and some of his men were getting out of the house through the back courtyard. As they dashed by, Justin Blair, the vehicle commander for one of the Strykers, began blasting the top floor and roof with his .50-caliber mounted machine gun. The thumb-sized slugs were blowing chunks of cement and other debris off the back of the house and it was raining down on Wells and his escaping squad. Wells later told me that the falling debris felt like manna from Heaven: he knew he was being covered at that point.

The men got word that they would have Apache Attack helicopter support coming in, so they marked the building for the pilots to make sure they hit the right house. At about the same time that Wells's unit was working its way to the front of the house, Lt. Seau's men arrived on foot to cover them. When they got there, the Apache was hovering over the house. There were a couple of soldiers at the front gate trying to treat one of their men who'd been hit. Seau ran up to Skip, who was assisting in the treatment of the soldier, and introduced himself. Skip informed him that there were still as many as six enemy fighters in the building and yelled, "Duane, where are you?"

Wells turned around and Skip gave him his signature bear hug. "You okay, man? You been hit?"

"I'm okay, Griff."

"Dude, I heard on the radio that it was you. I got worried."

Wells reassured him: "I'm good, I'm okay."

Everyone pushed back to their vehicles while they prepared for a coordinated assault on the house. Seau mounted his vehicle and radioed the chopper to suppress the building with everything it had. The Apache started laying heavy fire into the house with its thirty-millimeter chain guns. Shortly afterward, Capt. T.J. Siebold, company commander for Alpha Company of the 1–5 Infantry (Seau's boss), came on the net and instructed them to move on the house now as it was on fire.

The Stryker carrying Malich and the medic missed the entrance to the combat support hospital (CSH) and had to go around to the back entrance. En route the PA had instructed the CSH to be ready to receive their wounded. Miller and Shaver kept talking to Malich to keep him awake long enough to get to the CSH. There was a vascular surgeon on the airfield getting ready to fly home. The CSH team ran out onto the airstrip and got him off the plane and took him back to the CSH to wait for Malich. His collapsed lung was making it difficult for him to breathe. They punched him a couple of times in the chest with a needle to relieve some of the pressure. Malich remembers telling the PA and the surgeon, "I can't do this anymore."

The surgeon held his hand and told him, "Don't worry, we have you now."

Malich struggled as they put a mask over his face. The next thing he remembers is waking up in a hospital in Germany with his wife by his side.

Seau had his men dismount once again and head for the building along with Sgt. Wells's squad and the other recon soldiers. Seau remembers praying that the insurgents who had met the recon unit earlier with grenades and machine-gun fire were either dead from the Apache attack or had lost their will to fight. As they entered the house, it was completely dark, with water sprinkling down though the ceilings, smoke everywhere, and spots of fire burning throughout the structure. Sgt. Korey Staley's squad (first squad), part of Lt. Seau's platoon, quickly took control of the bottom floor. Skip asked Seau: "You want me to take my squad and clear the top floor?" He led the way, followed by Seau and the rest of his squad. They moved quickly up the stairs as water gushed down. At the top of the stairs, they saw two dead enemy fighters lying next to grenades, machine guns, and piles of unused ammo: they could have fought for hours more if the Apache hadn't shown up.

The entire building had been cleared when the platoon happened upon a group of women and children huddled in the corner of a room on the bottom floor. Miraculously, none of them were hurt. A small boy, not more than seven, came forward and pointed out where his dad—one of the dead men—had buried some weapons. They dug up more mortar rounds and suicide vests and other weapons. No one in Skip's platoon had been killed. He didn't find out that Malich was okay until they got back to FOB Marez for the debriefing.

About a week later, he called me from Mosul and gave me a blow-by-blow account of the battle. I asked him why the enemy hadn't just given up. "Most of the time they hit us and run to fight another day," he said. "This time they knew they couldn't win and had their families with them, but they started the fight anyway." They had a choice and they made it. They could have just surrendered. Once the grenade rolled down the stairs, they communicated their intentions and sealed their fate. Skip had written in his journal a bit of wisdom from Aristotle: "The vicious and the virtuous have not indeed power over their moral actions; but at first they had the power to become either the one or the other, just as one who throws a stone has power over it until he has thrown it, but not afterwards."

Skip was troubled by the fact that he was able to go through the house, clearing it and counting the bodies, without really thinking about the fact that they were dead people. His job was to assist Lt. Seau in making an accurate report. He had gotten used to participating in deadly duels and doing the paperwork afterward. "A lot of people think being a soldier is easy," he told me over the phone. "You know, like, ready, aim, fire." He had been reading Clausewitz's *On War.* "That book sums up why I pay less attention to the opinions of people who haven't been in war. This battle happened fast, without time for planning, and became complex quickly." He quoted Clausewitz: "'Everything in war is simple, but the simplest thing is difficult. The difficulties accumulate and end by producing a kind of friction that is inconceivable unless one has experienced war.'"

He also cited a passage from B. H. Liddell Hart's *Strategy*: "In war the chief incalculable is the human will." This war had had a long list of "incalculables." The enemy didn't have rules of engagement and didn't even know what the Geneva Convention meant. They had no problems using their family members as shields; they had no problems blowing themselves up. While American troops were fighting to live, many of the enemy combatants were fighting to die and meet Allah and get their allotment of virgins.

I ended our phone call as I always did: "We love you and we pray for your safety, comfort, and wisdom daily."

Chapter 11

Home Again

The 1–5 had completed its deployment in Iraq and Skip was headed home. We had been planning a homecoming for a couple of months. We had offered to send him and Diana anywhere they wanted to go on vacation. Skip asked if we could have a family reunion. It had been several years since we had the family together. My middle sister, Sharon Scollard, started planning the gathering. She found a house on the Delta in Central California that would accommodate all the relatives who would be coming. The Griffins were an odd assortment. There were the CPAs and lawyers. Then there were the ones with tattoos and piercings on various parts of their bodies, and I was never sure what they did for their livings.

A rule was expressly stated that everyone had to agree to before the reunion: *No drugs on the premises—If you feel the need to smoke grass, please do NOT do it on the grounds.*

A good portion of the family still smoked, so we wanted to make it clear that it would not be allowed at this function. Skip was proud of being a soldier and was very patriotic: he didn't want a raucous party. I asked him if he would give a short presentation about what the army was doing in Iraq and whether the media was presenting a true story. He jumped at the opportunity.

After dinner, Skip went downstairs and wired his laptop to the big-screen TV. We pushed the pool table out of the way and the whole family joined us. Some had kids on one hip; some had Buds or Coronas in their hands. Before bringing the images up to the screen, Skip said a little prayer for his comrades still in Iraq. This had been his life for a year. He announced that he would first show the G-rated version while the kids were still up. When the kids were in bed he would show the real version. He referred to it with a phrase he would often use: "War is bloody and dirty." The G-rated version presented the sanitized story that we see on CNN and Fox. There were photos of his squad carefully patrolling a street, him and his squad at the Tal'Afar castle, the Iraqi people—but no violence, no blood. A couple of times he even slid into his imitation of CNN's Anderson Cooper.

After the kids had gone to bed, Skip showed slides of the war we didn't see on CNN—the uncensored war. He hated the failure of the media to reflect the way things really were in Iraq. He was on a mission to show as many people as he could what the war looked like from a foot soldier's perspective—not from the perspective of some reporter holed up in the Green Zone.

It was too cold to use the pool at the house, but there were other activities. There was a tattoo contest and a piercing contest. I was a little shocked that we had so many relatives who had so much metal put through various parts of their bodies. I was amazed they could get through the metal detectors at an airport.

The 1–5 was scheduled to go to Germany in a few months but would eventually end up back in Iraq.

The year in Iraq had affected Skip. He was on edge and agitated a lot of the time. He didn't like being in groups of people. Loud noises bothered him. He had never raised his voice at me, but one time on the phone he got angry when I didn't agree with him about one of Nietzsche's books, *On the Genealogy of Morals*. I had noted that Hitler was a great fan of Nietzsche, and had used his work to justify anti-Semitism. Skip refuted me with his usual firm grasp of logic: Smith & Wesson makes handguns used by a number of police departments. Bad guys also use their handguns. Smith & Wesson is not bad just because bad guys use their guns. That Hitler had stolen Nietzsche's ideas and used them for his own purposes didn't mean that Nietzsche himself was anti-Semitic.

He was still as loving as ever, but the gore, the killing, the plight of the Iraqi people—all this had changed him. He seemed to have a need to constantly play certain scenes over again in our conversations. As we dissected these scenes into smaller and smaller pieces, his feelings of guilt began to percolate to the surface. He was still a hugger, still ended every conversation with "Dad, I love you and Mom. Give a hug to my babies [his little brother and sister]." Diana would wake up sometimes and find him sitting on the edge of the bed crying.

Diana was the center of Skip's universe, but he was often curt and distant even around her. I was worried that he wasn't decompressing properly. We convinced him to see an on-base counselor. It seemed to help, but he still wasn't the same. During a conversation at the start of 2006, he told me that being back home was hard, although he loved being able to go back to Diana after a day on the base, watch TV, play with his dog Luna, or sit in his study surrounded by his library. Once you have experienced war, preparing for war and practicing it is harder mentally and emotionally.

He was unnerved by the rituals of daily life. There were too many rules, too many working parts. When I asked him what he meant, he rattled off a list: traffic signals, groceries, paperwork, inspections, people walking around seeming not to care or know what was going on in Iraq. Skip's unit was preparing to relocate to Germany. They would spend a year there and then get deployed to Iraq. Diana was excited but apprehensive about going to Germany. She had never lived outside the country. We all talked about it a lot. His mom and I talked of visiting them once they got settled in. I didn't press the issue of working on our book. We were going to complete it over the summer. Skip was going to take a stab at writing an introduction and I was going to catalog the hundreds of photographs he'd taken in Iraq and attach notes to them. He was able to write about twenty pages.

In February 2006, Skip told us that his orders had changed. He was being transferred to Bravo Company and would be going back to Iraq sooner than originally anticipated, probably in June. What he didn't tell us was that he had requested to go back to Iraq with the 3–2 or any other unit going back sooner. Command Sgt. Maj. Freddie Du, his conduit for transferring units, asked him: "Sergeant Griffin, why do you want to go back to Iraq? You just came home. You want to be with your family." Du recalled that Skip's response was: "Sergeant Major, I just want to go back and be with the soldiers. I really want to go back with this unit that's going back." Du knew that Skip was determined and had an excellent record as a combat NCO, so he made it happen. The 3–2 was scheduled to return to Iraq in June of 2006. Now, so was Skip.

June was getting close, and Skip's mom and I wanted to go up to Fort Lewis to see him and Diana before he was deployed. We were juggling work schedules and time with our six kids. I could get off work, but Kim couldn't, so I flew up alone. Normally we would have a set agenda that revolved around the book, but now we just wanted to spend time together. Skip had worked through a lot of his issues after months of dissecting, digesting, and rethinking. He mainly wanted to talk through why he was going back, and in explaining his reason reaffirm the reason to himself. He knew he had to be tough while wearing his uniform in the streets of Iraq. He did have some inner doubts about being as rough as he was during the last tour. Would it have been better to ignore the occasional guy who gave the throat-cutting sign as his Stryker rolled down the street rather than stopping and kicking his butt? Did the confrontations that he had with these guys accomplish anything? Did it possibly make them stop and think before they tried to mess with the Americans? Was such a guy already an insurgent, or did this confrontation push him into becoming one? Did it have a greater impact on his male pride because he was Muslim?

Skip and I had a long talk about the different social customs in the United States and Iraq. What brought on this conversation was a photograph of kids and adults using the soles of their shoes to hit a statue of Saddam that had been ripped down. A peculiar custom to Americans (less so after an Iraqi reporter hurled his shoes at Bush during a press conference in Baghdad), but to those Iraqis it was the ultimate insult to Saddam. Skip felt sorrow for the Iraqis who had been caught in the middle of the war. He still remembered, all too vividly, the day he and Sgt. Ducre had walked into the room where the mother was holding her sick child with the bloated tumor. We talked about how it would have worked in Iraq if we had not gone in, guns blazing, but instead just cut off the head of the snake with assassin attacks and then spent some of the billions on sending teachers, doctors, and consultants to fix their infrastructure. We agreed that we would be less hated by the rest of the world, there would have been fewer deaths of Iraqi civilians and American soldiers, and Bush might have been loved rather than reviled worldwide.

My trip ended way too soon. We drank our merlot, had our discussions, went to Half Price Books. We promised that we would each work on our respective parts of the book. We would often split up at bookstores and then occasionally check in with each other to discuss our finds. I would drift from philosophy to math to business. Skip usually stayed in the theology and philosophy sections, occasionally drifting over to the history section. That day Skip bought Descartes's *Discourse on the Method* and *Meditations on First Philosophy*. I bought Thomas Hobbes's *Leviathan*. He had already read it and told me it was a good read; he quoted a line that had stuck in his head, about how the state of nature is "the war of every man against man, thus men band together in communities out of fear."

They took me to the airport. I hugged Diana good-bye. My son, SSG Darrell R. Griffin, Jr., and I hugged for the last time on this planet. I wish I could remember every detail of that last hug. I wish I could remember exactly where we were standing, what we each of us was wearing, and the last few words we spoke to each other. All I can remember is that we hugged.

Chapter 12

The Last Tour

Skip started his second tour, deploying in July 2006. As did almost all combat units going into Iraq or Afghanistan, they landed first in Kuwait at Camp Buehring and stayed there for about three weeks getting the troops ready for their stay in Iraq. During this period, they would site their weapons and be briefed again on the rules of engagement, general orders, and a host of other information that could help them accomplish their mission while in Iraq.

Skip brought in his own guns. That spring, he had talked Diana into letting him buy a new M-4, with a top-of-the-line scope, and a Beretta 9mm pistol. Skip had his personal version tricked out with a better scope, better butt stock, and a few other nominal enhancements. One of Skip's associates, who was a little jealous of him for some reason, decided that Skip's chain of command should know about his weapons. By bringing in his own weapons, Skip violated some pretty serious army rules and regulations: soldiers cannot supply their own weapons, which is considered behavior unbecoming for a noncommissioned officer, and in violation of international laws that regulate the conduct of warfare. There were also practical issues: weapons are standardized for a number of reasons, such as maintenance and interchangeability of parts. Skip's intention wasn't to violate any rule; he just felt he could do his job better with his own weapons. But it showed poor judgment, and his command had to act on the information they'd been given.

Once they were made aware of the existence of Skip's "special" weapons, his platoon sergeant and his first sergeant performed a complete search of everyone in Bravo Company and found and confiscated his weapons. Skip was immediately relieved of his squad in Bravo Company and sent to Headquarters Company to await full disciplinary actions against him. This could have ended Skip's military career, along with some serious jail time and a significant fine. He was assigned to SSG James Pelletier in HHC, pending determination of his punishment. Pelletier's first thought was, "Oh, great, another problem child."

Skip was assigned to sleep in Pelletier's fifteen-man tent. When Pelletier entered the tent, Skip was sitting on his newly assigned bunk with all his equipment laid out in a grid, doing a pre-combat inspection. Sgt. Pelletier noticed that on a number of Skip's pieces of equipment were the stenciled words: *Malleus Dei*.

"So you think you're the hammer of God, do ya?" Skip was surprised that Pelletier knew what *Malleus Dei* meant. From this first meeting in the tent in Kuwait, he and Pelletier became close friends. They worked together, slept in the same tent, ate together, worked out together, and spent hours in deep discussion. They discovered they had both read *Aristotle and the Arabs: The Aristotelian Tradition in Islam,* by F. E. Peters, which traced the transmission of the Greek philosopher's ideas through the medium of critical commentary by early Islamic scholars. Pelletier had majored in philosophy at the College of Saint Thomas More and had worked his way through the classics of Western thought. He and Skip would talk late into the night about the issues we had planned to address in our book. Pelletier stretched Skip's thinking process. Often, Skip's phone calls home would start with, "Hey Dad, my roommate Pelletier said . . ."

Skip insisted he was a Calvinist, but Pelletier didn't believe him: "For one, Griff didn't really believe in the total depravity of the human soul. For someone who was so dedicated and gave his life for humanity and not simply in the military as combat NCO, but also his time as a paramedic and a preacher—he constantly gave. Griff was an optimist of the human spirit, despite what he had seen. Not because of it, but in spite of it. Mr. Griffin, did you ever notice that whenever he would send you a group of horrific combat pictures that he always included some pictures of smiling kids?"

I could see why Skip felt like a Calvinist. Given what he had seen in the world, it seemed like a fitting piece of the puzzle; it made sense. Having been a paramedic in Compton, California, and an infantry NCO with two tours in Iraq, where poverty and squalor are on a level Americans simply don't understand, he found it easy to believe in—or at least accept—the depravity of man and the concept of predestination. The Iraqis hadn't chosen their fate; they were living with it.

Pelletier and Skip talked theology far into the night. They agreed that God knows all, but he does not cause by his knowing. God exists outside of time: "If you place God inside time as the first cause, as the prime mover, then everything He does know He causes," Pelletier wrote me later. They agreed (as did I) that the concept of God is outside of the real understanding of man, which doesn't mean that God doesn't exist. Our efforts to describe God only serve to put limits on God; but to try to understand God we must try to describe him. Man is a thinking entity, master of the world, subservient to God. Pelletier explained:

Philosophy, if properly practiced, leads to questions that philosophy cannot answer. Darrell and I were in love with the "Great Conversation," as he liked to call it. The Great Conversation is the ongoing search for truth through logical and reasoned observation of reality. The Great Conversation is philosophy, the love of wisdom. Conversation is, in fact, nothing, if not an attempt to gain or convey truth from one to another. The very words, "it is true that…" are assumed in every statement in every human language. When you say that you are hungry, what you intend to convey is that *it is true that* you are hungry. In fact, every sentence ever uttered or written has been a statement or interrogation of a quality or quantity of truth. It all comes back to this, and without an understanding of what truth is, there can be no conversation, and the constant attack on the absolute and immutable nature of truth threatens to end the Great Conversation in a Babel-esque confusion of semantic quibbles.

Darrell once posited that the root of most, if not all, of the problems of modern society was the attempt to make truth relative. I was intrigued and confused at first but it didn't take long for him to explain his position. Darrell stated, quite simply, that if we are not able to agree on terms, then we cannot communicate. If we cannot communicate, then we cannot convey truth, and if we cannot convey truth, the Great Conversation is lost. He was right.

Darrell often joked about some of the euphemisms that the military has used over the years, like the use of the term "controlled pair" in describing the technique that had been outlawed by the Geneva Convention called the "double tap." The techniques are identical in all but name, and if you read army doctrine today, the preferred technique for engaging an enemy in close quarters is the controlled pair. I caught myself in that last sentence using another euphemism designed to "soften" the impact of the military's mission. Instead of saying "killing," I used the more politically correct "engaging."

But who would want to cloud our ability to communicate? Who would intentionally deprive us of the ability to clearly, concisely, and precisely convey truth to one another? Darrell and I argued about this regularly. I was (and for the most part still am) of the opinion that there is a concerted effort being made by a class of people bent on the destruction of Western civilization as we know it. Darrell was slightly less dramatic than I in this case. He argued that this degradation of the truth was a byproduct of the "politically correct" movement. He insisted that the entire challenge to the immutable nature of truth was a result of the attempt at creating a universally inoffensive manner of speaking.

All of this leads back to what Darrell saw as the root of the problem, the supposed relativity of truth. If a thing is true, then its opposite must of necessity and by definition be false. This, however, is far from politically correct. You must, according to the "p.c." movement recognize that "your" truth is valid and true to you, and others may hold opposite, yet equally "true" beliefs. This relegates truth to a matter of personal interpretation, rather than an honest and objective observation of what *is*. If a thing is black, it is not white. If a thing is good, it is not evil. If a thing is true, it is always true; if it is false, it is always so.

On July 28, 2006, after a few weeks of preparation in Kuwait, the brigade flew on C130s to FOB Marez in Mosul, Iraq.

> *This is the city of Mosul. The signs of progress are definitely here as compared with my last deployment to this city. Much still has to be done in order for this city to function on its own. Electricity is still not in every home, sewage still runs into the streets and alleys where children play, and garbage is still just thrown into piles alongside the*

road or heaped into piles in the fields or burned, filling the air with a very unique smell. As far as I know, there are currently no exports leaving the country aside from oil. Whether or not these oil revenues trickle down to the masses in Iraq remains to be seen. In the other oil-producing states, the producers alone benefit from the sale of oil, because these states do not have any type of well-established textile base or GDP. This type of economic imbalance virtually guarantees the absence of a viable middle class in Iraqi society. Without this middle-class presence, the results are predictable for the foreseeable future.

Skip reported that we were making substantial advances in Iraq, but the enemy always seemed to be able to keep up. We would develop stronger bottoms on our Strykers and they would develop stronger IEDs. We developed the cage system around the Strykers to catch RPG rounds and they developed SVBIEDs:

On one occasion, a PUK [Patriotic Union of Kurdistan] HQ building in Mosul was completely sheered on its front side when armed insurgents engaged the gate sentries in order to distract them while one of these VBIEDs drove up the middle of the gate and, once close enough, detonated, killing almost everyone in the building. This is another advantage exploited with this type of weapon: being able to carry massive amounts of explosive material. Knowing this, we would look for vehicles whose rear tires seemed unusually low due to the weight of the explosives. However, some cars made into SVBIEDs, discovered before they were used, were found to have reinforced rear shocks, so that the sagging rear of the car wouldn't be noticed.

Another threat present in the battle space was precision small-arms fire. Vehicles, in addition to being used as explosives platforms, were also used as covert, stable firing platforms for snipers similar to the way in which the John Malvo/D.C. sniper used his car for a shooting platform. The Iraqi police had stopped a vehicle at one of their checkpoints, and upon closer inspection found a Sniper Variant, Draganoff rifle under the backseat. The right taillight was missing and the two holes for the rear taillights were used for a scope on top and the barrel to protrude through the bottom hole. The enemy we faced on a daily basis was always adapting, using the concepts of economy of force by employing stand-off weaponry, using stealth when employing sniper weapons, and most importantly, tactical patience. They had the advantage of having to get lucky only once. The other advantage exploited was based on how we would often be forced to respond to this type of attack by firing in the known or suspected direction of enemy fire, which increased the possibility of noncombatants being struck, which would in turn work in their favor by the negative propaganda generated. The political pressure created by this negative propaganda forced combatant commanders to severely limit the Rules of Engagement, which in turn created the potential for uncertainty and fatal-pause decision-making on the part of U.S. forces when

*having to return fire. If we couldn't see him we could
not shoot. If we did not shoot back we would continue
to be engaged. If the enemy could remain concealed
while firing we would not be able to at least return fire
in order to keep his head down. The guerilla warfare
practitioner has the distinct advantage of being able
to set the conditions in such a way that we are able
to only react. This is the ultimate advantage: being
able to act proactively while forcing your opponent to
respond reactively. This is insurgent warfare at its
finest. This was the enemy we faced.*

As part of Skip's disciplinary action over the gun-smuggling
episode, he was ordered to see the brigade psychologist,
Dave Cabrera. It was Cabrera's job to ensure that Skip
wasn't a danger to himself or others. This type of interview
normally took a solid hour, but after a few minutes of
discussion it was clear to Cabrera that Skip was no danger
to anyone. Cabrera told me: "We talked for an additional
hour with our conversation steeped in religion, ethics, and
philosophy." He recommended that Skip be put back in
charge of soldiers at the earliest possible time. He even
went so far as to write a letter to his chain of command to
recommend leniency. In Cabrera's opinion, they should
put him where he belonged: leading troops.

The army did a thorough review of Skip's background
before sentencing him. Based on the number of soldiers
willing to stand up as character witnesses on his behalf;
his prior service record, which included a Bronze Star with
Valor for saving the life of his first sergeant on his first tour;

and a stellar service career evidenced by perfect noncommissioned officer evaluation reports, they decided to go light on Skip. He would have to work in the Tactical Operations Center (TOC) for a period of at least six months before being allowed back into a combat role. TOCs have a very big job, tracking combat battalion soldiers on the ground and other resources deployed over miles of terrain. On any given day there are dozens of computers whirring, images flashing, printers running off reports, and phones ringing. Like a human brain, the TOC receives constant streams of data from several sources on all aspects of operations: troop movements, aviation assets, supply movements, intelligence, even the weather. The staff is required to analyze this data, process it, and send out directives or additional information to help the brigade carry out its mission. The TOC was the nerve center of the battalion and critical to the success of every mission, but this sentence was hell for Skip. He knew he'd gotten off easy, but he hated desk work. Eventually he would get back out into the battle space. This punishment would prove to be a valuable learning experience for Skip. As a squad leader, he was primarily concerned with his own team. At the TOC, he learned how a squad's mission fit into the overall mission of the battalion.

While assigned to the TOC, Skip made two new friends, Sgt. Freddie Rocha and Sgt. Samuel Armer. Skip and Rocha bonded immediately because of their Mexican blood (Skip was half Mexican) and they were both from Los Angeles. They both wore their "Los Angelesness" with pride, being from the "'hood." Skip would always make fun of "Roach" because he was Mexican but couldn't speak

Spanish. Rocha's 'hood image was just that: an image. He looked after his extended family, making sure they got a proper education in life and a roof over their heads. He liked to pretend that he was a "homeboy," but he couldn't shroud the fact that he was smart, responsible, and driven. The boy from the 'hood, with his "Yo" greeting and his arms extended in front of him like a rapper, was really a regular American guy.

Armer looked like he could be a Mormon missionary—this guy was wired tight. He always looked forward to breakfast with Skip. Not only did he get a generous helping of eggs, chipped beef gravy, and bacon, but also a daily discussion of politics and current events. Armer recalled: "Griff was very passionate about his views and he always could reference something to back up his standpoint. He would talk about great philosophers and the things that they had written about hundreds of years ago. I did not know much about philosophy, so I just listened."

One other soldier who became a good friend of Skip's was Victor Quinonez. "Q" was a well-educated guy who felt he had to give service to his country. He didn't fit the image the American public has of someone who voluntarily joins the army, an image perpetuated by some of our own politicians—most notably Senator John Kerry, who told students at Pasadena City College: "You know, education, if you make the most of it, if you study hard and you do your homework, and you make an effort to be smart, uh, you, you can do well. If you don't, you get stuck in Iraq." How does that explain Q or James Pelletier or Skip? They weren't "stuck" in Iraq: they *served* in Iraq.

Skip and Q worked in the TOC together for six months. People remember odd things for unknown reasons. Most people remember Skip for his philosophical discussions and physical strength. Q recalls one time when they got off work in the TOC at FOB Marez. They worked out at the gym, and then decided to borrow a golf cart and drive over to the PX to buy some sodas. They hopped in the cart wearing their army issue physical training T-shirts and shorts. As they drove, it got colder and colder, so they huddled together in the drizzly Mosul weather. In their little golf cart, they weaved in and out between the tanks and heavy-duty trucks on the narrow, muddy road to the PX. As they cut in front of a huge rig, the driver yelled out of the cab window, "Get out of the way, Dumb and Dumber!" This incident left a lasting impression on Q. It was a moment when life almost seemed normal, doing something goofy and laughing about it.

Skip and I had a long e-mail exchange about faith and doubt, a subject that preoccupied us:

Skip: How are you guys? Hopefully all is well back there. Well, things are going ok over here in Mosul. It's still dangerous over here especially with the mortar attacks but these are occasional and not on a daily basis. I wish that I could send pictures and fill you in on what's going on here but I can't.

Me: Sorry about the delay in getting back to you. I have been taking a tax course that is taking 20 hours a week and working three jobs.

Skip: I have started my book and it begins when my life took a turn that would change my life forever once I arrived here the first time when fighting was more intense than it is now. It will be a narrative concerning all the bad things that I witnessed and had to do in order to survive here with the men that I led. I will spare no details so that people will know what it truly means to experience the macabre reality of war as well as the emotional, spiritual, and mental costs. After laying this out I will attempt to make sense out of my time here and then attempt to offer a solution to the problem concerning how to leave here with our national dignity preserved to some degree. I miss you guys so much and realize that these two deployments have taken a lot out of me in many ways.

Me: Son you have given a lot to your country. More than most people ever dream of giving.

Skip: Being here has forced me to reevaluate everything I thought I knew about life and myself. I wish that I could say that my belief in G-d has remained but it has not.

Me: I think we agree that you cannot intellectualize your belief in God. You either have faith or not. I pray daily for your wisdom, comfort, safety, and a closer walk with God. I have been praying that all of my kids get closer to God. I was excited to learn about three months ago that Rene and JR [Skip's older sister and her husband] started attending church and they both have embraced a new love of the Lord. Sommer and Steve [Skip's younger sister and her husband] have also started walking closer to the Lord after finding a church home a couple of months ago. I never push religion on my children, but my faith in God has grown geometrically over the years and I have an inner peace that I never felt was possible. I have been a tortured soul most of my life. That began to change when I met Mom. It changed again when Kim got saved and I saw what the Lord had done with her soul. [Kim grew up agnostic without any real exposure to the Christian faith.] I had another big leap in my faith when you asked me to pray for you the first time you went to Iraq. I never really had a prayer life, but my praying for you daily tightened up my relationship with God.

Skip: I do recognize the utility of such a belief but can no longer apply it to myself. Faith in G-d has to come willingly, it cannot be forced any more than a person can force someone to love them. I have had many interesting conversations with local Iraqis, soldiers, my peers, and many others that run the entire gambit of topics and have become more and more interested in what others think about war, G-d, themselves, and the war in Iraq, as well as the destiny of our nation in the community of nations. I too am interested in what others think of G-d, but

I realize that my relationship with my G-d is mine and mine alone. These things will be reflected in our book and I can't wait to see where it goes.

Me: It sounds like you have the "fire in your belly" to get this book written and I am excited for you.

Skip: I love you guys with my whole heart and miss you greatly. Stay safe, stay alert, and vigilant in these uncharted times. Time seems to be on fast-forward in this world right now. I love you all.

Me: Skip, we love you more than you will ever know. We think about you all the time. We are incredibly proud of what you have accomplished in this world.

Skip had started a blog to get some of his ideas out. He fought daily battles during his first tour in Iraq, and didn't have a lot of time to write in his journals or his blogs. During his second tour, he was involved in fewer battles. He was in the TOC for six months, where he spent most of his time in front of computer screens, watching the blips of troops in the streets rather than fighting in the streets himself. During his first tour, it was emotionally easier for him to deal with daily contact with the enemy because he knew it was going to happen every day; there was no guessing or speculation. During his second tour, he said he was always waiting for the other shoe to drop, for a major battle to spring up out of nowhere. Anticipating battles was at times more difficult to deal with than the actual daily fighting of his first tour. Being a soldier didn't leave him a lot of time to write blogs, but his occasional posts helped him develop his thinking about the future. I learned from the entry below that when he got out of the army he was considering a career in politics.

From Skip's Reallifeblog.com:

"The Situation in Iraq from an Infantryman's Perspective on the Ground" Sunday, October 29, 2006

I am Staff Sergeant Darrell R. Griffin and am curr-ently deployed in Mosul, Iraq. This is my second combat tour here as an infantryman. I fought hard on my last tour and will soon show some photos of my last tour, compare the situation on the ground currently with my last tour, and discuss political issues that I feel are extremely important without the mudslinging and partisan infighting that kills any and all intellectual political debate. If I return home safely, I will run for office in some capacity and will introduce a long forgotten type of leadership. I will not trick people with "political speak" that politicians use stating the "what" of what they will do if elected as opposed to the "how" of what they will do.

I have dedicated fifteen years of my life to what some have called "The Great Conversation," studying philosophy in many venues. I was an Emergency Medical Technician in Los Angeles County for four years, have served in the military for nine years now as an infantryman and have faced insurgents on the field of battle, have had to kill some up close and have lived through the reality of war that you cannot put a spin on. I received the Bronze Star with Valor and have many other related campaign awards. I feel called to enlighten our nation. We must wake up. We lead the world in obesity while children starve throughout the world, movie stars starve themselves slavishly while children sit emaciated in a forgotten desert, and we have allowed both political parties to put us to sleep. We have been forgotten by our governmental parties because they are both too busy jockeying for position and are providing a sterling example of what the great sage Nietzsche defined the politician to be: dogs that fight over the collective scraps of humanity. I have much to say about the Manichean moral polarity of perpetual good vs. evil. Sometimes these two moral categories put up more walls than anything else and stultify the search for solutions globally and domestically. Diplomacy is also a form of strategy in the tradition of the great Sun Tzu and always fighting on the field of battle. I will speak again soon my friends.

He worked hard on his blog, but he wondered if anyone was reading it:

Is there anyone out there that cares enough to hear what I have to say. I'm not your typical talking head who attempts to legitimize himself just because he fights in war. I am starting the Progressive Party and will soon explain my manifesto for the American people.

From Skip's journal:

November 2006

A recent article in the Stars and Stripes *magazine stated that the current prime minister Nuri Al-Maliki (a Shia statesman openly supported by Moqtada al-Sadr) does not want U.S. and Iraqi forces to launch a military offensive against the militias (most if not all Shia in loyalty) that currently plague the country. Maybe this would defang the real power in Iraq, influenced by the unseen hand of Shia Islam of which Maliki is a devotee. Late last year, in 2006, his advisers said that the prime minister was urging the U.S. to combat Sunni groups while Iraqis focus on Shia militias. We would, in essence, be the culprit in getting rid of his enemies and not the real enemy plaguing Iraq, ALL militias.*

When I was down south in Najaf, we stayed at an Iraqi army compound and discovered that they had never been mortared or attacked in any way, shape, or form. The area that this compound was located in was predominantly Shia and we asked what sectarian affiliation the soldiers in this compound were and the answer was not surprising: they were Shia. However, up north in Mosul, a PUK was car-bombed killing scores, an entire Sunni neighborhood is disarmed by the Iraqi army with wild Iraqi army soldiers shooting up the neighborhood at night, and the prime minister asks us bluntly to first combat Sunni groups? We are being courted and coerced to take sides! The ideal military would not take sides, but the reality would argue otherwise. Who are we taking down when we kick down the door of an Iraqi home? Who are we fighting? Can the various factions in Iraq come together to form a unified government? This is the only solution. As of now, there is no sign that this is happening or will happen. Let us view the factions that are jockeying for dominance:

The Shia—This faction is said to be under the shadow of Iranian influence. An Iranian influence would foster sentiments of Theocratic rule as opposed to a Democratic form of government. The Shia also would not want the Sunnis to once again maintain the former position of political minority elitism. This would be too risky because of the Baath connection and the Sunnis. Would an Iranian-influenced Shia majority be willing to share power with their prior oppressors, the Sunnis? Iraq has long been ruled by a secularist Sunni government, despite its 60 percent Shia population (the Baath Party was secular and not Sunnis who made up the party itself).

Moqtada al-Sadr is still jockeying for a power grab and is the self-proclaimed religious leader of the Shia in the country. Whether or not he is being controlled by Iran is irrelevant to the situation on the ground in central Iraq.

The Sunni—Syria is a de facto Baath Party regime. All three branches of government are guided by the views of the Baath Party. Less than 1 percent of the country is Shia with the largest majority being Sunni. A dispropor- tionately significant role is played by the country's largest minority, the Alawis, however, the majority in Syria is Sunni. The center of gravity in Syria favors a Sunni/ Baath-centric trajectory geostrategically. Saddam was not the only loser of regime change. An entire regime became the loser. A Sunni/Baathist regime was deposed, and not Saddam Hussein.

The Kurdish—the Kurds have long wanted an independent state of Kurdistan. If this were to be done, Iran, Syria, and especially Turkey would end up with a Kashmir-like situation that exists between India and Pakistan. All countries bordering northern Iraq will not allow this to happen. The old border lines drawn by the British mandate when Iraq was created by them would have to be redrawn in order to facilitate this desired Kurdish state because if not, which of the three countries with Kurdish minorities would be willing to give up some of their sovereign territory to the Kurds and their desired state? Iraq cannot support an independent Kurdistan.

While Skip was in the TOC, he reported to SFC Hale, the night-shift Battle NCO for Headquarters Company. Under the best of circumstances, the trip to Baghdad from Mosul is a long and dangerous journey. Most soldiers would prefer to fly or take the trip in a Stryker. Skip volunteered to be the NCO who rode with a private in an unarmored vehicle. Sgt. Hale recalled:

When I would leave the wire, I would always include Griffin going with me. We would be up all night in the

TOC and then volunteer to go out with the TAC, just for the simple reason that we felt like that was the best way to help our buddies. One of the things that kept me going over there was the simple fact that when we were outside the wire Griff always had the biggest smile on his face, because he felt like he was doing everything he could do for his country. There was never a day when he would turn down a chance to get out there. The one thing that stands out in my mind when he worked in the TOC was when we were transferred to Baghdad. We needed an NCO to ride with a private in an FMTV [Family of Medium Tactical Vehicles, two-and-a-half-ton trucks that do not have armor]. Without hesitation Griff said, "I got it, Brother." Keep in mind that the FMTV is not as tough as the Stryker, but Griff said he wanted to go because if someone else were to get hurt he would not have felt he was giving his all. That was when I knew how great of a man, soldier, and friend that he truly was."

From: Darrell Griffin, Jr.
Sent: Monday, November 27, 2006
To: Darrell (DAD) Griffin
Subject: Re: Thanksgiving

Hey Mom and Dad just wanted to e-mail you one more time before I convoy down to Baghdad. I am very nervous about the ride down because that represents over 400 miles of chances to get blown up. I will be driving a humvee and not a Stryker. As soon as I arrive I will let you guys know. Keep us in prayer for the trip down. I miss you guys a lot and hope to see everyone again after this is all over. Please continue to call my baby doll because she loves to hear from you guys. I love you and miss you.

Skipper

Skip told me once on the phone from Mosul: "Dad, I know when I've been away from my books too long when my gun barrel is warm and my books are cold." (It got really cold in the winter months in Iraq.) This picture was taken by Skip once they were in Baghdad at FOB Striker.* The first thing he unpacked was his books.

---

* The name "Striker," given to the FOB, is sometimes confused with the name "Stryker," given to the fighting vehicle that the brigade used. No one is really sure where the FOB Striker name came from, but the vehicle is named for two American servicemen who posthumously received the Medal of Honor: PFC Stuart S. Stryker, who died in World War II, and Specialist Robert F. Stryker, who died in the Vietnam War.

From: Darrell Griffin, Jr.
Sent: Friday, December 08, 2006
To: Darrell (DAD) Griffin
Subject: (no subject)

Dear Mom and Dad,

I am convoying within hours and just want you guys to know that I love you and ask that you pray for me and believe for me because I can't right now. Keep all of us in prayer that we get to B==== [Balad] safely. I will e-mail as soon as we get there.

Skipper

From Skip's journal:

December 9, 2006
3rd Brigade is moved to Baghdad in response to sectarian
violence not being stopped in the city. Advance Guard
from 5–20 Sykes Regulars sustained two catastrophic
Stryker kills with one friendly KIA and seven WIA
[wounded in action] *within weeks of arriving in*
Baghdad. Our Battalion Commander LTC Huggins
has briefed us as to the situation as it is in Baghdad
concerning the dynamics guiding the sectarian violence
occurring in the city. Our Battalion will be occupying the
southwest portion of the city. We will have to determine
who our friends are in the midst of the chaotic fighting,
and will attempt to impose some type of order in order
to stop or slow the pace of the daily killings that produce
body counts on average of fifteen to twenty per day. One of
the initial difficulties that we have faced since occupying

our battle space has been the witnessed, overt support that the police provide to the Shia faction in the city. On or about Jan. 1st, our company, along with our Scout platoon, was conducting a SIGINT[signals intelligence] *operation in the Albayaa section of Baghdad. We had passed an Iraqi police station en route to our objective. Once our entire company had saturated a neighborhood that the SIGINT asset led us to, the entire neighborhood began to open fire with small-arms from every conceivable direction. While the melee ensued, our UAV*[unmanned aerial vehicle] *assets witnessed these same Iraqi police units that we had passed, assisting casualties sustained when we returned fire on suspected directions of enemy fire. We could safely assume that these police, like all others, were loyal to their sect more than the concept of neutral policing. In a section of Baghdad that we were patrolling, a Sunni neighborhood had suffered a loss of electricity because the police, who, for the most part, were in reality members of the Mehdi army loyal to Moqtada al-Sadr, had cut the power flowing into this area.*

I spoke to the wife of an Iraqi police officer who lived in this neighborhood and asked if her husband was Sunni as well. She said that he too was Sunni and I then asked her how her husband even survived in a Shia-dominated police force loyal to al-Sadr. Because of the language barrier and not having our interpreter with us, she could not respond. I became frustrated by my own question. Time after time, we have witnessed the police in Tal'Afar, Mosul, and Baghdad behaving in this same manner. Once again, the options open for picking friends are limited to the three conflicting parties of Sunni, Shia, or Kurd, who are more prominent in the north of the country.

The only Iraqis that I have time to speak with are interpreters hired through a private company called Titan Inc., who are usually from the immediate area in which we operate. They are all convinced, Sunni and Shia alike, that the only option for victory is to eradicate the militias that easily infiltrate not only the military but the police as well. This poses another problem, because sometimes neighbors band together merely to defend their respective neighborhoods from attack from militia groups, and in defending themselves for purely defensive and not sectarian reasons, are considered as militia.

One interpreter that I spoke with displayed a great deal of clarity when he stated that if the militias are not disarmed it will be Democracy by the gun, which is really another way of describing chaos. It seems that the sectarian strain runs too deep for any real cooperation between these conflicting groups. I was sympathetic to those who merely came together to defend their neighborhoods, but how can you tell on the battlefield where the militia ends and where neighborhood defenders begin? I will never forget, among so many other memories, the Sunni wife who was married to the Sunni police officer because of wondering how he even survived as a cop in a Shia/Sadr police organization.

I suffered a heartbreak at the end of our combat patrol in that neighborhood located in the area of Dora, south of the Green Zone, because upon leaving I was scanning rooftops from my air-guard hatch in our Stryker when I saw an old woman peering out of her window carefully and I saw the look of so much fear and uncertainty in her time-worn eyes that had probably seen so much. This is no way for a human being to live; living with violence and intrigue on every street corner, where you can't even trust your own neighbors for fear that they might be someone on the opposing side of who you are. Once again I had to push this heartbreaking thought deep into my heart because I was a Squad Leader leading nine heavily armed young men and trying to bring them home alive.

On December 9, Donald Rumsfeld announces his resignation as SECDEF. This changing of the guard takes place while the Iraq conflict continues. With a Democratic majority now in power and with the obvious difficulty that lies ahead for the party that ushered in

01/11/2006

the war to stay relevant in Washington, one cannot help but wonder how this will play out on the streets of Baghdad, and in the decision-making process of our elected officials involved in the complexities of this war. One has to wonder whether or not we have lost the political initiative in Iraq due to the fact that the American people have elected to change loyalties and perspective by bringing the Democratic Party into power once again. We are vulnerable right now politically because of the national elections so close at hand. No political party will stick its neck out, so to speak, concerning solutions as to the situation in Iraq because if it fails, their respective parties and jobs will be gone.

All are quick to say, "We need a different direction in Iraq because the current one is not working!" Ok, what does this different direction look like? What direction do we go in? We must discern between criticism and solution. We must not elect someone for stating the obvious! So, how do we proceed to victory in this country?

Chapter 13

The Battle of Najaf

Elsewhere in the area of Najaf on the morning of January 28, 2007, at about 7:00 a.m., the Najaf provincial governor and the police chief drove out to the compound of an Islamic cult group called the Jaish Alrad, "The Soldiers of Heaven." This was a group of six hundred militants defending a fortified chicken farm surrounded by a ten-foot berm, multiple trenches, and fighting positions throughout the compound. The group's mission was to attack Ashura marches and Shia leaders in Najaf. The insurgent group involved in this engagement was associated with the extreme Shiite religious sect led by Sheikh Mahmoud al-Hassani al-Sarkhi, known locally as al-Mahdawiyin. Among their intended targets were Grand Ayatollah Ali al-Sistani and Moqtada al-Sadr. The compound is about two kilometers to the north of Najaf.

When the governor and the police chief arrived at the compound, they were instantly ambushed with heavy machine guns and RPGs. There were numerous dug-in positions throughout the entire complex for resupplying the fighting locations, and big stacks of weapons and ammunition spread all over the compound. The Soldiers of Heaven had dug several mortar pits with sixty-millimeter and eighty-two-millimeter mortars. The governor and the police chief abandoned their vehicles and headed toward the river to the east of the compound, where they stopped to call for a QRF (quick reaction force).

SSG Ryan Wallace, an Air Battalion commander, was on the scene. His official MOS is Combat Controller. This MOS is a multidisciplinary job that integrates Navy Seals, Special Forces, and Rangers with the resources of air power. Wallace had come down to Najaf for some other missions, and he and his battalion were on their way home. As the assault against the governor and the police was unfolding there, a number of resources nearby got dragged into the fray: Iraqi police, Iraqi army scouts, a Special Forces Operational Detachment Alpha (ODA), a twelve-man Special Forces team, a contingent of Seals, and Hila (city) SWAT, an emergency team like the kind you would find attached to any American big city police department.

As soon as they rolled up, they came under heavy fire. Sgt. Wallace had two F-16s overhead, on their way back to Baghdad. When they found themselves in the midst of this unexpected battle, they started putting strafing rounds into the governor's and police captain's vehicles to preclude the enemy from stealing them. The responders were taking accurate sniper fire and machine-gun fire. The local Iraqi army ground force commander ordered to have the source of the fire, a mosque, destroyed. Air support dropped a five-hundred-pound bomb on the mosque, but it went through the roof and failed to explode. Sgt. Wallace imagined all the bad guys inside looking up at the mosque and praising Allah that they were still alive. About a minute later, another bomb came in and completely leveled the mosque: "The pilot of another flight calls in and says, 'Hey man, I've got thirty to forty personnel in a trench line.'" He is cleared to go hot. Whole pockets of insurgents got "taken out." Before they ran out of ammo, Wallace's air support had dropped four laser-guided bombs and four JDAMs (joint direct attack munitions, a guidance kit that converts existing unguided gravity bombs into all-weather smart bombs), and done multiple strafing runs.

Wallace looked up over the tree line just as the first Apache came in:

You could see his chin gun. It was pointed down at something. He rolled through dry. He had a malfunction in the gun from taking small-arms fire. Then his wingman came in right behind him, pointed at the same target, and then his rotors just stopped. They completely froze up. No smoke, no sparks, no fire. The rotors froze and the helicopter fell out of the sky from six hundred to seven hundred feet. As soon as it went behind the tree line, maybe fifteen seconds later, a big black cloud of smoke came up, so we assessed that those guys had died instantly.

When company commander Capt. Clemmer got the call, he decided to augment a few Special Forces guys to secure the helicopter (fallen angel) until it could be recovered. As C Company—Skip's unit—went rolling up to the crash site area, it became quickly obvious that the mission had morphed into something much bigger. The crash site had not been secured. The wrecked helicopter lay between the Special Forces guys and the insurgents. The Special Forces guys only had about ten Humvees, Clemmer recalled, and the heaviest weapon they had was a fifty cal. One of their vehicles was out of ammo. By the time Skip's unit arrived, around 4:00 p.m., they'd been fighting for eight hours. Clemmer had his full company with all platoons as he rolled toward the site, two kilometers away. Clemmer assessed the situation and told his platoon leaders, "We are going to seize that site." He pushed his platoons in between the downed bird and the insurgents and established a perimeter around the helicopter. Shortly thereafter LTC Huggins arrived on site to manage the entire battle space.

Here is Lt. Gregory Weber's (Skip's platoon leader) account of the Battle of Najaf:

We were told that an Apache had been shot down. It was unknown the status of the pilots, but that our company would move to secure while the wrecker team would recover the bird. We left about an hour after being alerted and en route were told that the pilots were KIA and that there is potential contact in the area. As always, we were joking and discussing random things during the drive down. Nothing ever scared us or got us too worked up (at least that we ever spoke out loud about to each other), it all was routine because we felt we were prepared for anything. As we got closer to the downed bird, the report came through that an Iraqi army platoon was ambushed there early in the morning and it sustained large casualties. In response, the IA moved out with more elements along with an SF team to regain contact. While doing so, that unit came under fire and called in for Apache support. It was then that the Apache had been shot down. That IA unit along with SF had been there since early morning in fairly sustained contact until we arrived sometime around sunset (1800ish). As we came toward the turn-off for the objective, Cpt Clemmer pushed 2nd and 3rd platoon forward to support the fight. As we moved in, we rolled down a road that had IA and SF engaging numerous targets off to east. Apaches were engaging with their hellfires, rockets, and guns at a number of insurgents within three hundred meters of us. Eventually, we were pushed forward to secure the south side of the downed bird...with 2nd plt to the east, 1st to the north, and MGS plt to the west. Second plt and 3rd plt were at the "front lines" of a village we couldn't see at the time.

In a very traditional army style, the platoon was on the ground dismounted, lying in a natural trench, holding the line for the recovery team to secure the bodies of the pilots and the aircraft. Throughout the entire night there was sustained small-arms fire whipping over our heads. Griff was at the forward-most position of ours with one of his teams. I was walking the line for most of the night between his position and another squad's position. Throughout that night we saw the most amazing display of aerial firepower. Within hundreds of meters from us, the air force dropped the largest amount of ordnance since the invasion of Fallujah. AC130 Spector gunships were firing their 40mm guns, 105m shells, and chain guns. A10 warthogs were doing chain-gun runs and dropped a number of 500 lb bombs and two 1000 lb bombs. Apaches were going black on ammo [running out of ammo], our mortar section was laying down 60mm and 120mm mortars, and our trucks [Strykers] were engaging with .50 cal MGs. It was a spectacular sight, something that C Co. [Charger Company] alone has only seen and hardly any other soldier in the service will EVER see. The fighting kept up like that until around 0100 hours where a surrender call was made from a couple trucks' PA systems. No response and some more bombing continued. Another surrender call was given around 0400, again no response. At 0600, C Co. was to move and clear up to the village perimeter. Moving from west to east up to the village was 1st, 2nd, 3rd, from north to south. I moved with Griff in the center, with 2nd sqd [squad] to our left, 3rd sqd to our right…trucks following behind us. We eventually made it up to the perimeter of the village where we saw nothing but burning buildings and destruction. As we lay against the berm of the village, there was a large cache that was still on fire, popping off rounds and eventually blowing up only 100m from us. Griff and I laughed because watching 2nd plt, who was closest to us, running for cover looked like something out of a movie to us. One by one men started coming out to the edge of the village holding up white flags. I got our terp [interpreter] on the PA system and told him to tell people to come out with their hands up and surrender. One or two starting coming out. Then small groups, then larger groups. Eventually 3rd plt had 200+ men sitting in front of us surrendering. I tasked Griff with the entry point to the detainee and casualty holding area that I had my plt sergeant establish. Griff was in charge of searching and clearing, one by one, the people coming into our lines. I called Cpt Clemmer letting him know of my situation and advised he move the Company effort to my position along with any and all medics available. We eventually had three hundred to four hundred wounded and nonwounded males being treated and separated in a makeshift holding area surrounded by C wire. Around 0800 to 0900 Griff, me, and a couple of Griff's guys moved across the street and into the village. We moved up and turned the corner to see a sight that will never be forgotten by me or Griff. We looked around and saw nothing but dead insurgents, all still holding on to AK-47s. Some of the bodies were mangled, some were burnt severely. Some you could barely make out because of how bad they were burnt. There were hand grenades, weapons, and RPGs all over. Houses were still burning; we were coughing on the smell of burning flesh. It was dangerous, to say the least, with how much ammo was still in there cooking off. As we bounded forward again, more people started coming to us, it was more families now, women and children, men that were too hurt to walk on their own. One man came up and dropped his young son on top of another dead body. The son was still alive but on his way out. Another woman was holding an infant who was purple from being deceased so long. Griff and his guys started helping people out of the village and pointing them to the medics. I was on the radio with the commander giving him an assessment and letting him know what we were doing. I eventually pulled another squad into the village with us to start clearing homes and gathering weapons. We began to pile weapons in one spot, dead bodies in another spot. As we continued moving on, helping injured people out, clearing weapons off dead bodies, pointing out RPG rounds and hand grenades to EOD, marking the dead women and children, we came up to a heavily bombed building that Griff and I assessed as being the enemy's casualty collection point from the night prior. There were enemy KIA all over, enemy WIA begging us to kill them, and a room that needed to be cleared that had bodies stacked so deep that we couldn't open the door. Griff was trying to open the door to this room when he started yelling, "Put the weapon down!" He could barely see into the room, but there was a WIA insurgent reaching for his AK-47s. Griff turned to me and said, "Sir, I got a guy going for his weapon, I gotta take the shot." I approved, he made the necessary steps to tell the guy to stop and escalated his force properly but had to engage to neutralize the threat. The day continued like that until around 1400. Nothing but dragging bodies out, clearing them, piling up weapons, getting wounded out to the medics. It was a grueling task. The boys were smoked and Griff and I were watching them closely because of how they were taking the horrific sight. Around 1400 came and IA showed up to take over the site. Griff, me, his sqd, and the rest of the plt withdrew to our trucks and grabbed an MRE [meal ready-to-eat] real quick. We drove out to get fuel at a fueler nearby and eventually made the trip back to FOB Kalsu. We were there by around 2200 that night.

From: Darrell Griffin, Sr.
Sent: Sunday, January, 28, 2007
To: Darrell Griffin, Jr.
CC: Kim Griffin
Subject: (no subject)

Hi son.

When you can, please give me a quick update on how you are doing. There seems to be a lot of things going on in your area of operation right now. Even if you just drop me and Mom a line telling us you are okay will do.

We love you and pray for you daily.

Love you
Dad and Mom

From: Darrell Griffin, Jr.
Sent: Tuesday, January 30, 2007
To: Darrell (DAD) Griffin
Subject: (no subject)

on 28 jan. we were spun up to guard an apache attack helicopter that was shot down south of the town of Hilla. as nightfall approached and the pilots' remains were being recovered we came under intense small-arms fire from a Shia religious compound. we called in airstrikes on their position and they were pummeled all through the night and they kept trying to mass their fires on one of my fighting positions. we returned heavy fire and kept them back all night into the morning. when daylight came we assaulted the compound and what we witnessed can only be described as apocalyptic. there were hundreds of blown apart bodies, including women and children mixed in with the men who wanted to fight. we spent the remainder of the day policing up hundreds of (not surprisingly) Iraqi army ak-47's, grenades, rockets, and heavy weapons. we also spent the day piling up bodies of the dead. i came into one room where it appeared to be an enemy casualty collection point that had been struck by a 500lb bomb and brought my squad in and a man reached for his weapon and tried to shoot me. i shot 6 rounds into his face and oddly enough he was smiling as i warned him to stop. It's as if he wanted to die so i obliged him. That puts my grand total at 8 confirmed kills up to this point in my 2 tours. Dad, I have seen what hell must be like when we assaulted this compound. i had to rotate out my guys because they were getting sick and horrified at all the wall-to-wall gore. there were fathers bringing up their dead babies to me and shoving them into my arms for help. i didn't know if these were bad guys or not and i had to see women blown apart and it appeared as if they were relaxing at the end of the day when their lives ended. the weird part about it all is that the Shia leader of this compound was believed to be by those living in this compound the final Mehdi or messiah who would usher in the golden age of Islam. i would compare this to the David Koresh incident in Waco, Texas. all the enemy dead had iraqi army weapons so I'm assuming that they were Iraqi army. and in these parts (the south) all the army are Shia. Our whole platoon is going to a mandatory combat stress meeting today. this is the heaviest fighting and most tenacious enemy that i have faced ever. i can't tell you enough how scared we all were when we had to defend and hold our positions throughout the night with no sleep at all. this has all taken place during the festival of Ashura, when all Shia Muslims commemorate the death of imam Ali Hussein who was martyred 1300 yrs ago by. I gotta go i'll get back to you.

Skip

Chapter 14

A Spartan Warrior Comes Home on His Shield

From: Darrell Griffin, Sr.
Sent: Friday, February 09, 2007
To: Darrell Griffin, Jr.
Subject: Thanks for calling us this morning

Son

I am so proud of you, but I also hate thinking of the fact that since you will probably be in the army for the next 20 years I will not be able to spend more than a handful of days with you before I die. Son, based on statistics, I have about 15 more years on this planet. This means that we may see each other another 15 times. Your Mom, Alexis, and Jordan and I do miss you. We pray for you daily. God has been very good to you. He has given you a very special wife and he has turned your life into a shining example of what a person can do with their life if they are determined.

The guy that gave you the iPod accessories asked if you could take a picture of the unit with you in your Stryker so he can show his friends.

We love you.

From: Darrell Griffin, Jr.
Sent: Wednesday, February 28, 2007
To: Diana Griffin
Subject: Re: Thank you MY LOVE

Hey honey I'm in Karbala and yes it's really f _ _ _ _ _ _ _ d up here so pray for us. I won't be calling you while I'm here so it will be 2 weeks before we speak again but thank god for e-mail. I love you and will send my e-mails as often as I can in case you have to go home to be with auntie Dora ok? [Diana had lost her mom to pancreatic cancer a few years earlier and now her Auntie Dora was ill.] If your family needs you make sure you go okay? They might need you because you are and have always been the strong soul in your family along with your cousins who are good open people and they will need you most okay? I love you and Allah or God willing things will work out as He wills them. They always do. I love you Diana and Luna [the dog]. I will check with you in a day or two okay?

When Diana shared this e-mail with me it made me feel uneasy. Skip always liked Diana to be at their home at Fort Lewis. It made me wonder what was going through Skip's head. What was he thinking?

> *February 2007*
> *As of this writing, the Iraqi military and police have taken more control of security and intelligence gathering. However, the Iraqi forces still will not conduct more invasive and audacious operations without requesting*

the assistance of U.S. forces and are very apprehensive when it comes to operating at night. Whenever an IED is reported by local nationals to the JCC [Joint Command Center] *at night, Iraqi EOD will not respond, thus leaving the IED until daylight. All in all, the Iraqi government is still heavily dependent on U.S. forces logistically and tactically. However, the local Iraqi government is trying its best with its own police and military still dying, killing but yet serving albeit with corruption still present within its ranks. The corruption became more palpable while operating in Baghdad and south in Karbala. Most if not all of the police are card-carrying members of the Mehdi army loyal to al-Sadr. Whenever we would travel the MSRs en route to an objective, you would see the police manning checkpoints along these routes. As soon as they would see our lead elements approaching, they would turn on their red/blue police lights as we passed, thus signaling their other fellow "officers," alerting them of our presence. They would, in turn, notify high-ranking political personnel working with the Jaish al-Mahdi (JAM) in their respective areas because we made it known that these were persons of interest to be either captured or questioned. We would arrive at the objective, raid a political office, and see no occupants in the building. Heaters would still be burning along with cigarettes still smoldering in the ashtray. The local infrastructure is still in its fledgling state, most palpably, the emergency medical services. Our brigade, in addition to combat operations, had been assisting in the rebuilding of the infrastructure in Mosul by acting as a quasi-911 dispatch assistance center. The JCC calls our brigade TOC with grid coordinates corresponding to emergency calls in the city. Ambulances are dispatched to the grid coordinates while grid coordinates are recorded in order to see if the same coordinates/locations are used frequently, which would be deemed suspicious in nature. The insurgents would use ambulances to transport weapons and would also use them to plant IEDs on the roads. Access to gasoline is still very limited in Mosul. Long gas lines, sometimes forty cars long, can be seen on any given day at the various gas stations. These long lines are potential threats to U.S. forces because stationary car bombs can be easily hidden in these lines.*

From: Diana Griffin
Sent: Monday, February 26, 2007
To: Darrell Griffin
Subject: Thank you MY LOVE

Hi My Stee Tee [a private term of endearment]

I just want to thank you for calling me twice to make sure I'm ok, with all that is going on with Auntie Dora… It brings back a lot of sad memories of my mom and how blurred that time of my life was, I'm so grateful that I have you as my husband who is so compassionate and understanding, even with you fighting a War you still think of me and comfort me… I love you so much Darrell more than you could imagine… I'm so nervous that you have to go back to that place Karbala?? Is that where you will be? I pray that He continues to protect you. Always look deep into my pictures and into the soul of my eyes and you will only see love that I have for you... God Bless you my love, my husband, I love you.

Love your baby doll

Diana and Luna

We found the tone of Skip's e-mails and phone calls disquieting, although we couldn't put our fingers on anything specific. There was a sense that events beyond our control had been set in motion, but we were all still participants.

From: Diana Griffin
Sent: Tuesday, March 06, 2007
To: Darrell Griffin
Subject: Are you OK?

Hi Honey,

Are you ok? I heard on the television this morning that 9 soldiers were killed North of Baghdad. Where exactly are you? I pray no one from your Company was hurt or killed. I get so scared when I hear this in the news. They also mentioned Karbala and something about Sadr City. Is this near where you are at? Oh honey I pray that you are ok. Please e-mail me as soon as you get this e-mail so that I know you are ok. I have an FRG meeting today at 6:30 (it is for C Company). I'm sure I will find out more info there... I love you so much honey... God's protection for you is all I pray for. God Bless you my love.

Love, your baby doll, Diana and Luna

From: Darrell Griffin, Jr.
Sent: Wednesday, March 07, 2007
To: Diana Griffin
Subject: Are you OK?

Hey honey, we are in Karbala still and we have been doing a lot of raids in the area. We saw a bunch of dead Shias floating in a canal last night, I'm ok so far. How is Luna? Are you going home to see Auntie Dora? I don't have a lot of time so I just want to say I love you and miss you a lot; we leave here on the 13th. G-d bless you…

One thing that helped Diana feel closer to Skip while he was deployed was the Family Resource Group (FRG). This is a nonprofit organization of soldiers' family members (primarily wives) that meets regularly to disseminate timely information about soldiers to their families and also provides support programs for their wives. Between the Web site, e-mails, and phone calls, wives and families are able to keep pretty close tabs on their soldiers. The downside is that if the communication gets interrupted for a few days, panic sets in.

From: Darrell Griffin, Sr.
Sent: Tuesday, March 06, 2007
To: Darrell Griffin, Jr.
Subject: No Subject

Hello Son,
    I have been watching the news a lot lately. It looks like we are taking steps to make Sadr less effective. I would person-

ally like to see him taken out of the picture completely. It is getting close to your birthday. I wish you were spending [your] birthday in California. I hope all is going well for you and your comrades. Things here are going pretty normal. Sometimes normal is a good thing.

We love you and miss you.

Here is Skip's e-mail to his wife, Diana. It was haunting in that he had never before told her to go home. There were so many things that pointed to the fact that Skip would not be with us much longer and the fact that he knew this.

From: Darrell Griffin, Jr.
Sent: Saturday, March 10, 2007
To: Diana Griffin
Subject: Your Honey

Sorry I got cut off. So anyway, really take it into consideration about going home to be with your family for your own sanity. But if not, don't get caught up into hiding out in the house. Get out and do things for yourself ok? I love you both and you already know by the pain behind my words how much I miss you.

Your husband, Stee Tee

From: Darrell Griffin, Jr.
Sent: Sunday, March 11, 2007
To: Diana Griffin
Subject: Your Honey

Hey honey,

We will be extended for 3-4 months here in Iraq. I can't expect you to be strong without us being together for so long. I'm sorry this has happened but there is nothing I can do about it. Do what you have to do in order to stay happy and not bored. All of us here have only each other to pick each other up because we don't have family here to reach out to. Go home and spend some time with your family because you have been away so long. I think it would be good for you to go home. Right now I have to draw strength from myself alone because I am the only one that will never let me down. When my year mark comes up, I want you to buy my pistol for me if you are still home ok? I would appreciate that. I will be conducting offensive operations for one week in and around B-dad. I go back to FOB Striker tomorrow and will be able to call you again. Take good care of yourself and Luna. I have no words to strengthen you Diana. We will both do what we have to do in order to survive and live while we live in two separate worlds. The lives of my men can get taken with a bright flash or a lucky shot, and this can take one second to occur. This is our reality. They are my family and my strength. You have to find what strengthens you and sustains you in your world. I have nothing but them. Deep inside, this is so hard for me to be here but I motivate my boys so much that I tend to forget how painful things are for me while being strong for others.

This is another of the e-mails where we sensed that Skip felt or knew that something was going to happen. Its tone was so different from the kind we were used to getting from him. What did he know that he wasn't telling us?

From: Diana Griffin
Sent: Sunday, March 11, 2007
To: Darrell Griffin
Subject: I Promise I'll Be Strong

Dear Honey,

I kind of expected that would happen. Mentally I'm somewhat prepared emotionally. I miss you so much my husband, but I promise to be strong for you and me… and yes it will be an entire year without seeing my Stee Tee…. But we both are strong in our marriage and we have a love that no miles will ever keep us apart. You are my heart and what makes every waking moment special. I love you so dearly Darrell, my love… I will keep our home filled with warmth awaiting for you to come home. I'm sure at our FRG meeting this Tuesday (our B-Day) we will get some information.

Honey stay strong and know I'm here for you waiting along with our little Luna. She misses you just as much as I do. Don't think I get bored because I don't. I've been doing a lot more yoga, and playing with our baby [the dog Luna] when the weather is nice. I will contact your dad about the extension. I am a strong woman honey. You stay strong too. I love you more than life itself and my prayers are with you. God bless you, my husband.

Love eternal,
Diana and Luna
I LOVE YOU xoxoxo

Skip called me and told me about this e-mail from Diana. He said it was one of the best he had ever received. We talked about the high divorce rate of soldiers who are deployed. I reminded Skip that his situation was different. For one thing, a number of the marriages that don't make it through deployments are between young people. The young brides buy into the romance of waiting for their soldiers but don't realize how hard it will be. They don't think of the fact that all of the family responsibilities will fall on their shoulders while their husbands are away.

> *Contemplating war in the abstract and actually fighting the war caused a change in my thinking and perspective from the inside out. Merely contemplating war limits one's perspective to the abstract, far removed from the smell of death, the screams of those who have lost their limbs in a blinding instant, and the screams of horror driven by sudden and violent loss of loved ones who were merely at the wrong place at the wrong time. Maybe those who have the power to send us off to war and an uncertain future should fight a war first and then consider foreign policy. The fact that violence occurs in combat does not, should not, preclude the act of war, but this violence should cause those who make these decisions to slow down and consider the awful burden of sending us off to kill and die if need be. They should also consider the potential for innocent noncombatants going to their deaths as well. If the cause is not just, then the blood of innocents will weigh heavily against them on the scales of Justice in a hoped-for reckoning, in a hoped-for conclusion to the*

human experiment. The blood of the infantryman will
not weigh against them because our blood has already
been spoken for in the necessity of war-making.

In late February and early March 2007, Alex Kingsbury from *U.S. News & World Report* was embedded with Skip's unit. With him was the photographer Max Becherer from Polaris Images. The subject that dominated much of their conversation was the fight near the city of Najaf that had happened just a few weeks earlier. Skip and his comrades spoke of Najaf often because the images were still so fresh in their minds. Skip told me that he would never be the same after witnessing the carnage.

Alex and Max went on a few raids with Skip and his men, but they didn't see a lot of action. Of one mission, Alex would write: "The raid was unremarkable. Griffin and his unit failed to nab their target, and the platoon—with a reporter and photographer in tow—spent a few hours chasing men who had fled the scene across open farm fields. Crunching through those fields, Griffin and I began talking about philosophy and politics of famous thinkers."

Alex was one of the few people who could hold his own in debate and conversation with Skip. He told me that the first time he saw Skip he gravitated toward him; most of the guys were sitting in front of their laptops watching movies or playing video games. Skip was over in the corner of the tent with his stack of books, reading.

I wondered what the higher-ups thought of soldiers clicking off so many digital pictures in Iraq. As Alex noted in *U.S. News & World Report*, "Many of the soldiers in

Iraq carry cameras. . . . Griffin went through three digital cameras during his two tours, once running through a hail of enemy bullets to fetch one he'd dropped in the sand." It was official policy, set in Washington, that photographers' access to the battlefront be severely limited; unlike Vietnam, "the living-room war," where the most grisly footage routinely made the nightly news, the Bush administration wanted Iraq to be the unseen war. The leadership on the ground in Iraq had a different view: "I hope, in the long run, that those pictures will help this generation to deal with whatever will have to be dealt with in the aftermath of this thing," Alex quoted Col. Huggins: "They will certainly never forget the things that they have done here."

Between raids, Alex interviewed Skip on video. They had borrowed a couple of plastic chairs from a nearby Internet café on the FOB, found a tent that wasn't being used, turned on the video, and started talking. During the twenty-six-minute interview, Skip mentioned to Alex that he was an atheist. This bothered me and his mom. We didn't want to think that at this critical time in his life he had lost his faith in God. All people at one time or another doubt their faith. I remember reading an article in the *Los Angeles Times* entitled, "Mother Teresa's Failing Faith." The article quoted Mother Teresa as saying, "If there be God—please forgive me. When I try to raise my thoughts to Heaven, there is such convincing emptiness that those very thoughts return like sharp knives and hurt my very soul." She recalled rejoicing that, in 1958, "that strange suffering for ten years" at last disappeared. But five weeks later, the article reported, she was "in the tunnel" again, and her dark night of the soul never lifted.

Skip called home on his birthday: March 13, 2007. It was a disturbing conversation. Normally he was full of energy and would try to cram a two-hour conversation into fifteen minutes or half an hour. Even when he was physically exhausted I could still see through to his sharp mind. This phone call was different. The first thing he said was: "Dad, I am so tired, I just want to come home." There was resignation in his voice. I wanted to try to cheer him up, but for some reason I wasn't sure that I should. It was as if this was the way this conversation was supposed to be. Skip's calls would normally come around two in the morning. I was usually a little groggy, but I had been anticipating this call because it was his birthday. "Dad, you know how you always pray for my strength, wisdom, and comfort? This time I really need it, so pray for me and my men."

Looking back, I see now that Skip was "in the tunnel" much like Mother Teresa had been. One of the few moments of Skip's adult life when he doubted God was captured forever on video the day Alex interviewed him. Not captured are the times he would say the blessing at our family meals, the times we would talk about God being outside of time, the times we would pray together on the phone. What also made Skip's mom and me feel a little better was the fact that in the taped interview Skip says, "I'm a Calvinist." A person cannot be an atheist and a Calvinist. If Skip were truly an atheist at that particular moment, would it destroy his years of loving his God?

Skip acknowledged that it is difficult to be a believer in a Supreme Being. I sometimes have doubts, but I do believe. Skip believed, but he doubted as well. In his journal, he quoted Pascal:

> *"Man is only a reed, the weakest in nature, but he is a thinking reed. It is not necessary that the whole universe arm itself to crush him. A vapor, a drop of water, suffices to kill him. But when the universe will have crushed him, Man will still be more noble than that which kills him, because he knows that he dies and the advantage which the universe has over him; the universe knows nothing of this."*

Then I go back to one of Skip's writings:

> *Is faith a type of knowledge superior to rational knowledge, or is faith a simple substitute for knowledge?*

Kim and I dissected his phone call. We were both bothered by it. It was not our normal Skip making that call. We were looking forward to his next high-energy, middle-of-the-night, I-have-just-read-a-new-book kind of call. Originally, Skip was going to come home in June, but they extended his tour to September. I hated hearing this because I was looking forward to spending a week with Skip getting the book organized. Kim started price-checking plane tickets and preparing her packing lists. She never did anything at the last minute. We were going to be ready to go visit Diana and Skip at Fort Lewis as soon as we got the word.

From Skip's journal:

A mother's memory that I want to honor comes from an incident that took place on 5 March 2007. Our company was conducting a raid in a city near Karbala in order to kill or capture a suspected intelligence officer associated with Ansar al-Sunna. We entered the home corresponding to the grid location given to us by our S2 [intelligence]. *His name was similar to the one we were looking for, but our interpreter informed us that we did not have the tribal name that corresponds to all last names of all Arabic people in general. We waited for two hours while his name was traced by our battalion S2, and to calm things down I spoke to the elderly man through our interpreter "Thunder." I asked him questions about himself, such as where he worked, what he thought about Moqtada al-Sadr, and other questions pertinent to all Iraqis.*

I noticed that one of his wives had been holding an infant that began to cry profusely. I asked if I could help in any way and the father indicated that the baby was hungry. I noticed the mother attempting to breastfeed her little baby and yet the baby continued to cry. Thunder, who is a certified and well-educated doctor of internal medicine educated in Iraq, told me that the mother, because she was very frightened by our presence, was not able to breastfeed her baby because the glands in the breast close up due to sympathetic responses to fear and stressful situations. I then tried to reassure the mother by allowing her to leave the room and attain some privacy so that she could relax and feed her child.

I felt something that had been brooding under the attained callousness of my heart for some time. My heart finally broke for the Iraqi people. I wanted to just sit down and cry while saying I'm so, so sorry for what we had done. I had the acute sense that we had failed these people. It was at this time, and after an entire year of being deployed and well into the next deployment that I realized something. We burst into homes, frighten the hell out of families, and destroy their homes looking for an elusive enemy. We do this out of fear of the unseen and attempt to compensate for our inability to capture insurgents by swatting mosquitoes with a sledgehammer in glass houses. The old man sitting down in front of me could very easily have been lying to us for whatever reason; we would never know. I would much rather keep a liar as a friend than have a liar pushed to the side of the insurgency. The mosquito represents the small, quantifiably inferior force that we are chasing; the sledgehammer represents the full weight of our military and the glass house represents the country of Iraq. May that woman's child have the life that he deserves, lived to the fullest.

From: Darrell Griffin, Jr.
Sent: Saturday, March 17, 2007
To: Diana Griffin
Subject: (no subject)

Dearest Diana, Spartan women of Greece used to tell their husbands before they went into battle to come back with their shields or on them because they died honorably in battle. But if they did not return with them, this showed that they ran away from the battle. Cowardice was not a Spartan virtue. Tell me you love me the same whether if I come back with my shield or on it.

Hope you enjoy reading the Newsweek [*U.S. News & World Report*] report that quoted me. I have the recording of the actual video interview. The night vision footage is of my squad! I LOVE YOU MY SPARTAN WOMAN OF STRENGTH AND VIRTUE.

It was March 20, 2007, and C Company rolled out as a company to do a mission in Sadr City. The company was required to keep a platoon at Combat Outpost Callahan manned by elements of the 82nd Airborne. The purpose of the COP was to enable soldiers to live in the neighborhood they patrolled, maintaining a constant presence. Before this one became a COP, it had been nothing more than the skeletal remains of what had once been a busy shopping mall in Baghdad's Adhamiyah District.

On this day, C Company was serving as the quick reaction force at COP Callahan. It had come down that there was an imminent threat to the COP via VBIED. The battalion felt the biggest threat was to the JSS (joint security station) in Baghdad, so Skip's platoon leader, Lt. Gregory Weber, was instructed to move his platoon to the JSS. Upon arrival, Weber reported to the site commander, an old Armored Calvary guy. He and Weber didn't get along from the start, and almost came to blows, which was unusual for Weber, who was generally cool and collected. When he walked into the commander's office at the JSS, he was told there was an imminent threat.

"The commander was talking real slow, with no sense of urgency," Weber recalled: "He said, 'What I want to do is pull my guys off the gate and I want you to use your Strykers and your men to watch this gate [the main gate leading into the JSS compound].'" Weber thought this was nonsense. The insurgents were going to drive up to the gate and blow it up. "'Sir, this is your compound. I don't understand it. Why are you having someone else guard your compound?'" According to Weber, it was a pride thing. "A compound commander would never ask someone else to guard his compound. You just don't put another unit at your main protection area." The commander told Weber he wanted a squad on top of the building pulling high-side security (the rooftop was a major advantage if the JSS was raided). He wanted another squad at the gate, and one watching a corner of the building. He thought insurgents were possibly going to rappel the fifteen-foot-high concrete T barriers.

Weber pulled his squad leaders aside. He was honest with them about how he felt about the assignment. He told them he thought it was nonsense. Weber told me that Skip always said, "Screw it, we gotta do it, we gotta do it." Skip agreed to take high-side security. The 2nd squad of the Third Platoon, led by SSG Standly Villiers, took the gate; another squad watched the corner of the wall. They sat there for a while, planning how to work rotations and how to sleep and grumbled a little more. Skip tried to cheer everyone up by telling them what a great mission this was: "We are going to get in a fight tonight."

They had consolidated their trucks into the motor pool area. They were dead tired. None of them had gotten any real sleep the night before. Weber had forgotten his poncho liner to wrap up in so that he could sleep on the ground. Skip offered to share his. It was bitter cold and the poncho liner wasn't really big enough for two guys. After about an hour, Weber got back in the Stryker and tried to sleep there.

The next morning, the rest of C Company came back out from doing their mission. Weber's platoon was designated the QRF while the rest of the company was on a mission. The QRF could be called in the event something happened and the company needed more resources.

Weber was not really a cigar smoker, but he took Skip up on his offer to smoke one this morning. Skip and Weber finished smoking their cigars just as Capt. Phillips and the rest of the company returned from their mission. They were all still grumbling about the miserable night. Weber recalled that Skip was in a great mood. Weber asked him why. Skip said, "I don't really know, but I think God has something special planned for me today."

They left the JSS at about noon for the drive back to FOB Striker. Weber's platoon was the lead platoon. Skip and Weber were in the second Stryker. Behind Weber's platoon was the new company commander, Capt. Stephen Phillips, and his contingent of Strykers. Skip and Sgt. Charles Sims were standing in the back hatches serving as air guards. Their jobs were to provide security to the rear of the vehicle, and assistance when maneuvering it backwards.

The company was about fifteen minutes from the front gate of Striker when they heard a distinctive small-arms round followed by some more sporadic rounds. According to Sims, there were a few seconds of confusion as they were trying to determine where the fire was coming from. Sims saw Skip duck and say, "What was that?" Sims was scanning the horizon. Sgt. Christopher Pacheco noticed that Skip was still standing in the hatch, but his legs were limp. Specialist Robert Spracklin could see blood dripping heavily from Skip's helmet as he leaned forward in the hatch. Pacheco yelled, "Sergeant Griffin's been shot!" Sims and Specialist Christopher Mueller pulled him down into the Stryker and laid him on Sims's lap. He was still breathing. They found the wound, got the first aid bag out and wrapped his head in gauze. Sims kept pressure applied to the top of his head. Skip was breathing in a labored, erratic, and deep manner. Pacheco and Sims held his hands and started speaking to him, telling him to hold on, trying to calm him down. While the guys in the truck were caring for Skip, Weber called Capt. Phillips on the radio and reported that they had received small-arms fire and there was a casualty. Phillips quickly got the convoy out of the kill zone and brought the entire company to a halt. He would later tell me that this radio call would be forever burned into his memory. He said that what felt like minutes were really only a couple of surreal seconds. He snapped back into real time and told Weber he needed a status of the severity of the casualty and the battle roster number. Weber responded, "It's very severe."

"Get me the battle roster number." Phillips ordered 1st Sgt. Viriato Ferrera's Stryker, which contained the senior medic team, to push forward and get next to the lead vehicle where Lt. Weber, Skip, and his squad were. Phillips ordered an immediate casualty transfer from Skip's infantry carrier Stryker to the first sergeant's Stryker, an armored mobile treatment platform known as a Stabilized Medical Variant. As the transfer was happening, Phillips got a third call from Weber informing him of the wounded soldier's battle roster number. He knew who it was. He didn't have to pull out the battle leader's booklet that he always carried in his shoulder pocket. It was Darrell Griffin. They rushed the medical evacuation vehicle (MEV) and the rest of the company to the combat support hospital located in the Green Zone. Eleven minutes after being hit, Skip was on the operating table. Ferrera, Weber, Phillips, and the company medics waited in the operating room lobby. They were at the CSH for about two hours. It took forty-five minutes for a helicopter to land, and another forty-five minutes to move him by air because the treatment team was stabilizing him for the flight to the military hospital in Balad, just north of Baghdad, where there was a specialist in head trauma. He died en route.

After the helicopter took Skip away, the company stayed in the Green Zone for a while to allow the soldiers to take a deep breath and come to terms with what had just happened. The mission was still not over. They had to ride back to FOB Striker, through the same kill zone where Skip had been shot. As the company pulled into Striker, Phillips instructed the driver to let him off at the battalion's TOC. He walked into the TOC to talk to the operations officer on duty. Maj. Scott Green, the battalion executive officer, put his hand on Phillips's shoulder. Phillips looked at him and said, "It happened, didn't it?"

Diana's response that Skip never saw:

From: Diana Griffin
Sent: Saturday, March 17, 2007
To: Darrell Griffin, Jr.
Subject: How Exciting

Honey, How exciting to see your words on paper! I'm going to e-mail the journalist, Alex Kingsbury, and ask if he has any pictures of you. I watched the video and I think I could hear your voice. I'm sure of it. I think there is one part where you are by an Iraqi woman near a door. Is that you honey? Do you know if that article will be out this week's coming issue? I'll be in line to buy a couple of copies for our memories in the future. It's ironic how during your first deployment your pictures were in "Getty Images" and now "U.S. News" has your words. I feel so proud being your wife for many other reasons as well, my Soldier, my husband.

I love how you refer to me as your Spartan woman, those words are so beautiful. I know you will come back to me with your shield in hand, with honor and humbleness. That is the man you are, my husband. "Strength and Honor and Virtue."

I sent your package this afternoon. They didn't have the gloves in tan so I sent black. They don't carry the ACU light-green color T-shirt, they said it's the Marines or Navy who wear that color. I found the Ranger pants, & I sent the Oakley Boots. You should get the package by the end of next week.

I went to the FRG potluck. As you said, nothing was mentioned about you guys moving, so I didn't say anything. I didn't want to get everyone upset or get you in trouble. Did you send the link to your dad about the article? Are you using AKO? Should I send e-mails to AKO or AOL? Did you get the password for My Pay? Enough questions Diana, I'm so silly. I miss you so much, I love you so much. I hear your voice in my mind. May God keep his hedge of protection around you. God bless you my love. I LOVE YOU.

LOVE, YOUR SPARTAN WOMAN OF STRENGTH AND VIRTUE

Greek Goddess DIANA and Luna

This is the e-mail Diana sent to Skip the morning of the day that she was visited by two army sergeants in dress green uniforms who came to inform her that Skip had been killed in action:

From: Diana Griffin
Sent: Wednesday, March 21, 2007
To: Darrell Griffin, Jr.
Subject: Where's Stee Tee??

Are you okay??? I haven't heard from you since Sunday and it is now Wednesday. I know you said you were going on a dangerous mission. I get so nervous when I don't hear from you. Call me or e-mail me. I just hope and pray you are okay honey.

I bought the issue of U.S. News with the article you are quoted in. First page second paragraph in big bold lettering. I bought 4 issues. One to show, and the rest for memories of our journey in the military. Honey, please let me know you are okay. I love you so much and my heart aches for you. I am praying for you my love along with everyone else who is sending prayers your way. God bless you my Stee Tee, I love you.

Chapter 15

Last Journey

March 21, 2007, is a day I've tried both to forget and remember everything I can about. I have wanted to forget because it was the worst day of my life, and to remember because it still doesn't seem real. I only know it is real because I can't pick up the phone and call Skip anymore. He doesn't call us anymore. Diana has been tormented by the feeling that maybe it's all a mistake. She sometimes feels as if she's having a bad dream and will wake up and it will turn out the army got it wrong and he's still alive. Kim often awakes in the middle of the night and says, "He's not going to call any more, is he?" We used to get so excited and he would laugh at how groggy we were when he called. I wish I had recorded all of his calls. There is something about a recording of a voice that a picture can't give you. I recorded his voice on his answering machine at his house at Fort Lewis.

The few days after Skip's death were possibly worse than the day of his death. After the first day, we knew it was real and not some nightmare that we were sharing.

March 22, 2007
Kim stayed home from work. Jordan and Alexis stayed home from school. I don't really remember much except for

getting lots of calls of sympathy. All of my relatives called. My cousin Rick told me through his tears that Skip was his first real hero. He said, "We now have left our family blood in the sands of Iraq."

I had often passed a large cemetery on the 405 Freeway near UCLA. I Googled "Federal Veterans Cemetery" to get the contact information and called them. The lady at the other end of the phone line said that I should give contact information to the casualty officer working with us at Fort Lewis.

Diana also asked me to find a mortuary near our church. I called my good friend Rick Kasel, the pastor of my church, Shepherd of the Hills, in Porter Ranch. He put me in touch with Lara Morris, who worked in the Pastoral Care Department. She said she wasn't allowed to recommend any one specific mortuary, but she could coordinate with the one we selected. I Googled mortuaries near the church, and we settled on Crawford Mortuary in Northridge. It was close to home and located near the church. I knew that relatives would be coming in from different parts of the country and would want to visit with Skip before his funeral and burial. Before sending this information to Diana, Kim and I wanted to check it out first. How does one check out a mortuary? Crawford Mortuary seemed a little small, but since there wasn't going to be a viewing, we decided it was adequate.

March 23, 2007
Kim went to work, and Alexis and Jordan went to school. I stayed home and sat in my underwear in our darkened

bedroom. I put blankets on the windows to black out the light. I didn't feel like doing anything, not even brushing my teeth, taking a bath, or brushing my hair. I finally got up at about 2:00 p.m. and showered because Kim called to say that she was going to come by for me so we could pick up the kids. She said I needed to get out of the house.

I talked to Megan Garvey from the *Los Angeles Times.* She wanted to get some information to do a "soldier's obituary" for Skip. I told her Skip was my best friend as well as my son. I said Skip was the smartest man I ever knew. I told her that I was blessed with being able to talk to Skip on his birthday a week before he died. The last words I said to him were: "I love you and I pray for your safety, comfort, and wisdom daily."

Diana told me that Alex Kingsbury, the reporter who had interviewed Skip in Iraq the week before he died, had called her and told her that he had twenty-six minutes of video and audio footage of his interview with Skip. He offered to bring the tape to Diana at the official army ceremony at Fort Lewis, Washington. She had told Alex that Skip was writing a book and that I was going to finish it. She said he offered to help.

Kim's mom, Kiyo, lives close to us. It seems customary for people to bring food to those who are grieving and in the process of burying a loved one. Kiyo brought us a complete dinner of fried rice, chicken, and vegetables, and a pie for dessert. I had three glasses of brandy to help numb myself. As a diversion, we took the kids to Borders to buy books. I came home and had a few glasses of wine and settled in for bed. Kim had all of us sleep in the living room because the kids didn't want to be alone—none of us did. I went out to the garage and retrieved four mats and Kim made them into beds.

The wine seemed to numb my emotions a little, but the memories of Skip were still playing over and over in my head. Nothing I did (sitting in my bedroom in my underwear in the dark, drinking a bottle of wine) seemed to soften the pain. The only thing that seemed to help was to pray. I prayed that I would stop drinking so much and that I would be able to deal better with Skip's death. I did stop drinking so much, and I began to have conversations with Skip. I am not a nutcase, as far as I can tell (do crazy people know when they are crazy?), but these conversations were a great help to me. Sometime later, he began to speak back to me and help me through critical sections of the book. Between talking to God and my son, I was barely able to cope with losing Skip, but I was able to stumble through each day.

March 24, 2007

I got up at 7:00 a.m. Kim had to go run some errands. She was expecting a busy week as we continued to work on Skip's funeral. I was waiting for Kim's mom to bring her cement guy over. A few weeks earlier, Kim and I had taken the pebble coating off of the front porch, and she wanted to have it covered before people started arriving for the funeral.

March 27, 2007

I needed some photographs for a collage about Skip's life for the funeral, so I called Linda Romano (Skip's birth mom) to see if she had any pictures of Skip before he turned four. It had been maybe thirty years since I had last seen her, and probably twenty since I had last spoken to her. She said, "I only ask you one favor. I ask that I get to see my son." I told her that he might not be in a condition to be seen. She said, "I've worked in a doctor's office, I have seen some really bad situations." I told her I'd think about it.

Today was the day I started working with Pastor Rick Kasel and the casualty assistance officer from Fort Lewis to set up the funeral service and burial. I felt I should be at work, because once Skip was buried I would still have to earn a living. Life does go on, but it's different. What about the other kids? I don't want them to feel less important to me. I have this burning need to stand in the same spot where Skip was shot. Can I arrange this? Should I try to arrange it? Is it odd? Is it necessary? Would it help me to deal with his loss?

I wanted to give Skip two last gifts before I finally said good-bye to him. One of them was to find a way to complete the book we had started. I felt that he could live on past March 21, 2007, if I could make the book happen. I had always planned to die before my children, so I could look down from Heaven (or up from Hell, if I had misjudged my standing with God) after they buried me. World events changed all that.

The other gift was to give Skip the send-off that I feel he would have wanted. We had talked a number of times about how he would like his final ceremony to be if something happened to him. He wanted a traditional military ceremony, including bagpipes. I was grateful when Diana called me and asked if I would make the funeral plans.

The first thing I did was to go through Skip's files at home. We probably have every report card that he ever received. I always thought I would throw them out, but now I am so glad that I didn't. Every scrap of paper, every object that touched Skip's life, is precious. At times I feel guilty that I didn't realize this before he was killed. When I came to the section in Skip's files labeled "ART," I got chills up my spine. When Skip was older, we often talked of the dark side and our belief that there is such a thing as evil. We also discussed the phrase *Malleus Dei*, which is Latin for "The Hammer of God." Skip came across this term as he was reading Kierkegaard's *Repetition*. Kierkegaard talks about the biblical Job in this book: Were the calamities that befell him the result of the "hammer of God" or simply the "natural" power of universal and necessary truths? According to the Bible, it was God who tested Job as He tested Abraham. But we cannot "know" this. We must have faith. While he was still living at home, Skip drew this picture. He walked into my study and said something like, "Dad, here is Man." Twenty years later, I now know what he meant. There is the Hammer of God and there is evil.

James Pelletier, Skip's roommate and fellow philosopher, wrote me a few months after Skip died:

It was effortless to love Darrell, and even more so for me as we shared so many experiences in common. He and I shared

a love of philosophy and a joy in honest and open discussion of truth that I have been unable to find in my almost eight years in the army. Self-taught and well read, Skip had a better understanding of truth and knowledge, honor and love, faith and justice than I had been able to grasp through years of formal private education. He was a considerate man not only in his dealings with people, but in the most basic meaning of the word. Everything he did and said was carefully considered, and he reviewed all of his actions, thoughts, and words in the harsh light of his understanding of reality. He and I had conversations and arguments that lasted for days on end, sometimes weeks, ranging in topic from what our mission was here in Iraq, and whether it was truly just and necessary, to the nature of God and faith, and the apparent disparate gap between faith and reason.

Many who knew Darrell only in passing thought his enthusiasm for his vocation borne out of naïveté. Those of us who knew him well knew that his dedication to ideal was in spite of, or perhaps even because of his experiences on the battlefield, and in his time as a paramedic. Darrell and I shared more than just our love of learning. As a sniper team leader, I have been exposed to the basest truth of war: people die in war. There are very few ways to keep sane in the face of the inhumanity that men in our profession are immersed in, and must of necessity participate in. Most soldiers simply cannot be concerned by questions of things greater than themselves, or of their immediate circumstances. Most are content with providing themselves safety and sanity by not considering what they have seen. Then there are those who consider their actions and the actions of others who are not able to process it with any reason or intellect. These men satisfy themselves with transferring what should be known to what they 'feel.' They cannot begin to take what they have lived and analyze it in the light of faith and reason. Then there are men like Darrell.

Darrell analyzed every thought, word, and action, and was able to, with great faith and intuitive reason, understand everything. I remember one conversation I had with him over an essay that I have been writing for years about the importance of the infantry. I remember it most because I saw a light in his eyes and heard an excitement in his voice that I had never experienced from any other person over something that most deemed mundane. I remember explaining to him that I was taking great pains to view the modern world of soldiering through the eyes of classical wisdom, and seeing a passion well up in him. We discussed the ideas of ancient Greek philosophers and how they applied to what we chose to do as men and as soldiers. How the infantryman must be ever adaptive to an ever-changing battlefield because, as Heraclitus told us, everything is in flux, and heat is the catalyst for that flux, and where else is there more fire and change than on the ever-mutable battlefield?

I know you read this and I imagine it is difficult for you to share the passion that this subject brings to my heart, but I know you also know how much it enthralled him, because that is who he was. That is how we cope. That is how the thinking soldier, like Darrell, deals with the misery and suffering of 'man's inhumanity to men,' as he often quoted. We analyze it, and we judge it, and we take it in the light of faith and wisdom, and we act on it. Darrell had difficulty on many occasions, as have I, justifying war in general, and specifically the war we fought side by side, and on those occasions, we spoke. When words were done, we thought. And on more than one occasion, together we cried. He was my strength in what I have lived, and his memory is my strength as I continue.

The army flew Skip's body to Dover, Maryland, for an autopsy and final preparations, and then flew him home on a private jet a few days before the funeral. One of his best friends in the army, SFC Duane Wells, accompanied Skip from Dover to the Burbank, California, airport. Sgt. Robert Hansen flew in from Oklahoma to be with the family.

I hadn't seen Skip's birth mom, Linda, for thirty years. I had invited her to Skip's funeral, but I wasn't sure she would show up. I had to get to the church early on the day of the funeral to make sure everything was ready. As I walked into our church auditorium at Shepherd of the Hills, there was a person sitting alone at the front of this huge gathering place. It was dim in the sanctuary, so I couldn't really make out who it was. As I got closer I saw that it was Linda. We hugged but didn't speak.

Skip had told me that if anything happened to him he would like one of my friends to be the officiating minister. I asked Pastor Rick Kasel to preside over the funeral and burial. A number of people spoke at Skip's service. Ryan Ramirez, Diana's nephew, talked of Skip being a father figure to him; Rene read the Spartan Woman e-mail that Skip had sent to Diana days before he was killed; Guillermo Salazar, a close relative, read e-mails from some of Skip's comrades; Michael Smythe, now a philosophy professor, who had been a clerk at Archives Bookshop in 1999 when Skip came into the store, recalled their heated theological debates; Alex Kingsbury, the reporter from *U.S. News & World Report*, remembered Skip's last few days in Iraq; and Brig. Gen. Robert Cone presented the U.S. flag to us. I delivered the eulogy.

The procession from the church to the cemetery required us to go down the twelve-lane 405 Freeway, one of the busiest in the world. We were accompanied by a motorcycle brigade called the Patriot Guards. There had been incidents of people throwing red paint on the families of fallen soldiers. According to an obscure Kansas-based Baptist congregation, soldiers killed in the war are being punished by God. I didn't want anyone disrupting my son's funeral, and it was the mission of the Patriot Guards to keep the crazies away.

The Los Angeles Police Department shut down three lanes from the church to the cemetery. You would see the best and the worst of people when this happened. Some flashed peace signs; some stuck their hands out of their car windows and gave the "One Way with Jesus" sign, pointing their index fingers to the sky. Then there were those who flipped the bird: the motorcade had slowed them down.

We buried Darrell R. Griffin, Jr., on April 6, 2007, at the Westwood National Cemetery.

First Lt. Gregory Weber, Skip's platoon leader, wrote the following tribute to Skip in *Patriot*, the battalion's newsletter:

Staff Sergeant Darrell Griffin arrived at Charlie Company in December, where he was assigned as the Squad Leader of 1st Squad, 3rd Platoon. SSG Griffin had little time to gauge his men before he was tasked to begin combat operations. He immediately demonstrated that he would prove to be an instrumental soldier, leader, and friend to the men of 3rd Platoon. SSG Griffin's first mission as squad leader was when 3rd Platoon was tasked to clear a large apartment complex in the Dora neighborhood of Baghdad. As the main effort squad of 3rd Platoon, SSG Griffin led his Soldiers through a grueling twelve-hour nonstop mission to clear the area. It was here that Darrell demonstrated his physical and mental toughness when he went apartment to apartment, showing no signs of fatigue.

Everyone that knew SSG Griffin could tell countless stories of how motivated he was to be a hardened soldier, but few knew him as the scholar and intellectual that 3rd Platoon came to know him as. SSG Griffin was constantly reading books about political climates between countries, international diplomacy, and world affairs. One particular book, *Islam*, was among his favorites. He was reading the book for the fourth time when the Company was working out of FOB Kalsu in February. Sometimes soldiers can lose sight of how different our culture is compared to that of Iraq, but not when SSG Griffin was nearby. While reading this book, SSG Griffin would spend hours discussing culture and his desire to help the people of Iraq with the local national interpreters. This type of behavior was typical of him and it improved soldiers' understanding of being here tremendously. SSG Griffin shared a Stryker with Sergeant Foster, Sergeant Pacheco, Specialist Novoa, Sergeant Sims, Specialist Fernandez, Specialist Spracklin, Private First Class Smith, Specialist Mueller, Specialist Guajuardo, and myself. We spent the most time together and worked as a close-knit team, given our proximity. Many times on missions, the Company would face either a long drive or a long duration of sitting idle in a blocking position. With conditions like that it was easy for us to get complacent; SSG Griffin wouldn't let that happen. Whether he was making a joke about something he saw, explaining his newest theory on international relations, or discussing new tactical entry techniques, SSG Griffin kept everyone around him in good spirits and ready to accomplish whatever was thrown at them. As SSG Griffin's right-hand man, Sergeant Pacheco recalls how unconditionally giving SSG Griffin was. "Regardless of what he had, Griff would constantly give to the soldiers." SSG Griffin made it his mission to gather soldier-needed items in order to help someone out. "It was amazing how he never once thought about himself, it was always about the soldier," said Sergeant Pacheco. Because of that trait, the leaders of Charlie Company will always remember what they are serving for and how the memory of SSG Griffin will constantly remind them to devote themselves unconditionally to their soldiers. SSG Griffin began every mission with the words "Strength and Honor" on the internal communication system and then would yell it down below to the guys. Regardless of the danger the men faced, those three simple words brought peace of mind to them all. Griff, the Fighting Hellfish will miss you always and will carry you with them in their hearts forever. Strength and Honor, SSG Griffin, Strength and Honor.

Command Sgt. Maj. Victor Mercado called me some time in April to say he was going to be in town and would like to visit Skip's grave. I gave him the address and agreed to meet him there. I got there before he did and was kneeling in front of Skip's grave. It had only been a couple of weeks since he was put in the ground, so the grass had not yet started to grow back over it. The headstone hadn't come yet. The only thing to show that Skip was buried here was the index card that said: *Grave No. A 15, Section 89A, Darrell R. Griffin, Date of Death, 03/21/2007.*

When Victor arrived, he knelt down beside me and prayed, putting his fingers to his lips and then to Skip's temporary grave marker. I got up and leaned against my car while he stayed there for a few more minutes. Before he left, we talked about unimportant things for a while. He said don't be disappointed if you don't get to go to Iraq because the army just does not allow parents to go there, especially not to the battlefield.

I had been e-mailing back and forth with Alex Kingsbury of *U.S. News & World Report.* He said he wanted to do an

article about Skip and that his editor might make it their cover story. It was May 21, 2007. I took Alexis and Jordan to Borders. I was looking at the magazines when I saw Skip's face looking back at me. His face was on the cover and there was an eight-page story about him in the issue. I bought a couple of issues and left the store with the kids. It was several months before I could bring myself to read the story that Alex wrote.

Copyright 2007 *U.S. News & World Report*, L.P. Reprinted with permission.

Chapter 16

A Father's Last Gift

Even before Skip's burial I had started checking into the possibility of visiting his comrades in Baghdad to gather information for the completion of "our book." I was also hoping that visiting the last place my son ever saw would bring me some degree of closure. People around me kept talking of closure. What is closure in relationship to the death of my son? Does closure mean that his loss will not constantly haunt me? Does it mean that I won't think about him daily? I wish I knew what closure was; then maybe I could achieve it.

Arranging My Trip to Iraq

I wrote to everyone I could think of: Congressman Howard Berman, Alex Kingsbury, even General David Petraeus, commander of U.S. forces in Iraq. The general wrote back to me right away.

Dear Mr. Griffin, thanks for your note and, more importantly, thanks for the sacrifice your family has made. Though I do not recall meeting him, Griff was, by all accounts, a great soldier and leader. And I can fully understand why you would want to visit places where he served, talk with some of his comrades, and get the closure that this might help bring.

Having said that, supporting a visit like this is a challenge due to the need for security, transport, billeting, etc. And due to the high operational tempo associated with the ongoing surge, we currently have a ban on visitors for the next month or more—though some obviously are still supported. Knowing the meaning of this to you and the sacrifice your family has made, we will see what is possible.

I have shared this with my Chief of Staff and his deputy, Maj Gen Moore and COL Jim Hoy, and they will help you link up by e-mail with Griff's unit and also see what might be possible.

Finally, thanks, in turn to you and your family, for allowing Griff to serve our country and for supporting him so magnificently.

With best wishes from Baghdad
—Gen Dave Petraeus

I was encouraged that someone this high up in the chain of command was at least listening to me.

Congressman Berman called me in June 2007 from the floor of the House and told me that he was working on getting me to Iraq. One possibility was to get me to Northern Iraq through some Iraqi governmental connections that he had. First he wanted to try to work with his connections at the Department of Defense (DOD). On July 12, he wrote a letter to Assistant Secretary of Defense Robert Wilkie, telling him about the book Skip and I were working on and recommending that I be granted permission to travel to Iraq. He expressed concern that my trip could possibly set a precedent but said that he felt that my situation was unique. The congressman also mentioned in the letter that I had been in touch with Gen. Petraeus.

Toward the end of July, I finally got permission from the Department of Defense to travel to Iraq. This did not mean buy a ticket and hop on a plane. There were several other issues to resolve if I was to have a safe trip.

Things started to move pretty fast during the first week of August, when the DOD assigned Traci Scott from the Office of the Secretary of Defense to my project. She started contacting the appropriate people in the military to get my visit moved up on their priority list. She was e-mailing me several times a day to bring me up to date on the status of my trip. On August 4, she sent me the link for the embed forms that needed to be filled out online, and instructed me to send a copy to the embed unit in Iraq. I would be issued my visa once I got to the Kuwait City International Airport.

On August 15, Traci Scott e-mailed me: "Buy Your Ticket to Kuwait!" That same day, Sgt. Jonathan Bell from the Iraqi embed group (MNF-I Media Embed NCOIC) e-mailed me to let me know that I had been approved. This meant that I would have someone to meet me at the Kuwait airport upon my arrival. It also meant that, as long as I got myself to Kuwait, the army would take care of getting me from Kuwait to Iraq and back again under relatively safe conditions.

On August 16, Gunnery Sgt. Chris W. Cox, from the Coalition Forces Land Component Command Public Affairs Office in Kuwait, e-mailed me asking for the details of my trip and listing the documents I would need. Time was of the essence, as my son's unit would be leaving Baghdad and going back to Fort Lewis, Washington, around the middle of September.

The Flight to Kuwait

Once I got the okay from the embed group, I worked on getting my round-trip tickets to Kuwait. I shopped around Orbitz and Travelocity and found a fare for $2,263 with a layover in Amsterdam.

I was amazed at the amount of food that's served on international flights. I was used to the peanuts and soda served on domestic airlines, so I asked the flight attendant if I could get a bag of peanuts. I was nervous. I was hoping that I had all the pieces in place and wouldn't get stranded in Kuwait or Iraq without any contacts. It was a little spooky going into this part of the world by myself. I am not a tough guy like Griff. I was a fifty-five-year-old, out-of-shape dad.

I arrived in Kuwait on time. This is when it hit me that I was really on my own. Most of the men at the airport wore the traditional Muslim attire, and I noticed that women were very subservient to their men, walking behind them and not daring to look in my direction. I was obviously an American. The airport itself was a modern structure that would rival anything in the United States. Most signs were in English and Arabic. I went to get my visa at the Kuwait airport security, picked up my luggage, and headed for the Starbucks where I was supposed to meet Sgt. Cox. As I was wandering through the airport, I got excited when I saw the familiar Starbucks logo. It was like seeing the American flag. There was the same blond wood furniture, the same condiments bar and baristas. The first thing I did was order an iced coffee, unsweetened, with room for cream. It was reassuring just to ask for my favorite concoction.

I noticed a number of other Americans, most of whom were contractors, but no one named Sgt. Cox. Finally a man tapped me on the shoulder, introduced himself as SFC David Choi, and asked if I was Darrell Griffin. I was really glad hear someone say my name: I had been at the airport for a couple of hours by this time and was a little concerned that I couldn't find my contacts.

SFC Choi was in civilian clothes; Sgt. Cox had warned me that the Kuwaitis didn't like to see American soldiers. He was joined by Lt. Kim Cruz, an Asian woman about twenty-five years old. As she walked toward me, I could see the men in the immediate area follow her with their eyes. She was one of the few American women in the airport, but she would have stood out even at the Los Angeles International Airport. We were joined by a couple of Swedish journalists and escorted out to a van.

David and Kim were national guardsmen assigned to the Third Army Public Relations group. David was from the California National Guard and Kim was from the Alabama National Guard. At home Kim was a nurse, and David was a student at University of California, Davis, studying international affairs.

Once we were past the last airport checkpoint, they pulled over to the side of the road and strapped on .45s. Here were a nurse and a college student strapping on their pieces for our drive to the middle of the desert. This was when I realized we weren't in Kansas anymore. The ride from the airport to our first destination, Camp Ali Al Salem, took about forty-five minutes. If we had continued on the same road we were on for a couple of days, we would have eventually hit Baghdad. Only heavily armed convoys take this route. Camp Ali Al Salem is called the Gateway to the Theater. Anyone (military or civilian) legally entering Iraq or Afghanistan will normally enter through this camp.

On the way to the camp there were a number of enterprising merchants by the side of the road selling orange sodas, and odds and ends such as blankets, boots, and uniforms that obviously came from questionable sources. Other than these green-lit "hodgi" stands along the way, there was only desert and silence and an occasional checkpoint. No one seemed interested in stopping us; one guard got mad when we pulled up to his barrier and woke him up.

We drove for about an hour and pulled into the heavily fortified check-in area of Camp Ali Al Salem, where we were ordered out of the van and instructed to stand behind a thick concrete barrier while the guards gave the van a complete security check. We then proceeded to tent #2, which housed the public relations office, the passport desk, and the in/out processing groups for the various branches of the military.

The tent was packed with soldiers headed for various cities in Iraq and Afghanistan.

There were also a lot of contractors. You could easily tell the soldiers from the contractors, and not just because of their uniforms. The soldiers were clean-shaven and in pretty good physical shape, and they always said "sir" at the end of every sentence. Most of the contractors were overweight and stubble-bearded, and every other word out of their mouths was a four-letter expletive. Some of them had knives strapped to their legs and wrap-around sunglasses that they wore even at night.

Kim took us over to the passport desk, manned by contractors, where we had to leave our passports and visas. For some reason, our passports had to be sent back to Kuwait City for review and more stamping. (Since we had to pay for this stamping service, it's my guess that it was just another way of filling jobs and generating revenues.) We wouldn't get them back for at least twenty-four hours. Kim gave us each a temporary pass card that we hung around our necks; it gave us entry to the dining facilities and the PX. Then she took us over to the billeting trailer for our tent assignment.

Camp Ali Al Salem is really a tent city in close proximity to an Air Force landing strip. Behind the tents were separate men's and women's latrine trailers, shower trailers, laundry trailers, the dining facility, the PX, the Internet trailer, the phone trailer, and various fast-food trailers: McDonald's, KFC, Hole 'n One Donuts, and some pizza place. Scattered between the tents were smoking shacks on elevated platforms, which resembled bus shelters on stakes. (I wondered why they were built off the ground, since no one had to worry about floods.) The facility was well fortified with razor wire, concrete barriers, and hard-looking guards.

Specialist Choi showed the Swedes and me to our tent, Papa 5. On the way, he explained the procedure: once we got our passports, we would be required to check in at 6:00 a.m. in the morning and at 3:00 p.m. in the afternoon each day to see if we had been selected to get on a plane or helicopter headed for Baghdad.

When we got to our tent, we claimed our bunks. I was glad I had brought along a flashlight: the tent was pitch dark. All around us we could hear the snoring of the contractors and journalists who had arrived before us. There were no blankets, only a bare mattress. The floors were cement. At least it was cool: each tent had a large-capacity air conditioner attached to it, which made the tents look like inflated kids' jumpers.

One night, the Swedes and I walked over to the dining facility (DFAC) for chow. The food was actually pretty good. Just outside the chow hall was a big metal barrel. As they approached the front door of the DFAC, the soldiers would point their weapons into the barrel, cock them, and examine their firing chambers to make sure they were safe. After we had our badges checked, we were allowed to go down the chow line and select our courses. I found an empty seat at one of the picnic-bench tables. Everyone was glued to the flat-screen TVs placed around the dining hall. President Bush was on the screen, meeting with the troops in Fallujah.

I got my fill of chicken strips and started back to my tent. Passing a latrine trailer, I ducked into a stall. I peeled my trousers down my sweaty legs and sat down. The walls were covered with graffiti. My eyes were drawn to a phrase scrawled in black Magic Marker: "If it doesn't kill you it will make you stronger." A previous visitor to this particular toilet stall, noticing that the writer had gotten Nietzsche's famous quote wrong, had crossed it out and replaced it with the correct version: "That which does not kill us makes us stronger." The editor had signed his name as "Skip."

The Swedes and I were at Camp Ali Al Salem for two days before we were able to fly out. I eventually got put on a flight (an Air Force C130). Kim and David had managed to procure for me a Kevlar helmet and a complete set of body armor that felt liked it weighed a hundred pounds. The temperature outside was about 120 degrees Fahrenheit. Before getting on the plane, we were equipped with two large bottles of water. They didn't want anyone passing out from the heat or dehydrating.

The body armor and Kevlar helmets were mandatory as the planes were known to attract small-arms fire along the way to Baghdad. The temperature in the C130 was about 140 degrees while we sat on the runway. It did cool down a little once we were in the air. I was afraid to drink too much of the water I had brought with me because, at my age, I have to pee more frequently. I asked one of the soldiers where the bathroom was. He said, "Back at Ali Al Salem." I wouldn't need one anyway, he assured me. "You'll sweat it all out." He was right. By the time we arrived at the Baghdad airport, I could have wrung a cup of water out of my shirt.

A group of DynCorp contractors was on the flight. I had a conversation with one of these guys. His mission was to train local police departments. I was appalled by how ill-prepared he seemed for the job. He was sixty-seven years old, obese (he couldn't close his body armor over his stomach), had no background in police work, and had been a low-ranking border patrol agent. He commented to me that he was going to "ride this gravy train for four years" at a cool $130,000 per year.

DynCorp had gross revenues of over $2 billion in 2007. Their most recently filed 10-K (annual Securities and Exchange Commission report) showed that revenues from their Middle East contracts accounted for approximately 46 percent of their total revenues. Most of their contracts are on a cost-plus basis, which means that the more they pay their staff the more they get as a percentage markup. DynCorp profits from an extended war, and it's unlikely that our soldiers will be able to rely on the Iraqi police it "trained" for some time to come.

Here is a statement from DynCorp's 10-K:

Increased Spending by Our Customers—The DoD budget for fiscal 2008, excluding supplemental funding relating to operations in Iraq and Afghanistan, has been proposed to Congress at $481.4 billion, representing a 62 percent increase over fiscal 2001. The U.S. government budget for international development and humanitarian and international security assistance coordinated by the DoS has grown from approximately $15.0 billion in fiscal 2000 to a projected $25.0 billion in fiscal 2009 (a compound annual growth rate of 5.2 percent). As a result of the U.S. military's presence in the Middle East and abroad, we believe that this trend will continue for the foreseeable future and that we are well-positioned to benefit from this trend. Among the factors that could impact U.S. government spending and that would reduce our U.S. government contracting business are: a significant decline in, or reapportioning of, spending by the U.S. government, in general, or by the DoD or the DoS, specifically.

My son died in Iraq. He died for the idea that he was helping the Iraqi people achieve democracy and freedom—not so that a huge corporation could rake in billions.

From Camp Ali Al Salem to Baghdad International Airport

The flight from Ali Al Salem airfield to Baghdad took about an hour.

We had to keep our body armor on for the entire ride. The U.S. Army portion of BIAP is really just four large tents that are used for processing contractors, reporters, and military personnel into Baghdad. When I got to BIAP, there was no one to pick me up. I sat down on a bench to rest, uncertain what to do next, when an Iraqi drove up in a small Opel pickup and asked me in broken English if I wanted a ride somewhere. "Absolutely!" I replied. I was tossing my luggage into the back of the pickup when, all of a sudden, I felt uneasiness about the situation. I said, "Look, I'm new here, so can you come inside and check in with the security desk?" I could barely get my baggage out of the back of his truck before he sped off.

Shaken, I found someone in the main tent who would give me a ride to the Rhino Stables. The Rhino is a highly armored vehicle that looks like a Winnebago on steroids. It only runs at night for security and safety reasons. The Rhino is used to cross over the various red zones that are not under coalition forces control.

I had to cross a red zone from BIAP to Baghdad to get my press credentials—you need them to be embedded with any combat group in Iraq. I boarded the Rhino with a pack of journalists and we made our way under cover of darkness to the Combined Press Information Center (CPIC) offices, located near the old Baathist Headquarters in the Baghdad Green Zone.

At the CPIC offices, we unloaded our luggage so that it could be sniffed by army-trained dogs. Since it was late at night, we were shown to a room where several other journalists were sleeping and waiting until morning to be processed. I was lucky to find a mattress on the floor that had a blanket on it. I pushed the blanket off the mattress because it smelled like it had been there for a while. The mattress wasn't much better, but it was softer than the linoleum floor.

There wasn't much available for breakfast, only a couple of boxes of dry cereal. Just as the journalists were waking up, an army sergeant came into the room and told us we were under lockdown and wouldn't be able to leave the area. Apparently a suicide bomber had gotten through the checkpoint and was on the loose in our facility. I was probably the only one there who wasn't battle-hardened. The journalists just shrugged their shoulders. One of them said, "Let us know when he blows himself up or you kill him so we can get to our destinations." We got our credentials, but just as we were getting ready to leave there was another delay: a bomb found at another nearby checkpoint had to be checked out.

The next day, the CPIC office staff took us to Landing Zone (LZ) Washington near the CPIC offices, where we boarded a Black Hawk helicopter for a short ride at low altitude to LZ Victory. This landing zone is a short and relatively safe drive to Camp Striker, the base of operations for my son's unit. At LZ Victory, I was greeted by two men from Skip's unit, Maj. Robbie Parke and another soldier. They drove me in a Ford Explorer from the LZ to Camp Striker, where I was met by Sgt. Freddy Rocha. Freddy was one of Skip's friends from Headquarters Platoon and worked in the TOC with Skip before he got his own combat squad.

Freddy showed me to my sleeping quarters, a small prefab metal unit called a Container Housing Unit (CHU) set behind thick, thirty-foot-tall concrete barriers. When I got there, Freddy introduced me to Capt. Phillips. When the captain noticed that I didn't have any bedding, he gave me a poncho to use as a cover and a pillow. I went out to examine the wooden porch of my CHU. It was strange: I had a photograph of Skip building one of these very porches. I grabbed a cigar and sat on the stoop and smoked it just like I imagined Skip doing.

I had limited time with my son's comrades, so I wanted to set up as many interviews as I could. Freddy loaned me his cell phone so that I could keep in touch with the battalion. I unpacked all of my gear and fell into bed for a couple of hours' sleep. The next morning, the guys in my son's combat platoon assembled for a group picture.

Interviews in the Combat Zone

I recorded all my interviews with Skip's mates on videotape. I wanted to hear their views on the Battle of Najaf and Skip's last day alive. I was also interested in finding out what Skip was like other than how I knew him as his father.

During my three nights and four days on the FOB with Skip's comrades, I was able for a brief moment to experience life as a soldier, the life that Skip loved so much. There were the showers I took in the poorly constructed shower facilities, the good food from the dining hall, the AT&T pay phones that he used to call home, the PX where he used to buy necessities.

One night I couldn't get to sleep. It was about midnight. I got up and got dressed and walked out into the warm night air. The base wasn't well lit; there were large areas that were totally black. There was no activity, so I assumed Skip's company was out on a mission. I maneuvered around the cement T barriers and decided to walk over to the DFAC to see if I could get a cup of coffee. I had been there enough times by now that I could find my way in the dark. During the day, I felt pretty safe because soldiers carried their weapons everywhere they went. There were no soldiers around now. All I could hear was the crunching sound of my boots on the heavy gravel that was laid down everywhere to lessen the blowing of the sand by the erratic winds. I could see a light in the distance and started walking toward it. Suddenly, I heard another set of boots crunching on the gravel right beside me. The sound startled me. I looked over and there was Skip. "Dad, what are you doing here?"

he said. "You know it's not safe here. I can't believe you did this." I couldn't speak. "Dad, I love you. Don't worry. I am in a good place. Please get back to your CHU; it's not safe out here at night." He walked beside me with his hands in his pockets, his shoulders slightly stooped. He looked strong and healthy.

I stopped to say something to him, but he was gone. I said: "I love you, son." Then I was alone again. I bent down and picked up a handful of gravel from where he had stood and put it in my pocket. As I made my way toward the dining hall, I could hear only one set of boots crunching the gravel.

On the last day of my stay, I went to the FOB post office to send my clothes home, so I wouldn't have to lug them around on my trip back to the States. While I was standing in line, I called Battalion on a phone borrowed from the TOC offices to see if they had manifested me onto a flight from Baghdad back to Kuwait. Maj. Parke told me I had forty-five minutes to get to the airport. I ran from the post office to my quarters and packed for my trip home. I asked one of Skip's comrades who was cleaning his gear if he would see that my clothes got mailed out from the post office. I gave him a hundred dollar bill and told him to keep the change. All of my son's other comrades were elsewhere on the base making preparations for their return home. I jumped on a shuttle bus that was going to the airport.

I got manifested for a flight to Kuwait by showing my passport and orders at the desk run by private contractors. There was a military flight counter and a civilian flight counter run by a private firm that contracted with the U.S. military. It wasn't hard to tell which one I needed to check in at: it was the one with the guy standing behind the counter wearing a Hawaiian shirt. He was short and balding, with just enough hair to pull back in a thin ponytail. In the baggage processing area, there were bins for Mosul, Kuwait, Tal'Afar, and other cities in Iraq.

The next day, I flew out of Kuwait to Frankfurt, Germany, and on to Los Angeles.

My pastor, Rick Kasel, had warned me not to expect too much in the way of closure. As he put it, "The untimely death of a child is not like a rash that goes away. Over time you may learn to deal with it as a reality, as a part of your life that's gone, but you will never get over it." My trip to Baghdad didn't bring closure, but it helped me gather facts for our book, and I believe it helped my son's comrades to talk about Skip's last days. It also helped me understand where and how Skip lived and worked during his last days on earth.

President Bush's surprise visit to Iraq had disrupted my plans to meet with Gen. Petraeus in Baghdad, so he invited me to his home in Fort Myer, Virginia.

On the day of the meeting, Col. Mike Meese picked me up at the Pentagon City Ritz-Carlton and drove me to the general's house. He lived on the grounds of Fort Myer, the army post adjacent to Arlington National Cemetery, in a modest two-story brick house with a wraparound porch. We sat on the porch and he offered me an iced tea. I asked him if his life had changed since he appeared on TV

testifying before Congress. He said the biggest difference was that he couldn't go into Barnes & Noble without being recognized.

Gen. Petraeus is not a big guy physically, but he has a comfortable, nonconfrontational intelligence that somehow disarms you. I could sense that he's intuitive about people. He seemed to be analyzing my thoughts before I even verbalized them. On TV he looks bigger than life, but he's shorter than I am. He's in great shape from running. His voice and measured way of speaking immediately put me at ease. I could imagine him standing in front of a history class giving a lecture.

He had read the article about Skip in *U.S. News & World Report* and he told me that I should be proud to have him as my son. He asked me some questions about Skip, about what made him who he was. He showed me some cluster graphs that analyzed the violence occurring in various regions of Iraq—the same graphical analysis that he had presented to Congress a few days earlier. It showed a definite drop in violence for most areas of Iraq.

As I was leaving, the general gave me an Iraqi Freedom Medallion. Inscribed on the coin were the words *Iltizam Mushtarak*, which means "United Commitment" in Arabic. Col. Meese then drove me back to my hotel.

Later that day, I went to Arlington Cemetery with a group of Gold Star Parents—parents who had lost a child in the war. One woman was crying over her son's grave. I gave her the medallion that the general had given me. She poured her son's favorite Irish whiskey, Bushmills, into shot glasses and we all drank to her brave son. A couple of weeks later, I wrote to the general and told him what I had done with the medallion. He replied: "We'll send a coin, Darrell; in fact, we'll send a few, in case you run into more parents . . ."

Two days later, another coin arrived in the mail.

Appendix

Skip's Incident Reports

All b(3) exemptions refer to 10 U.S.C. 130b.

SECTION IV - FINDINGS (para 3-10, AR 15-6)

The (investigating officer) (board), having carefully considered the evidence, finds:

On 21 1620 MAR 07, C/2-3 IN was returning from completing a mission in Sadr City when third platoon was attacked by Small Arms Fire (SAF). SSG Darrell Griffin was assigned to Charlie Company (C CO) Third Platoon 2-3 Infantry of 2-2 Stryker Brigade Combat Team (SBCT). SSG Griffin's company was attached to 2/82 Airborne Division (Fort Bragg, N.C.). SSG Griffin was manning the right rear air guard hatch of a Stryker M1127 Infantry Carrier Vehicle bumper number C 31 when he was struck by enemy fire. The order of march for the vehicle movement of the platoon was C 32, C 31 (SSG Griffin's vehicle). C 33 and C 34 was the trail vehicle. SSG Griffin's Stryker Vehicle (C 31) was struck by enemy Small Arms Fire (SAF). One round struck SSG Griffin below the helmet approximately 300 meters North of a well traveled route by Coalition and Iraqi Forces. SSG Griffin sustained a Gunshot Wound (GSW) to the head by a burst of 3-4 rounds while he was manning the right air hatch. The platoon leader asked the member of his crew for a situational report (SITREP). (TE)(G) when he noticed that SSG Griffin was slumped over with blood leaking from his helmet. (TE)(G) pulled SSG Griffin down into the vehicle to assess SSG Griffin's wound. (TE)(G) applied pressure to the wound as the Combat Life Saver (CLS). (TE)(G) placed a pressure bandage on SSG Griffin wound. The platoon leader informed his company commander of the injury SSG Griffin sustained. The company commander instructed the platoon leader to turn his vehicle around with the casualty and link-up with the Medical Evacuation Vehicle (MEV). The MEV was called forward and SSG Griffin was placed into the Medical Evacuation Vehicle (MEV) with a faint pulse. The platoon escorted the MEV to the International Zone (IZ). Upon arrival at 28th Combat Support Hospital (CSH) SSG Griffin was immediately moved into the Emergency Treatment Room (ETR) where he was found to be unresponsive. SSG Griffin was immediately moved to radiology for a CT of the head. Following SSG Griffin's CT scan, his vitals were stable and SSG Griffin was transferred via Air MEDEVAC to the Theater Neurosurgical Facility at the 332nd Expeditionary Medical Group (EMOG) in Balad Airbase for neurosurgical evaluation. SSG Griffin's respiratory effort was weak, and in consultation with the treatment team it was unanimously decided that SSG Griffin's wounds were not survivable. At 21 1750 MAR 07 Dr. Teff the neurosurgeon was unable to detect any vital signs or other evidence of life and formally pronounced death at that time.

Conclusions:
I find no fault or negligence in the Death of SSG Griffin. The platoon conducted the proper battledrills, medical aid and evacuated SSG Griffin immediately to a medical facility.

Enemy small arms fire (SAF) continues to be a major threat causing serious injuries, and in some cases death against Coalition and Iraqi Security Forces (SF). Coalition Forces are conducting the proper tactics, techniques and procedures to reduce the threat of SAF. Some of these measures are, but not limited to, ensuring that soldiers ride in the Strykers at name, tape dutilade and the addition of the sniper screen (camouflage net draping the top of the Stryker vehicle supported by iron/metal bars to conceal the soldiers). These measures have increased the service members ability to maintain situational awareness, provide security, and provide concealment from the enemy. The platoon did a great job and conducted the proper procedures when they received a casualty on the battlefield.

SECTION V - RECOMMENDATIONS (para 3-11, AR 15-6)

In view of the above findings, the (investigating officer) (board) recommends:

The positioning of the vehicles and crew was approved by the Troop Commander. The platoon appeared to follow all troop leading procedures and tactics techniques and procedures within the troop when conducting their operation. The platoon was well rehearsed in their battledrills against small arms fire attacks. The investigating officer recommends that no further actions be taken against the platoon or crew and that this case be closed.

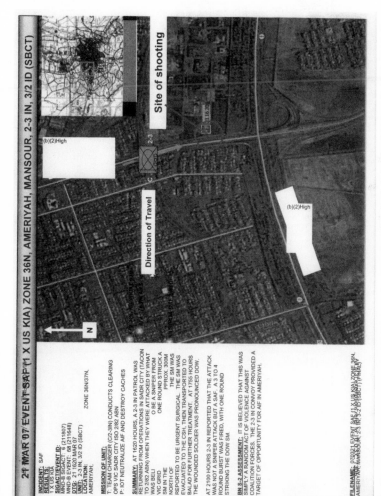

21 MAR '07 EVENT SAF (1 X US KIA) ZONE 36N, AMERIYAH, MANSOUR, 2-3 IN, 3/2 ID (SBCT)

INCIDENT: SAF
RESULTS:
1 X US KIA

SIGACT/EVENT ID:
MND-B SIGACT: 6 (211807)
MND-B EVENT: 68 (211648)
DTG: 21 1620 MAR 07
UNIT: 2-3 IN, 3/2 ID (SBCT)
LOCATION:
AMERIYAH;   ZONE 36N37N,

MISSION OF UNIT:
T: TEAM CHARGER (C/2-3IN) CONDUCTS CLEARING
OPS VIC SADR CITY ISO 2/82 ABN
P: !OT NEUTRALIZE AIF AND DESTROY CACHES

SUMMARY: AT 1620 HOURS, A 2-3 IN PATROL WAS
RE TURNING FROM OPERATIONS IN SADR CITY (TACON
TO 2/82 ABN) WHEN THEY WERE ATTACKED BY WHAT
WAS BELI   O BE A SNIPER FROM
SM IN THE   ONE ROUND STRUCK A
NORTH OF   PPROX. 300M
REPORTED TO BE URGENT SURGICAL. THE SM WAS
EVACUATED TO THE CSH, THEN TRANSPORTED TO
BALAD FOR FURTHER TREATMENT. AT 1755 HOURS
THE WOUNDED SOLDIER WAS PRONOUNCED DOW.

AT 2100 HOURS 2-3 IN REPORTED THAT THE ATTACK
WAS NOT A SNIPER ATTACK BUT A SAF. A 3 TO 4
ROUND BURST WAS FIRED, WITH ONE ROUND
STRIKING THE DOW SM.

BN S-2 ASSESSMENT: IT IS BELIEVED THAT THIS WAS
SIMPLY A RANDOM ACT OF VIOLENCE AGAINST
COALITION FORCES. THE 2-3 IN CONVOY PROVIDED A
TARGET OF OPPORTUNITY FOR AIF IN AMERIYAH.

FILENAME: 070321 EVENT SAF (1 X US KIA) ZONE 36N,
AMERIYAH MANSOUR 21 IN 3-2 ID (SBCT) (PPT)

All b(3) exemptions refer to 10 U.S.C. 130b.

DEPARTMENT OF THE ARMY
HEADQUARTERS, 3RD STRYKER BRIGADE COMBAT TEAM, 2ND INFANTRY DIVISION
UNIT #43318
FOB LIBERTY, IRAQ APO AE 09344

REPLY TO
ATTENTION OF

ARROWHEAD
STRYKER BRIGADE

AFZH-IN-MD   28 March 2007

MEMORANDUM FOR RECORD

SUBJECT: Combat Injuries Sustained by SSG Griffin, Darrell Ray Jr.

1. On 21 March 2007, at approx 1620, SSG Darrell Ray Griffin Jr.,   (9)(4), C/2-3 IN, was reportedly manning the right rear air guard hatch of a Stryker M-1127 Reconnaissance Vehicle (RV) traveling South on   (6)(d)(2)(q) when the vehicle was attacked by small arms fire. SSG Griffin was struck in the head, and immediately transported to the 28th Combat Support Hospital (CSH) in the RV. A dressing was placed on his head wound en route.

2. On arrival to the CSH at 1634, SSG Griffin was immediately moved into Emergency Treatment Room (ETR), where he was found to be unresponsive (Glasgow Coma Score of 3), and was immediately intubated using a rapid-sequence induction technique. Labs were drawn as intravenous lines were started and a foley catheter placed. He was immediately moved to radiology for a CT scan of the head, which showed a left high parietal entrance, explosive calverial fracture pattern, hemorrhagic path involving the left deep nuclei and traversing the superior saggital sinus, and blood in the left lateral ventricle.

3. Following CT scan, his vitals were stable, and he was emergently transferred via air MEDEVAC to the theatre neurosurgical facility the 332nd Expeditionary Medical Group (EMDG) at Balad Airbase for neurosurgical evaluation at 1651.   (9)(4) (c)(4) SSG Griffin's company commander, was present at the CSH for this initial resuscitation, and confirmed that the Soldier identified on documents from the 28th CSH as Trauma Number 101-00-0018 was SSG Griffin.

4. On arrival to EMDG at 1720, SSG Griffin's head dressing was saturated with blood, and on exam by the neurosurgeon (a)(4) (c)(4) he was found to be bleeding profusely from the left parietal entrance wound. His skull was noted to be unstable. No pulse oximetry was attainable, and his systolic blood pressure was <90mm Hg. Arterial blood gas showed a PO2 > 60, hemoglobin was 60, and Prothrombin Time was off the upper scale, indicating a profound coagulopathy. Reversal meds were given IOT perform a better neuron exam, which revealed positive corneal reflexes, but no oculocephalic, gag or cough reflex. His respiratory effort was weak, and in consultation with the treatment team, it was unanimously felt that SSG Griffin's wounds were not survivable, and the team decided to cease aggressive resuscitation and provide palliative care.

5. SSG Griffin was moved from the Emergency Department to ICU-1 at 1740, and was noted to be in agonal cardiac rhythm, with fixed pupils bilaterally. At 1750,   (9)(4) (c)(4) was unable to detect any vital signs or other evidence of life, and formally pronounced death at that time.

KIA (GRIFFIN)_2-3 IN, 3/2 ID_21 MAR 07

All b(3) exemptions refer to 10 U.S.C. 130b.

SWORN STATEMENT
For use of this form, see AR 190-45; the proponent agency is ODCSOPS

PRIVACY ACT STATEMENT

AUTHORITY:	Title 10 USC Section 301; Title 5 USC Section 2051; E.O. 9397 dated November 22, 1943 (SSN).
PRINCIPAL PURPOSE:	To provide commanders and law enforcement officials with means by which information may be accurately identified.
ROUTINE USES:	Your social security number is used as an additional/alternate means of identification to facilitate filing and retrieval.
DISCLOSURE:	Disclosure of your social security number is voluntary.

1. LOCATION TASi	2. DATE (YYYYMMDD) 27 MAR 07	3. TIME 1508	4. FILE NUMBER

5. LAST NAME, FIRST NAME, MIDDLE NAME	6. RSN	7. GRADE/STATUS (g)(q) '(c)(q)

8. ORGANIZATION OR ADDRESS
Cco 2-3 IN

9.
I, _____ (g)(q) '(c)(q) _____, WANT TO MAKE THE FOLLOWING STATEMENT UNDER OATH:

After performing Clearing operations in (g)(q) (c)(q) Sodr City and pulling a night of QRF, I (g)(q) '(c)(q) Along with 1st Sgo. Headed Cwb Callihan For a few hours. After this the Company Headed back to Striker. We were Heading South on (g)(q)(z)(q) Approximately 300m from the (g)(q)(z)(q) Approximately 40mph When we Heard a round Fired outside. I was Riding on the Left bench and was the Second person from the hatch. (g)(q)(z)(q) As King for a sit. Rep. When I looked At SSG. Griffin He was (g)(q) '(c)(q) was standing up with His Head Leaning down. Seconds later I noticed Blood pouring out from the Front of His Mich. I started yelling to pull them down. This is when Lt Reported a casualty and asked for this Status. (g)(q) '(c)(q) was Checking His pulse and if He was Breathing while I (g)(q) '(c)(q) was Holding SSG Griffin and (g)(q) '(c)(q) taking off His Mich. I then yelled to (g)(q) '(c)(q) for thr Aid Bag, He passed it to me and I was passing Gauze to (g)(q) '(c)(q) and them and were putting Pressure on the wound. (g)(q) '(c)(q)

10. EXHIBIT	11. INITIALS OF PERSON MA _____ (g)(q) '(c)(q) PAGE 1 OF **3** PAGES

ADDITIONAL PAGES MUST CONTAIN THE HEADING "STATEMENT OF _____ TAKEN AT _____ DATED _____

THE BOTTOM OF EACH ADDITIONAL PAGE MUST BEAR THE INITIALS OF THE PERSON MAKING THE STATEMENT, AND PAGE NUMBER MUST BE INDICATED.

DA FORM 2823, DEC 1998   DA FORM 2823, JUL 72, IS OBSOLETE   USAPA V1.00

KIA (GRIFFIN)_2-3 IN, 3/2 ID_21 MAR 07

Military Abbreviations and Acronyms

1SG	First Sergeant
ACU	Army Combat Uniform
AIT:	Advanced Individual Training
AKO:	Army Knowledge Online
AWOL	Absent Without Leave
BIAP	Baghdad International Airport
BSM	Bronze Star Medal
CAO	Casualty Assistance Officer
CASEVAC	Casualty Evacuation
CHU	Container Housing Unit
CIA	Central Intelligence Agency
COL	Colonel
COP	Combat Outpost
CP	Command Post
CPIC	Combined Press Information Center
CPT	Captain
CSH or "cash":	Combat Support Hospital
DCU	Desert Camouflage Uniform
DFAC	Dining Facility
DOD	Department of Defense
DOS	Department of State
E-4	Enlisted (pay grade 4)
EMT	Emergency Medical Technician
EOD	Explosive Ordinance Disposal
FMTV	Family of Medium Tactical Vehicles
FOB	Forward Operating Base
FRG	Family Readiness or Resource Group
GDP	Gross Domestic Product

HHC	Headquarters Company
IA	Iraqi Army
IED	Improvised Explosive Device
ING	Iraqi National Guard
IP	Iraqi Police
JAM	Jaish al-Mahdi
JCC	Joint Command Center
JDAM	Joint Direct Attack Munitions
JSS	Joint Security Station
KIA	Killed in Action
LAV	Light Armored Vehicle
LT	Lieutenant
LTC	Lieutenant Colonel
LZ	Landing Zone
MAJ	Major
MEV	Medical Evacuation Vehicle
MGS	Master Gunnery Sergeant
MOS	Military Occupational Specialty
MOUT	Military Operations Urban Training
MRE	Meal-Ready-to-Eat
MSR	Main Supply Route
NCO	Non-Commissioned Officer
NCOIC	Non-Commissioned Officer in Charge
NGs	National Guardsmen
NTC	National Training Center
ODA	Operational Detachment Alpha
PA	Physician's Assistant
PCI	Pre-Combat Inspection
PFC	Private First Class
PH	Purple Heart

PID	Positively Identified
POI	Point of Impact
PUK	Patriotic Union of Kurdistan
PX	Base (formerly Post) Exchange
QRF	Quick Reaction Force
RPG	Rocket Propelled Grenade launcher
S2	Intelligence
SAW	Squad Automatic Weapon
SBCT	Stryker Brigade Combat Team
SECDEF	Secretary of Defense
SF	Special Forces
SFC	Sergeant First Class
SGT	Sergeant
SIGNIT	Signals Intelligence
SITREP	Situation Report
SPC	Specialist (military rank)
SSG	Staff Sergeant
SVBIED	Suicide Vehicle-Borne Improvised Explosive Device
SWAT	Special Weapons and Tactics team
ROTC	Reserve Officer Training Corps
TNT	Trinitrotoluene
TOC:	Tactical Operations Center or Top of Command
TTPs	Tactics, Techniques and Procedures
UAV	Unmanned Aerial Vehicle
WMDs	Weapons of Mass Destruction

Acknowledgments

This book was very difficult to write on a number of levels. I could not have written it without the help of a great number of people.

I would like to thank my wife, Kim, our children Rene, Sommer, Christian, Alexis, and Jordan, and Skip's wife, Diana, for putting up with my crazy hours, mood swings, and moments of depression during the writing and editing.

I would like to thank my agent at William Morris, Mel Berger, for directing me to one of the best publishers in the world, James Atlas of Atlas & Co. I would also like to thank Lukas Volger from Atlas & Co., who worked many long and hard hours on the design, layout, and production of *Last Journey*.

In his journal, Skip transcribed quotations from the books he read, sometimes at length. These were for his own use, to guide him while he wrote his book. I've tried to find the original sources wherever possible, and to distinguish the words Skip wrote from the words he quoted.

I would like to thank SSG Duane Wells for accompanying Skip's body on his last journey home, and I thank him and SSG Robert Hansen for staying to be with the family during Skip's funeral and burial.

And I cannot forget to thank Maj. David Cabrera, who served as the primary casualty assistance officer. He helped make this painful time tolerable by making all the planning of the funeral and burial go as well as possible. He was also always there for Diana during her time of grief. I would also like to thank SSG Willie Holifield for serving as the family's casualty assistance officer.

The Patriot Guard Motorcycle Club served to make sure that the funeral and burial were not disturbed and that we were able to honor Skip's last request for the funeral and burial that he wanted.

People Who Helped Me Get to Iraq: Parents are not allowed in combat zones. I was told this on a number of occasions. Once these people heard my story, they worked to help make it happen: Alex Kingsbury, *U.S. News & World Report*; General David Petraeus; Congressman Howard Berman; Gene Smith, Fred Flores, veteran affairs officer, Van Nuys; Margaret Mott, Van Nuys; Robert Wilkie, Assistant Secretary of Defense; Traci Scott, Office of Secretary of Defense; MAJ G. Scott Taylor, U.S. Army; Max Becherer, photographer, Polaris Images; MAJ Everett S. P. Spain, U.S. Army, aide-de-camp to the Commanding General, Multi-National Force-Iraq; MAJ Robbie Parke, U.S. Army; Gunnery SGT Chris W. Cox, Third Army, USARCENT, Public Affairs; CPT Michael Signori, Multi-National Force-Iraq, embed coordinator, Combined Press Information Center; LTC Barry Huggins, Skip's last battalion commander; MAJ Steven C. Phillips, Skip's last company commander; and CPT Gregory Weber, Skip's last platoon leader.

Soldiers Who Spent Many Hours Helping Me Gather, Assimilate, and Interpret Information: SPC Matthew Briggs; CPT Gregory Weber; CSM Victor Mercado; CPT Lewis Seau; MAJ Stephen Phillips; SSG Duane Wells; SSG Korey Staley; MAJ Brent Clemmer; COL Todd McCaffrey; SSG Robert G. Hansen; SSG Duane Wells; SPC Gregory Perrault; SGT James Pelletier; SSG Anthony Ducre; CSM G. Joseph Martinez; and LT Steven Willis.

Soldiers Who Were Always There for Quick Questions: MAJ Gene Agustin; SSG Samuel Armer; MAJ Christopher Bachl; CSM Alan Bjerke; CPT Erica Borggren; BG Robert B. Brown; MAJ David Cabrera; CPT Donald Carrothers; CPT Jarrel Delottinville; SSG Erick Svanoe; SPC Jose Fernandez; SFC Chris Gordon; SFC Douglas Hale; SPC Justin Hoover; MAJ Michael Klein; SSG Nicholas Malich; SGT Kevin Mcculley; 1SG Jerry McCullough; CPT Elizabeth McNally; COL Michael Meese; SPC Jason Mitchell; SPC Chris "Irish" Mueller; SPC Chris Oliver; SSG Christopher Pacheco; SSG Victor Quinonez; SSG Gary Robinson; SSG Fred Rocha; SFC Benny Salas; MAJ Curtis J. Sawyer II; PFC Jae Shin; CPT T.J. Siebold; SSG Charles Simms; SPC Rob Spracklin; SGM Charles Stanley; SSG Standly Villiers II; and SSG Patrice White.

I would also like to thank rest of Skip's fellow warriors of the 1–5 Infantry of 1st Stryker Brigade Combat Team,

25th Infantry Division, and the 2–3 Infantry of 3rd Stryker Brigade Combat Team, 2nd Infantry Division, for always being available to answer my many questions.

Friends and Family Who Were Always There to Answer Questions and Give Me the Support I Needed to Finish the Book: Babsi Arn; Barbara Bacon; Richard Barchard; Curt Edmondson; David Ross Griffin; Shelia Griffin; Sandra Hoffman; Kim Houser, Director Home Front Ministries; Curt Jensen; Sue Jesse; Pastor Rick Kasel, Shepherd of the Hills Church; Fred Kramer; Carie McCarter; Robin Mercado; Michelle Miller; Joe Neulight; Executive Pastor Dudley Rutherford, Shepherd of the Hills Church; Guillermo Salazar; Sharon Scollard; Michael Smythe; David Straus; Rene Tamayo; Pastor Shawn Walden, Shepherd of the Hills Church; Kelly Wells; Aunt Patsy Yates; and Nouriel Gino Yazdani.